Volume Four

Inspired learning through great books.

Ages 9-10

Second Edition

By Jane Claire Lambert

Five in a Row Volume Four

Second Edition

ISBN 978-1-888659-25-2

Published by:
Five in a Row Publishing
312 SW Greenwich Dr.
Suite 220
Lee's Summit, MO 64082
816-866-8500

Send all requests for information to the above address.

Lovingly dedicated to ...

... my husband Stephen
and my daughters Becky and Carrie
who all worked so far beyond the call of duty

... to Lynn and Carol
who have faithfully stood beside us

... and to all the children who have loved their
rowing experiences!

Contents

Introduction

Good books have always been the doorway to learning. That doorway leads to growth and an appreciation for the wonders around us. Come along on a learning adventure using picture books to open the door to art, history, vocabulary, geography, science, human relationships, applied math and writing!

No matter how young, children get a substantial educational head start from books. *Five in a Row* was created to bring excitement and fun to learning and to enrich children's lives through wonderful children's literature. These lesson plans are simple in concept, but rich in results. Read the chosen book in its entirety each day for a week.* After each reading, choose an exercise to share with your student, and watch their world expand as you begin to show them facets of the story they would never have recognized without your purposeful guidance. As a teacher of this material, you will find that you become excited and interested in a variety of subjects too. You'll rediscover the joy of learning and you'll build a special bond between you and your student as the two of you go on a learning adventure together.

This curriculum is intended to be extremely flexible, allowing you the option to do any combination of the exercises for each story. You may elect to skip over certain lessons which do not fit the needs of your student and you may place additional emphasis on certain ones which seem appropriate. You will find more exercises than you can use in a week,* so enjoy choosing just the right lesson elements for your students.

You can adjust school time to fit your needs as well. By using only one lesson element each day, you can work through *Five in a Row* in as little as 30 minutes daily, including the time to read the book. If you choose to use all of the lesson elements, field trips and follow-up exercises, you could easily spend several hours daily. Use *Five in a Row* however it best suits your needs and the needs of your students.

The technique of reading the same story for at least five days in a row is one that I have tested in teaching for many years. I continue to be amazed at the effectiveness of this technique! Each book will become very special to the children. They will remember more and more about the story, but more importantly, they will begin to think more critically as they begin wondering how certain portions of the story came to be, or how the characters solved a certain problem. These results could never be achieved in just one reading.

Students will see how the illustrator accomplished certain effects and they'll be encouraged to begin exploring those techniques in their own art. You'll see your students learning about science, history and applied math through everyday discussions. Your students will have the opportunity to try new activities they read about, or to learn more about a variety of people, places or animals. You'll also discover your student asking more questions than ever before. By the end of the week, a new book will have become their friend for life.

Perhaps the most valuable benefit of using *Five in a Row* is that young students learn to fully evaluate a work (with your guidance), and that skill will serve them well as they learn to read for themselves. Your students will begin looking to see whether a book is a Caldecott or a Newbery medal winner. They'll quickly classify a new book as either fact or fiction. They'll be able to articulate the point of view from which the story has been written. They will know about a wide variety of literary techniques and learn to recognize them for themselves. You'll be delighted when your students begin to evaluate the illustrator's medium and technique.

All of this is imparted in an enjoyable learning environment. Students think you're just reading them a book, but they're learning so much every day! The more lessons you do together, the more skills your young students will acquire; skills which will benefit them through high school, college and throughout life!

Welcome to the wonderful world (and the second edition!) of *Five in a Row*. Even though our world has changed greatly since the first edition, the purpose and mission of this highly effective curriculum remain the same: to provide students with a quality educational foundation for their elementary years with "inspired learning through great books." This second edition is up to date regarding today's technology while continuing to base learning on high-quality, carefully chosen books and lessons—including all-new activity sheets following each title. You are the leader for this adventure, so gather the children around you and have a great time!

Jane Claire Lambert
May 1994; January 2021

*Volume 4 differs in some ways from Volumes 1-3. See "What's Different About Volume 4?" on page 21 for more details.

About the Books Themselves

"The goal of our instruction is to lead children to fall in love with good books and and to embrace the joy of learning."

Sutherland and Arbuthnot write in the classic children's literature textbook *Children and Books*, "Aesthetic satisfaction comes to small children as well as to adults, and the development of their taste depends not only on their initial capacities but also on *the material they encounter and the way in which it is presented.*"* (emphasis added)

If you're like most of us, you can directly attribute a lifelong interest in at least one topic to the quality and creativity with which some particular teacher or a parent introduced the subject to you as a child. Likewise, you may well have nurtured a lifelong distaste for certain subjects for the same reason: an unpleasant early experience.

Sutherland and Arbuthnot go on to suggest that by selecting excellent children's literature and reading it together each day, children have the opportunity to "catch a new theme, savor the beauty, the subtle humor or a special meaning that eluded them at first."

"Sometimes," the authors continue, "an adult has the privilege of seeing this discovery take place. The children's faces come suddenly alive; their eyes shine. They may be anticipating an amusing conclusion or a heroic triumph. There is a sudden chuckle or breath is exhaled like a sigh. The book has moved them, perhaps even to laughter or tears; in any case there is a deep inner satisfaction and they will turn to books again with anticipation."

Sutherland and Arbuthnot conclude, "Once they have experienced the joy of reading they have acquired a habit that will serve them all their lives. It is important, therefore, that those who guide their reading select wisely."

It is within this context that the titles for *Five in a Row* have been chosen. In each case, content was of supreme importance. Books were chosen that showcase close family relationships, personal triumphs, and persevering in times of trial. There are books with people characters and stories with animal characters, but in all the stories the characters touch the reader's heart and demonstrate life's truths. Please remember, however, that our selection of a particular title by an author does *not* mean that we necessarily endorse *everything* from that author. We're aware of several cases where authors have written marvelous books and very questionable books as well. Please take the time to review any book you bring home from the library *before* reading it to your children!

In addition to content, the books also cover a wide range of artistic expression: from the charming, old-fashioned illustrations of Barbara Knutson to the hilarious oils of Brad Sneed; from the exquisite colored inks of Demi to the textured colored pencils of Jim LaMarche. Each title was selected for a diversity of magnificent art, beautifully rendered for the utter appreciation and enjoyment of children. Art to appreciate, art to learn from and art to be remembered for a lifetime!

It has been said some stories must be talked over or listened to while *someone who knows and loves them reads aloud.* If *you* come to love the stories, your student will too.

With these standards in mind, we hope you and your student find a special place in your heart for these stories and for the concept of *Five in a Row.*

*Sutherland and Arbuthnot, *Children and Books*, Harper Collins Publishers, 8th ed., 1991.

How to Use Five in a Row

Note: If you've already used FIAR Volumes 1-3, you can skip directly to the end of this section. Look for **What's Different About Volume 4?** for information and tips on how best to use this volume! If you are new to FIAR with Volume 4, please read this entire section.

First, select a book to study with your student. There is no right or wrong order for covering the material. Some of the books have overlapping lesson material, and there are references to remind your student of other books' lessons that have a similar theme, artwork, or lesson topic. But don't worry if you haven't read the other book mentioned yet—just skip that reference. These types of connections will soon become second nature to you and your student and you'll find yourselves making them on your own!

Some teachers will choose to purchase each book as a valuable addition to their permanent library. Most public libraries should have (or be able to request) the titles in this book. (Exceptions might be the Bonus Unit Studies in this volume. See "Finding the Books" at the end of this manual for more information.)

Important Note: Please take the time to read the book aloud to your student at least several times in your two weeks of study. The repetition is essential to your student's learning process, and the time you spend reading together is just as important as the lesson material itself. For more information on why to read the story for several days in a row, and suggestions if you have a child who resists this idea, see "Reading the Stories Five Days in a Row" later in this section.

Following the story units in this manual, you will find a sample planning worksheet for a two-week study of *The Pumpkin Runner*. You'll also find a blank worksheet which you can reproduce and use for each FIAR story that you study. The sample sheet shows how to correlate the teacher's guide suggestions and plans to the 10 days that you will study each particular book. Or, feel free to design your own worksheet. Some teachers don't care to use planning sheets at all, and just work directly from the *Five in a Row* manual. Do whatever works for you!

Notice that the sample lesson plan is outlined briefly and gives you a quick reference for the week. Not every lesson suggested in the manual under *The Pumpkin Runner* is listed on the sample lesson—there are too many lesson options available. So you will choose the ones that are especially suited to your student and list them on the blank planning sheet. While the subjects Math, Science, Art, etc., do not have to be used in the same order every week, remember that when planning a unit, the curriculum builds on itself. Whatever you study on Monday will be recognized by your student when you read the story again on Tuesday. When you read the story a third time on Wednesday, the lessons you introduced on Monday and Tuesday will not escape the student's notice as he hears or sees the examples again. So each lesson, except the one for the final day, gets at least one review and some lessons get several reviews. The topics you think are most important, therefore, should be scheduled toward the beginning of your study. It seems as though Art often gets tagged in the last slot. Try using this topic earlier in your study so your student can study the pictures for several days as he hears the story read and reread.

Also following the story units, you will find a sheet of story disks. These are quick, symbolic representations of titles included in FIAR Volume 4. They are meant to be used in conjunction with a laminated world or U.S. map. First, color the disk and put the name of the book on the back of the disk. For greater durability, laminate the disks before you cut them apart (or use clear contact paper after cutting). By placing a Velcro® dot on the disk and the other dot on the map where it goes, you can quickly take it off and put it back on each day (tacky putty will also work). Eventually you will be able to track the stories you have read all over the world. Even young students will learn some map basics. Any stories with fictitious settings can be placed in the margins of the map as the "Land of Make Believe."

There is also a page of blank disks so you can make your own pictures for these stories, or replace a lost disk. You might also like to make disks for other stories you read outside of *Five in a Row.*

Social Studies

Many different topics are included under the heading of Social Studies. Each story has a specific geographic area, and often the culture of that area is discussed. Making a flag is fun and informative, and you'll find flags to color in most units, as well as a "Parts of a Flag" reference sheet at the end of this manual. Geography also includes the mention of oceans, continents and geographic regions. (An excellent illustrated children's geography book is *Rand McNally's Picture Atlas of the World*, illustrated by Brian Delf. You'll find it informative and fun!) Under the topic Social Studies, you will also find lessons about town rules, stamps and the Postal Service, living on an island, Eastern and Western cultures, city living, trains, and sheep ranches. In addition, the Social Studies unit includes history. Under this heading, you will see lessons which create opportunities to discuss Daniel Boone, life in the early 1900s, statehood and U.S. history, the Old West and cattle drives, Native American culture, World War II, and the history of the Jeep. Social Studies also includes many lessons about people and their relationships to one another. In this category, you'll find subjects such as problem solving, being away from home, friendship, fears and compassion, grieving together, and disagreeable people—just to name a few. As you can see, a wide variety of subjects is included under Social Studies.

Choose the topics you'd like to discuss and either mark them in the manual or write them on the Planning Sheet under whichever day it seems best to cover them. If you use the Planning Sheets, be sure when presenting the material to tie it in to the story.

Language Arts

There are many techniques for learning Language Arts using children's literature. Increasing vocabulary, learning literary devices, learning list-making skills, composing short stories and acting out dramas are just a few of the ways. Teaching Language Arts is a natural extension of the enjoyment of children's literature.

Vocabulary is enriched by hearing new words like arborist (*The Tree Lady*), attire (*The Pumpkin Runner*) or trestles (*Mailing May*). A child's vocabulary is much greater than just the words he can read or spell, and reading a story which contains new words several times in a row will help increase his recognition and understanding of those words.

Two methods for organizing vocabulary words are the file box and the notebook. The file box method uses four-by-six inch, unlined index cards with alphabet dividers. Either the teacher or the student can print the word at the top left of the card. Write in a short definition at the left, and either draw an illustration or print a picture to show the word visually. Keep the words alphabetized and encourage your student to go through the cards frequently. This will help him remember which story each word was from. (To help in remembering the source, write the name of the book on the back of the card.)

A second method of keeping track of vocabulary words is to list them on a page in the Language Arts or Vocabulary section of a notebook. Print the word (large, if necessary) and illustrate with a drawing or picture as a visual reminder. Lists can be alphabetized or organized by FIAR title. Review these words from time to time while remembering your favorite incidents in the corresponding stories.

A notebook is good for more than just vocabulary words. In fact, it's a great way for a student to keep his work organized and ready for quick review and easy reference. For the grade-level student, this will likely come naturally. But for the very young student, to have his own notebook is special. For him, use colored dividers so he can find the subjects, even if he cannot yet read. In this way, he can proudly find his Science section and show someone his drawings or projects. He'll be able to look up his Vocabulary section with illustrations and share his art work with others.

List-making is another Language Arts skill that develops vocabulary, memory, associations and creativity. It is also a skill that has lifetime value in many different areas, from grocery lists, lists of people to invite to a party, "to do" lists, lists of ways to solve a problem, to descriptive lists that inform. There have been great, eloquent lists made by famous people of the things they liked, disliked, or the things they wished for. Once, while travelling together in a car, a friend's family began an oral list of methods of transportation. Many miles down the road, the list had grown to gigantic proportions with the hilarious inclusions of walking on stilts and walking on your hands added to the regular methods of riding in a car, bus or taxi. What began as a list-making exercise became entertainment. The art and skill of good list-making is included in this curriculum to provide both a learning experience and a good time.

There are many **literary devices** explained in FIAR and tied in to the lessons from children's literature. You probably will not cover them all, but they are included to remind the teacher of them and give opportunities for casual inclusion in the reading lessons. (Also see the Literary Glossary at the end of the manual.)

As you come to each new literary device, a list can be made with examples and pictures. Keep your list in the Language Arts section of the student's notebook. For instance, personification (giving human qualities to non-human things) might be defined and illustrated with a picture of the Pillsbury Doughboy® or Lightning McQueen from the movie *Cars*. Other literary devices can be illustrated, as well. Keeping a chart or list of these words makes review easy and interesting and can be used by the student as an inspirational list when he is creating his own works.

Ideas for leading your student into writing include letting them record their stories, which you then transcribe. Often the student will enjoy listening to his story in his own voice. Writing rebus stories, where pictures take the place of certain words throughout the story, is an interesting way to begin writing skills. As you follow the curriculum, you'll find lessons in what makes a good story, and ways to achieve variety. Your student will begin to appreciate the choices an author makes to create a story and the careful thought that goes into writing.

Many times in this curriculum these type of questions are asked: "How does the author make the story exciting? What words does he use? How does he ... ?" Eventually, as he sees these techniques modeled before him, the student will begin to include such elements in his own writing. The suggestion after every lesson to imitate an aspect of the author's work is optional, depending on the interest and abilities of the student. See if your student enjoys imitating the author's techniques. If not, just concentrate on appreciating the lesson. In time the rest will follow.

If, however, your student enjoys writing "after the manner of," imitating aspects of the author's story, he will like the suggestions to try a fable, an instructional story or a poem. He'll also begin to include a good setting, interesting characters, an exciting climax, or an important denouement (final outcome) in his own stories. Each of these is a separate lesson in the curriculum. Again, keeping a chart or a good notebook list filled with definitions and examples will give your student a ready reference when he is writing his own stories and makes review easy. Just add to the list or chart on an ongoing basis as you come to different lessons.

Remember, there are too many language arts topics to be covered in a single day. Choose the ones appropriate for your student and jot them briefly on the planning sheet under the day(s) you think best. Also remember, if you are going to teach vocabulary it is a good idea to do this near the beginning of the unit. As the book is read and reread, your student will see familiar vocabulary words again and again, providing a built-in review. Depending on your child's age, you may want to choose only a few words from each story.

Art

When you choose good children's literature, you will frequently discover exceptional illustrations, as well. Watercolor, pastels, charcoal, beautiful colors, active lines, funny characters and balanced compositions are all parts of fine illustrations for children. Furthermore, they can be used to introduce even young children to fundamentals and techniques of art.

Appreciating art is learning to recognize the many techniques and concepts which combine to produce effective art while learning what you like and why. Some pictures have a rhythm, balance and choice of color that combine to make them pleasing. Some illustrations are meant to evoke strong emotions or to provide information. Even young children can begin to identify great art wherever it's encountered. They'll also begin to know why they like it. By teaching about the artist and their methods, your student's taste in art will expand to include a rich and wonderful variety of work.

As you look at illustrations with your student, ask, "What do you think the illustrator used for his medium?" Sometimes it's hard to tell (check the copyright page of the book, which sometimes will provide this information). There are combinations of pen and ink with watercolor washes, etchings with strokes from oil or acrylic and the wet, transparent blends of watercolors. Look for the shading in a charcoal or pencil sketch, or the buildup of color by successive layers of colored pencils. Learn to identify the deep texture of pastels.

After you've discussed the medium, ask "why and how" questions. "Why do you think the illustrator chose this medium, color, style, viewpoint, etc.? How did the artist make it look like nighttime, etc.?" These kinds of questions will open a doorway to art appreciation for your student.

Let him study the illustrations as he tries to answer your questions. You may want to suggest some answers as you discuss the methods the artist used and how the illustrations help tell the book's story. Does the artist's work provide additional story information not included in the text? Does the choice of color palette convey the tone of the story?

Asking lots of questions will cause your student to look with a more critical eye. He will pore over the pages to find answers and he will gain a love of art based on newly-discovered information. This will lead to an emerging appreciation for great illustrations. Don't ask all the questions at the same time. Bring them up conversationally from time to time as you study each book.

One of the best techniques for teaching art fundamentals is to imitate a particular technique from the painting or drawing of a known artist. In *Five in a Row*, the lessons attempt to identify and single out a specific artistic element and to encourage imitation. Your student will be invited to mimic specific styles, colors and designs. Remember that appreciation usually precedes imitation. Therefore, look for examples of the element you are studying in other books or online. Let him examine and enjoy these additional examples before he begins experimenting with the technique himself.

In order for you to be ready to meet your student's needs, you may want to have certain supplies on hand:

Kneadable eraser

Drawing pencil or #2 lead pencil

Charcoal - (**Teacher's Note:** Supervise the use of charcoal, since it can get messy!)

Oil pastels - The favorite medium of many young students. They don't smear as much as chalky pastels. (**Adult supervision required.**)

Markers

Colored pencils - Look for good colored pencils. They make a difference.

Crayons - Look for "name brand" crayons.

Watercolors - Prang® brand is good, or tube watercolors are extremely easy to use for mixing exercises.

Acrylics - Not necessary, but it gives your student a chance to paint layer upon layer using lighter colors on top.

Brushes - You'll need brushes with several different bristle lengths and widths. If you want to paint fine-lined tree branches, you'll need the right brush!

Watercolor paper

Canvas paper for acrylics

Drawing tablet or paper

Tracing paper

Ruler

Templates of various geometric shapes cut from cardboard or cardstock

Above all, remember that creative art is an intensely personal subject. If you wish to demonstrate a technique, do it on a separate piece of paper—never on your student's own work! Be wise with your criticism of his progress. Grant him the respect you would grant any artist. Go slowly, letting him catch the enthusiasm for the ideas you present.

Math

In many of the books chosen for this curriculum, children will enjoy finding practical ways to use the new concepts they learn in math. These lessons are "applied math," developed from the story to show children how math is used in their everyday world. Many story units have multiple applied math lessons to choose from, depending on the ability and interests of your student. For example, your student may study the number of months and days on a calendar in *Roxaboxen*, fractions in *The Tree Lady*, and metric units in *The Pumpkin Runner.*

Note: The FIAR applied math lessons are not a substitute for a regular math curriculum. You will still need a math program for your student addition to the practical, everyday math lessons in *Five in a Row*.

Reading the story all the way through while enjoying the closeness of the teacher and the entertainment of the book establishes a good environment for presenting a math lesson derived from the story. Even the lesson will be a shared experience. If there are more math ideas than are appropriate for one day, choose the ones you wish to cover and write them on the planning sheet for the day(s) you wish to cover Math.

Science

Open wide the door to children's literature and find within the stories a vast array of scientific educational potential: from learning more about seasons and biomes, to discovering the science behind steam power and mountain engineering, to tides, falling stars, skeletons, oxidation, bamboo, peppers and paprika, friction, flora and fauna, human anatomy, and much more.

After reading the book for the day, bring up conversationally the science topics suggested in the lessons and other ideas that you may have. Don't try to use all the topics. *The Pumpkin Runner*, for instance, includes science topics of flora of Australia, botany (pumpkins), buoyancy and density, fauna of Australia, physics (hot air ballooning), the anatomy of running, and physical fitness. Just choose the ones you think are appropriate and mark them on the planning sheet on whichever day(s) seems best.

When presenting your science lesson, be sure to tie it into the story. For instance, in *Albert*, you might say, turning to the first page, "Remember how Albert lives in the middle of a city? What kind of things might you see and hear in a city?"

A science section in your student's notebook with pages for Ocean Life, Simple Machines, etc., will help in reviewing lessons he's studied. If he likes, let your student illustrate the topics with his own drawings of the story. This could be part of a beloved notebook by year's end.

Note: *Five in a Row* was created to be gender-neutral and you'll find a wide variety of fascinating lessons that appeal to both boys and girls. Don't assume that a boy may not enjoy a story that has a girl as the main character, or vice versa! And, please note that we've referred to "teacher and student" in the singular. Many of you will have more than one student.

Reading the Stories Five Days in a Row

This section explains the reasoning and philosophy that went into creating lesson plans in which the story is read over and over ("five days in a row"). It details benefits and what to do if there is resistance from your student.

Before you make a decision to read the selected story less than five days in a row, it may be helpful to know why the curriculum was developed this way. Then you have the background knowledge necessary to decide how you want to use it with your student.

Some children read a story only for the plot. When they "know what has happened," they are ready for a new book. The plot is all they know to find in a book. It takes a bit of creativity and planning for these children to experience the richness of a good story—to find out how much more than just the plot can come to them through a great book!

Thus, the *Five in a Row* curriculum was designed to find many treasures in every story—across several academic topic areas—and to provide a built-in review every time you reread the story. Each day as your child hears the story again, he is saying to himself, "Oh, there is the personification!" or "Oh, I see how that artist balanced the picture ... I remember that from yesterday." The repeated opportunities for your child to apply what he has learned as he hears the book over again is an important part of this curriculum.

In addition, each day as you read, your child will hear the sentence structure, syntax, mood and style of a story written by a great children's author. This repetitive reading of a story for five days can make a huge difference in your child's ability to read and write (at the proper time). His ear becomes used to good sentences—he may not have memorized them, but hearing them five times works almost as well. Again this will help in both reading and creative writing in the future.

Seeing the great works of art, several times in a row, in the illustrations of the *Five in a Row* selected titles, works in much the same way. Your student's eyes are being trained not to rush from one set of illustrations to another, but to observe different details each day as he listens to the book.

There truly was a great deal of thought that went into how this particular curriculum was created and structured, for the maximum benefits to occur. It isn't just a curriculum that recommends a book, has you read it once, and then moves you along.

Suggestions for a Resistant Student

Because there are significant benefits to reading the story over multiple days, we have some suggestions for those who might have a more reluctant student. Read the story on the first day. The second day you can just say you are going to read it again, but this time you are going to leave out a part and see if they can catch you. (This technique is also good on day three or four.) Or you can add in a character or line and see if they can catch it!

Another day you can say that you are going to read the story again, but today your student can be looking for... (something in the art lesson you are going to do. For example, ask your student to look for every picture that has both orange and blue in it—since later that day you will do a lesson in complementary colors.)

You could also have your student draw something about the story while you are reading one day. This is not ideal, since they aren't looking at the pictures, but it's a good option for one day.

If you do a lesson on onomatopoeia one day, the next day have them listen for the examples and raise their hand or clap when they hear one. In this way, you are using the previous day's lessons to spur yet another reading of the book.

With the above ideas and approach, you are retaining the right to say what you will do for school in a gentle, friendly way: "This is what we are going to do," while at the same time caring for your student enough to create a helpful environment in which he can get over the hump of the problem, and learn to hear a good story for five days. Then you have a win-win situation.

I think you will find that after a few units, you won't have to do as much of this type of "leading" because your child will be used to reading the book five days in a row and he will actually be enjoying it!

All that said, you are the teacher and you will make the final decisions for your family on how to use FIAR. I just thought you might want to know why *Five in a Row* was created in this way and how this method will benefit your child's learning.

What's Different About Volume 4?

If you've used Volumes 1-3 of *Five in a Row*, you're probably used to "rowing" a book for five days in a row. You've also noticed that you can move within Volumes 1-3 with no noticeable change in difficulty; the books do not get "harder" from one volume to the next. One significant difference between this volume and previous volumes is that the picture books in Volume 4 have **greater complexity and depth**, making them ideal for older elementary-aged students.

Because the books are more complex, the lessons are, as well. You'll find more lessons in each subject area, with topics designed more for older children than those for Volumes 1-3. For this reason, you'll **row each title for two weeks instead of one**. You may do this however you wish (two days in a row on social studies, one day on language arts, three days on science, etc.) depending on the lessons you want to cover with your children. **Note:** You will likely *not* read the book 10 days in a row; you may read it four or five days in a row and then once or twice the following week. It's a good idea to read it at least several days in a row the first week, though; see the reasons in the section above for the many advantages of this method of teaching and learning.

Volume 4 has been designed to continue the highly effective, enjoyable studies of FIAR Volumes 1-3, while at the same time preparing your older child for the next step in the FIAR curriculum: a transition to chapter book studies using a very similar approach to learning that students and teachers have come to love. After completing Volume 4, you and your student will be ready to take this next exciting step with Volume 5 of *Five in a Row*.

Roxaboxen

Title: *Roxaboxen*
Author: Alice McLerran
Illustrator: Barbara Cooney
Copyright: 1991
Summary: Roxaboxen, where children take a real place and enormous imagination and create an incredible town of their own.

22

Social Studies: Geography - Arizona

The author's text of *Roxaboxen* does not tell exactly where the story takes place. Perhaps this is the author's way of keeping Roxaboxen the universal play place—an extraordinary place for play that could exist anywhere! Many authors choose to treat their settings in this manner. Talk with your older student about authors' choices. One choice authors make is the setting of their story. Some writers choose to write their stories in the context of a real setting while some choose a fictional place. Yet there is still another option. A writer may also choose to never actually mention where a story takes place—either a real-life setting or a fictional one. Remind your student that he can make these same choices regarding *his* setting, as he writes *his* stories.

Only in the afterward of the book do you find that the original Roxaboxen actually did exist in Yuma, Arizona! Find Arizona on the map and place your story disk there. Arizona is considered one of the Southwestern States. The terminology *southwest* generally refers to the states of Arizona, New Mexico, Texas and Oklahoma. Phoenix is the capital of Arizona, while Flagstaff, Tucson and Yuma are other important cities.

Arizona was the 48th state, admitted to the union of the United States of America in 1912. The name Arizona comes from a Native American word *arizonac* meaning small spring. In fact the names of twenty-six of our fifty states in the U.S. are named for Native American words or tribes! There are many Indian reservations in Arizona including a large Navajo reservation in the northeast corner of the state.

Arizona has many different kinds of cactus, lizards and snakes, as well as the spectacular Grand Canyon, and Monument Valley that includes the Painted Desert and Petrified Forest areas. Find a book on Arizona at the library, or help your student search online to see the interesting and magnificent sights of Arizona.

Does your student know that Arizona is one of the "Four Corners" states? Arizona and three other states (New Mexico, Colorado, and Utah) have shared boundries that all touch at a single point. Look at a map and discover how this works. A person can stand at one place and technically be in all four of these states at once!

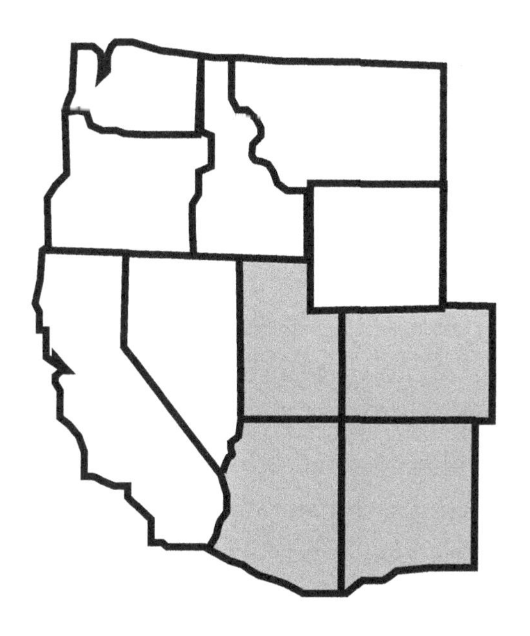

Social Studies:
Towns with Rules and Consequences

If you have used *Five in a Row* Vol. 1, you have probably explored lessons on "towns" in *Katy and the Big Snow* and in *Mike Mulligan and His Steam Shovel*. Roxaboxen also becomes a town with the addition of shops and homes, a mayor, police and a jail. Have you ever engaged in such wide scale pretending in your childhood? Has your student? This type of play promotes physical health as well as lots of enjoyment and actual learning experiences. Acting out scenes from life has always been an important part of playing pretend. If your student is interested (and especially if he has someone to create a town *with*) he could use large boxes to make store fronts and buildings for his town. Or he could just line out a town (outside with chalk or rocks and inside with pillows or tape) and use prepared signs to designate the buildings. He could pretend being a police officer, firefighter, shopkeeper, etc.

Does your student think the town of Roxaboxen runs well? (It seems the inhabitants of Roxaboxen are happy living in their homes, buying and selling and driving everywhere. Except maybe for the times of war, in general, the town runs well, in an orderly and enjoyable way.) Does your student know what a mayor does? A mayor, usually an elected official, is the head of a city or town government or municipality. The mayor is responsible for conducting the business of the city, seeing to its laws as well as its growth and well being. Remember when Frances moved to a new house on streets that were added later? This is an example of town growth. Is there an area of new construction and growth near you where your student can watch over a period of time as his own town grows? As a town grows it needs more shops, police stations, fire stations, post offices, libraries, hospitals, disposal services, etc.

Explain the beginnings of town politics in this simple way: In the town of Roxaboxen (as well as in real towns) people get along with each other because there are some basic rules and people follow them. Most of the rules have to do with treating the citizens of the town just like you would like to be treated. This includes such conduct as keeping your word, and not harming other people or their property. If the rules are not followed there are consequences. The consequences usually consist of having to pay for something damaged or having to give up some of your own time, money, and/or freedom to repay a wrong done. The consequences exist to help people remember *not* to break the rules. Talk about the fact that it is this idea of consequences being a deterrent that makes Roxaboxen humorous when little Anna May is always speeding. The story says "you'd think she liked to go to jail." In real life it would be unusual for anyone to enjoy being in jail; perhaps she just liked going fast. So, there are rules (or laws) to help keep order, and consequences like fines or jail for the public protection if someone cannot seem to keep the rules. The rules are set by the people of the town through the voting process.

Also, a town has a government structure with a person who acts as head of that government, usually called a mayor. Often the building where the mayor works is called the town hall. In *Roxaboxen*, Marian was the mayor, perhaps because she was the oldest or maybe because she had natural leadership skills. Are you more of a leader or a follower? How would your student describe himself in this area of relationships? How about others you know? What attributes do you and your student think make a good leader? A good follower? Both good leaders and good followers are needed to make a town (or any group of people) run smoothly!

Language Arts: Writing a Story from Third Person Point of View

Alice McLerran writes the story of *Roxaboxen* from the **third person point of view**. Your student may have studied some of the *Five in a Row* story lessons on first person point of view in *Night of the Moonjellies* (FIAR Vol. 1), *Owl Moon* and *All Those Secrets of the World* (FIAR Vol. 2), and *The Wild Horses of Sweetbriar* (FIAR Vol. 3). If you have any of these books available, read a few pages of the story to remind your student what first person point of view sounds like. Such a story is told by a character in the story using words like "I," "mine," or "it happened to me."

However, in *Roxaboxen* the story is *not* told by a character but rather by someone outside of the story. That someone is called the story's narrator. In other words, someone outside the story is telling or narrating the story. Read some of *Roxaboxen* and then part of another story written in first person and see if your student can easily tell the difference. If your student is able to understand the difference, let him write a paragraph or short story from third person point of view like Alice McLerran did in *Roxaboxen*. But, if the lesson is still too difficult, let it be just an introduction to the idea of third person point of view.

Language Arts: Reading - Inferring, Wondering and Exploring

Marian digs up a box filled with black pebbles. Ask your student how he thinks the box of pebbles became buried. Where did they come from? Let him consider the question for a moment. (It could be a child from years ago had played in the same place and buried his box of treasured black pebbles. Unless Marian hid the box to find it and surprise everyone, no one else had known that the box of stones even existed. If they had, they would have said so.) You may never know exactly how the box of stones came to be there, but isn't it fun to wonder?

Did you ever find a buried treasure of any kind? Has your student? We never know when, but if we are observant we may find something special, too. Has your student ever seen someone using a metal detector to find items buried beneath the ground or on the beach? Many types of items have been discovered in this manner!

Art: Inspiration and Memories

Don't miss the fact that Barbara Cooney took the then-eighty-year-old Frances back to Roxaboxen to help the illustrator imagine what Roxaboxen must have been like from a true Roxaboxenite! This information is found in the artist's information at the end of the book. Discuss with your student how difficult it would have been for an artist to capture the wonder, color, action, excitement and imagination of Roxaboxen if she had never been there. Does your student think Barbara Cooney's pictures are better because she went to all the work to visit the actual site and listen to Frances' memories before she drew the pictures?

Artists often get inspiration from visiting a locale in person before illustrating a story. (Garth Williams visited every site where Laura Ingalls Wilder had lived before illustrating her *Little House* book series.) Maybe your student would like to pick a topic to write about—one where he can visit before he writes or illustrates his story. For instance, if he wanted to write an article about fishing at a certain lake, he could visit the lake before he wrote the story. Or perhaps a new store he has wanted to visit could be the theme of his story. Have him outline what he thinks he might write about and then after visiting and writing, have him look back and see how much richer his work is because of the first-hand visit.

If you have more than one student doing this assignment, let them compare their work to notice what different things they each see at the site.

Art: Traditional Colors of the Southwest

With your student, spend a few minutes enjoying the picture on the title page. It is rich in the colors of the Southwest, mountains in the background and ocotillo bushes on each side. Isn't it a beautiful picture?

Traditionally there are certain colors associated with the Southwestern states of the United States. In art, pictures of home decorating in the Southwestern style, and in advertisements for products and places of the Southwest you will often see some traditional colors used. These colors tend to be the colors Barbara Cooney uses on the title page illustration, the illustration showing the jail, and throughout the scenes of *Roxaboxen*. Often traditional colors of the Southwest are rich in oranges, reds and terra cotta, browns, teal and dark blues, pinks and purples, sage and dark greens, which reflect the colors of the sunsets and dawns and the various plants that grow there.

Using a large box of crayons, a large paint chart (from an art supply store), or paint chips from a home improvement store, have fun trying to match the colors from Cooney's paintings to the sample colors or crayons. For added fun, use a large set of watercolors (such as the Prang 16-color set) and try mixing to obtain the colors you wish to match.

Again, as you and your student see examples of Southwestern color combinations in art, advertising, decorating shows and stores, stop and enjoy the colors and reminisce about the desert sunsets in *Roxaboxen*!

Art: Detail

By the end of the week your student may be able to look back at the cover of this story and now be able to identify the ocotillo spears. Your reading student will perhaps see the flag that says Fort Irene.

Art: Design Your Own Roxaboxen

Even if you choose not to play pretend and set up a similar play town like Roxaboxen, your student might enjoy drawing such a town, designing the buildings and thinking about town growth. You could design your town in an aerial view as seen from above, or in perspective drawing with different pages for different directions. Your student could also have different pages to reflect the original site and then town growth in various stages. Let him design the town any way he wishes and have fun in that place of imagination!

Just as Frances designed her own space when she moved to her new house, your student can also do a drawing plan for just a single home space and decorate it any way he likes.

Math: Grouping, Borrowing and Skip Counting

Marion digs up a box filled with round black pebbles. Find some kind of round-ish black stones (gardening store or hobby store), black beans, etc., and put them in a tin box. Let your student use these *Roxaboxen* units to work on appropriate math concepts. Math is more *fun* (that means easier to learn) when it is tied to something that stirs the imagination!

Math: Seasons - Numbers in Months and Days

Since Roxaboxen talks about the seasons, use this as a springboard to review number concepts about days in a week, in a month, in a year, and also in a season (like from September 21 to December 21. Don't forget the month of February during leap year!)

Science: Rivers in the Desert?

Marian names the curving road, River Rhode, because it is like a curving river. Then the text says you have to ford the river to reach Roxaboxen. Maybe there was a real river or stream in that place or perhaps a dry stream bed that only has water during brief thunderstorms. However, it is also possible that River Rhode is strictly an imaginary river and they only pretend to cross or "ford" the river to get to their play town.

Either way, what does it mean to ford a river? To ford a river is to cross it by means of walking, driving, floating a raft, etc. Sometimes it isn't safe to ford a river by walking, driving or swimming because of the strong currents that rivers often have. Assure your student that it is *extremely important* to find out about any water that he might have to cross. He might ask people who know the river to tell him about any dangers, or be able to find information at a conservation headquarters.

How else can you cross a deep river? You can use a boat, a raft, or a ferry. (If you want to extend this list in humor, you could also swing over the river on a rope or vine, wear stilts, develop some type of hovercraft or an airboat like they use in the Everglades, etc.) If you must walk across unfamiliar water it is essential that you take along a staff or walking stick to continually probe the water ahead of you to test for depth.

Science: Desert - Biome

Though many think the defining characteristic of a desert is a place of extreme heat, the first factor is actually the amount of rainfall. Deserts receive very little rain. There are some deserts in the world with no recorded rainfall. The necessary moisture for these areas to support any plant or animal life comes from thick fog that occurs now and then. Other desert areas have short, sometimes violent periods of precipitation and then long stretches with no rainfall at all.

Find a simple children's book on deserts and read through and discuss the many facets of desert life: heat and cold, plants and animals that can live with little water, animal behavior in extreme climates, the places of deserts in the world, mirages, etc.

In the story of *Roxaboxen*, some of the elements of desert life you can talk about, search for, and identify are: large expanses of dirt (sand) and stones, ocotillo plants, various scrub brush type plants, prickly pear cactus and other cacti, and succulents, a lizard, and a hummingbird.

Science: A Simple Machine or Not a Simple Machine?

Previously in *Five in a Row* Vol. 1, we've talked about simple machines. Simple machines help us do work more easily. Can your student remember some of the six simple machines and give an example of how they are used? They are: lever, wedge, wheel and axle, pulley, inclined plane, and screw (spiral inclined plane).

Does your student remember Big Jim in *Who Owns the Sun*? (Vol. 1). Big Jim uses a lever to pry up and move large rocks. Big Jim also uses an ax to cut down trees and the ax head is a wedge. You may not have talked about the wheel and axle which moved *Mr. Gumpy's Motor Car* (Vol. 2), or about the fact that places which are wheelchair accessible often make use of the inclined plane in place of steps, like in *Gramma's Walk* (Vol. 3), but you can mention these uses of simple machines now.

In *Roxaboxen*, we see children running around holding wheels and pretending to be driving. The question is, are these wheels a simple machine? Ask your student if the wheel can actually do any work or is there some part missing. For wheels to be a simple machine they need an axle to actually get any work done.

Science: Seasons

As the story of *Roxaboxen* is a reminiscing style of story, Alice McLerran chooses to tell the memory through the passing of the seasons. In this book we see the passing of the seasons of nature and also the different seasons of life from childhood to old age. Ask your student to name the seasons. Can he tell you what three months traditionally are included in each of the four seasons? If he doesn't know, just introduce this concept now.

Take a moment to discuss the seasons of nature. You could have your student fold an 8 1/2 by 11-inch piece of paper into half and then into half again to make four boxes. In each box have him write (and he may also want to illustrate) six natural elements of each of the four seasons. For instance, in the spring box one student might put: first flowers blooming, warm days/cool nights, heavy precipitation, new leaves on trees, birds' first nesting, peas and new potatoes from the garden. A winter box might include: bare tree branches, cold days and nights, snow, many birds have migrated, gray clouds, brown grass. Obviously the things observed and noted by your student will reflect what the seasons are like where he lives, since fall in southern California is not the same as fall in Vermont.

Another way to study this topic is to take a single season and study it more thoroughly than you have before. One of the ideas you might bring up is the terms **autumnal** and **vernal equinoxes** (the first day of fall and spring) and of the **winter** and **summer solstices** (the first day of winter and summer) and their approximate dates.

If you have already done these types of lessons before and had a quick review, you may wish to introduce the idea that the seasons are reversed in the Southern Hemisphere. (The first day of the summer season is around Dec. 21.)

Science: Precious Stones and Desert Glass

Remind your student of the part in *Roxaboxen* where Frances makes her home surrounded by desert glass and it is called a house of jewels. Your student may be interested in the fact that blowing, moving dirt and sand can wear away rough edges of glass and leave rounded pieces of colored glass which sometimes *look* like precious stones or jewels.

When people speak about precious stones (which are called gemstones when they are cut and polished) they usually mean those which are the most rare and therefore the most expensive, such as diamonds, emeralds, rubies, and sapphires. Semi-precious stones might include topaz, opal, amethyst, etc.

What the children find in the story *Roxaboxen* is desert glass: ordinary pieces of bottles, etc., and pieces of glass that have been smoothed and polished by the grit, and sand over long periods of time. They may have the colors of some semi-precious stones but they are just glass. These bits and pieces of glass are not exceptionally valuable except to those with imagination!

Go-Along Story: *My Great Aunt Arizona*, by Gloria Houston. The connection to *Roxaboxen* is only the name of the state—Arizona. The character in this go-along story is given her name by her brother who is living in Arizona and thinks it a beautiful place. This girl, who is named for the state, never lives there. But with the connection of the name Arizona it makes this a great time to read *My Great Aunt Arizona,* which is reminiscent of *Miss Rumphius* and *Island Boy* by Barbara Cooney.

Teacher's Notes

The *Five in a Row* lesson options for each unit in the manual are all you need to teach your child. The additional resource area provided below is simply a place to jot down relevant info you've found that you might want to reference.

ROXABOXEN

Date:

Student:

Five in a Row **Lesson Topics Chosen:**

Social Studies:

Language Arts:

Art:

Math:

Science:

Relevant Library Resources: Books, DVDs, Audio Books

Websites or Video Links:

Related Field Trip Opportunities:

Favorite Quote or Memory During Study:

Name:
Date:
Geography: **Arizona Flag**

The flag of Arizona is divided in half horizontally. The top half looks like a setting sun, consisting of thirteen (these represent America's thirteen original colonies) alternating red and yellow rays (starting and ending with red). The bottom half of the flag is the same blue color as the blue in the United States flag. The middle of the flag has a copper colored star centered over the top and bottom half. The copper color represents Arizona's copper production which is the largest in the United States. Your student might also enjoy drawing and coloring the Fort Irene flag from the story! *For more information, see Parts of a Flag on page 266.*

Color in the Arizona flag below.

Name:

Date:

Social Studies: **Geography - Four Corners Monument**

Four Corners Monument

Does your student know that Arizona is one of the "Four Corners" states? Arizona, New Mexico, Colorado and Utah have shared boundaries that all touch at a single point. Look at a map and discover how this works. A person can stand at one place and technically be in all four of these states at once!

This is a great opportunity to take a virtual field trip and explore the Four Corners Monument. Help your student search online for photos or use Google Earth to see the place where four states meet.

Print your photos and add them in the spaces below.

Name:

Date:

Science: **Desert - Biome**

Below you will find questions that can be used to learn more about desert biomes.

1. What causes a desert biome ecosystem to form?

____

2. What percentage of the Earth is made up of deserts?

____

3. What are the four major types of deserts?

    1. ___________________________________
    2. ___________________________________
    3. ___________________________________
    4. ___________________________________

List any additional facts or information you have learned about desert biomes below.

____

____

____

____

____

____

____

____

____

The Tree Lady

Title:	*The Tree Lady*
Author:	H. Joseph Hopkins
Illustrator:	Jill McElmurry
Copyright:	2013

Social Studies: Geography - Northern California

Katherine Sessions' childhood and schooling years were spent in Northern California. The area is typically defined as the area north of the Tehachapi Mountains (although there are other ways that the area is sometimes divided). Today, it includes the San Francisco Bay area which includes the cities of San Francisco, Oakland, San Jose and Sacramento (the state capital).

Northern California's diverse geography ranges from sandy beaches along the coast to the snow-capped Sierra Nevada Mountains. Yosemite National Park (displayed on the back of the California State quarter) and Kings Canyon/Sequoia National Park are just two majestic and beautiful areas you can find in Northern California. This area is where Katherine first learned to love nature.

Social Studies: Geography - Forests - Redwoods

Katherine Sessions loved trees! *The Tree Lady* talks about many different kinds of trees. At the beginning of the book when Kate was growing up in Northern California, she collected needles from pines and redwoods. Redwood trees are from the sequoia tree family which include giant redwoods and giant sequoias. Both trees occur naturally only in California.

These two trees differ in the climate they require to grow well. Giant redwood trees thrive in moist conditions and therefore grow closer to the Northern California coastline. Giant sequoia trees thrive in higher elevations (5,000-7,000 feet) and only grow naturally on the western foothills of the Sierra Nevada Mountains.

Redwoods can grow up to 378 feet tall, while sequoias grow up to 311 feet. Sequoias claim the largest tree in the world, known as General Sherman; this tree weighs in at 2.7 million pounds! It's 275 feet tall and more than 100 feet wide at its base. Wow, that's big!

Take a second and think about these trees compared to something your student might be familiar with: a football field. A football field is 360 feet long and 160 feet wide. Redwoods can grow taller than the length of a football field!

Social Studies: Geography - Southern California (San Diego)

When Katherine had graduated college she moved to Southern California. Today, this area includes Los Angeles and San Diego as well as other metropolitan areas. It also includes the coastline from Santa Barbara to the Mexico border. The area is typically defined as the area south of the Tehachapi Mountains. Its diverse geography ranges from sandy beaches along the coast to mountain ranges and desert areas which include Death Valley and the Mojave Dessert.

Social Studies: Geography - Desert Regions

When Kate moved to Southern California she found her natural environment desert-like and very different from what she knew growing up in Northern California. Desert areas are areas of land where little precipitation occurs. What does your student think of when she pictures a desert? Sand dunes, perhaps? Some deserts are entirely sand while others are rocky and some even have large areas of drought-resistant plant life.

Deserts often have extreme temperature differences between day and night. This extreme shift from hot to cold plays a part in the formations of the desert. Rocks become hot during the day and then as they quickly get cold at night it strains them and they break apart, creating dust and sand.

Plants and animals that live in desert regions have special ways of conserving water. Most desert plants are small and wiry having few or no leaves. Some long-living plants have very deep roots that tap into underground water sources. Desert animals have special ways of dealing with the heat and lack of water, as well. Some are nocturnal, staying underground or in shade during the daytime heat and venturing out at night when it's cooler.

The kangaroo rat is a wonderful example of a desert animal that has special ways of dealing with its habitat. It doesn't ever have to drink water because it's able to get all the liquid it needs from its diet of seeds. They also have special pouches on the outside of their cheeks for transporting seeds back to their burrows

A great resource book to read and study with your student if she wants to learn more about deserts is *Cactus Desert: One Small Square* by Donald Silver.

Social Studies: What Defines a Park?

"From her school, Kate could see City Park in the hills above town. It was called a park, but it didn't look like one."

Ask your student if she agrees with Kate that the view from the school window doesn't look much like a park. The bare brown hills with trash and cows certainly don't resemble what we think of as a park. Ask your student to make a list of what things she thinks make an area into a park. The list might include grass, trees, play equipment, etc. Have your student draw or paint a picture of what she would want at a park—it can be simple or elaborate.

A dictionary definition of the type of park described in *The Tree Lady* is "a piece of public land in or near a city that is kept free of houses and other buildings and can be used for pleasure and exercise."

Technically, City Park was a park but it lacked the beauty that Kate had grown up with in Northern California. Kate knew what City Park could become and she worked hard to make it a place where people could come and walk in cool shade and see beautiful trees. She created a space that would be a pleasure to those using it. Balboa Park (previously City Park) is world renowned today because of Kate's vision and perseverance to create a beautiful park for San Diego. Be sure to look online for pictures of what this famous park looks like today!

Social Studies: History - Timeline of Katherine Olivia Sessions' Life

Your older student might enjoy making a timeline of important dates in Kate's life and the story. If she researches other female contemporaries of Sessions (as in the next lesson) she can plot their lives out along the same timeline.

1857 - Katherine Olivia Sessions was born
1860s - Growing up in Northern California
1881 - Graduated from University of California with a degree in science; took job in San Diego after graduation
1909 - Announcement that the Panama-California Exposition was coming
1915-1917 - Panama-California Exposition was held
1940 - Katherine Olivia Sessions, known as the Mother of Balboa Park, died.

Social Studies: History - A Female Contemporary of Katherine Sessions

Older students might want to check out books or do research on a few of Katherine Sessions' female contemporaries. Below is a story of a woman that lived, studied and worked around the same time as Katherine Sessions, and she too persevered despite delays and difficulties to do what she loved.

Lucy Hobbs Taylor (1833–1910) was the first American female to become a dentist. She worked as a teacher for 10 years before deciding she wanted to be a dentist. She was denied admittance to dental school (because she was a woman) but began an independent study with a professor from the Ohio College of Dental Surgery. She opened her own dental practice in 1861 and four years later was admitted to the Ohio College of Dental Surgery. She earned her doctorate in dentistry there in 1866. Just 34 years later, in 1900, almost 1,000 women had followed her into the field of dentistry.

There are many, many women during the 1850-1950 timeframe who pushed through difficulties and opposition to follow their dreams and open doors for the girls and women who followed in their footsteps. If this topic interests your student, help her research other famous women and their accomplishments.

Social Studies: Career Choices

Katherine loved trees, even as a child! She loved science and learning and after graduating she became a teacher. Becoming a teacher was a good career choice because it was something that was readily available to women at the time and brought her love of science and learning into her job. However, she *really* loved trees! After teaching for two years, she was able to become a gardener. This gave her an opportunity to work around and with what she loved most.

We aren't always able to choose our career based purely on doing something we love, but we can always try to find a job that includes bits and pieces of things that are important to us.

Discuss with your student what things she loves doing (make a list or draw pictures) and discuss how those passions might be found or incorporated into different careers or jobs (make a list of possible jobs). For example, if your student loves drawing and painting, she could become an artist, illustrator or graphic designer, or she might become an art teacher!

Social Studies: History - Place Names

San Francisco is near the college where Kate graduated. After college Kate took a job in San Diego. "San" is Spanish for Saint. This is a great opportunity for older students to explore the Spanish influence in California including the missions, as well as the resulting city names. If your student likes making or reading lists, she might also enjoy looking online to see the long list of cities in California (or in the U.S. in general) that begin with San, Santa, or Saint.

Social Studies: History - World Expositions and Fairs

Katherine learned there was to be a Panama-California Exposition coming to City Park, later known as Balboa Park. World expositions (also called Expos and World's Fairs) originally began in Europe and later came to America as a way to encourage tourism and as a chance for people to see what was happening in the wold of industry, trade, art and design. Inventions such as the telephone, the zipper, electricity and the x-ray machine were all introduced to the public at World's Fairs or Expos.

Some of your student's favorite foods might have been invented because of a World Fair. The ice cream cone, for example, was first introduced at the 1904 St. Louis World's Fair. Several vendors at the fair decided that they needed an ice cream container that people could take with them and not have to bring back or throw away, and thus the ice cream cone was introduced.

The hot dog bun was also introduced at the 1904 St. Louis World's Fair. A sausage vendor asked his brother-in-law to create a sausage-length bun after he ran out of gloves that he gave to people to keep their hands from becoming greasy as they ate the sausages. Now we can hardly imagine having a sausage/brat/hot dog without a bun.

Social Studies: Asking for Help

Kate knew that Balboa Park needed more trees, "thousands more," to make it beautiful and shady for the people who would be coming to the fair. She knew that she couldn't plant that many trees alone. Kate knew that if lots of people helped, then they could work together and plant all the trees they would need.

Ask your student what she would do if she had a big job that she knew she couldn't do by herself. Discuss why sometimes asking for help can be hard. We might wish that we could do it ourselves. We might not want to inconvenience someone else. We might think that they won't want to help us.

Kate was a leader! People followed her example and wanted to help her. Being a leader doesn't mean you can't or don't ask for help; it means that you're able to show others what needs to be done and ask in a way that others want to follow you and help.

Kate did an amazing thing ... she didn't just ask for help planting trees, she planned tree-planting *parties*! She made it fun! It says, "Again and again, people volunteered to help." People wanted to help and even helped many times because Kate made it enjoyable.

We can't always make it fun for those helping us, but it's a great thing to remember and try to do when we can. Discuss with your student ways you could make helping each other fun. What do you need help with and how could it be fun? Maybe you could plan a time to work together cleaning the house—you could make it a dance cleaning party and play fun music loudly while you pick up or dust!

Social Studies: Perseverance

The last two sentences of the book are the perfect example of Katherine's perseverance. "Back then, few could have imagined that San Diego would become the lush, leafy city it is today. **But *all along, year after year*, Katherine Olivia Sessions did**." Katherine never gave up.

After graduating from college, Katherine took a job in Southern California and found herself in a place that she never thought she'd be: a city with very few trees. She loved trees! Ask your student if she can think of something she really loves? (a kind of food, a special place, forests, mountains, or the ocean if you live near those things). Then have her imagine moving to a place and the thing she loves isn't there ... how would she feel? What would she do?

Look at the illustration of Katherine as she arrives in Southern California. She has her back to us and is looking out onto the desert landscape. How does your student think she might be feeling?

Perseverance is defined as steadfastness in doing something despite difficulty or delay in achieving success. Katherine had perseverance. After reading through the book several times, have your student make a list of the times when Katherine did something even when others said she shouldn't, couldn't or that it wouldn't happen.

Examples: Kate got dirty even when girls weren't supposed to. Kate studied science when most girls were discouraged from doing so. Almost every page ends with an example of Kate's perseverance!

Language Arts: Using a Short Sentence for Emphasis

There are many different ways for an author to emphasize a point when writing: repetition, active voice and exclamatory sentences are just a few. The author of *The Tree Lady* has chosen to use very short sentences at the end of each page to put emphasis on Kate's perseverance throughout her life.

A short sentence must include a subject and a verb to be a complete sentence. Using a very short sentence will grab the reader's attention! Because the reader is used to longer sentences that flow, a short sentence is almost a jab to our senses—it startles us and makes us take notice.

Have your student point out the shortest sentence on each page of *The Tree Lady*. She will likely see the pattern form: the shortest sentence on each page is the last sentence. Have your student dictate or write a short paragraph about something she loves and end it using a short sentence to create emphasis. It's fun!

Language Arts: Repetition

The author of *The Tree Lady* also used repetition to emphasize Kate's perseverance. The final sentence (or idea) on each page throughout the book is short and repetitive. "But Kate did."

This sentence appears, word for word, five times in the story. Variations of it, "But she did," "they did" and "it did" also appear many times. The repetition used in *The Tree Lady* creates a literary refrain—that refrain is, ***she did***. Kate was active, she didn't sit around and wish things were different, she did things, despite the fact that they were discouraged ... Kate *did* things, she persevered despite opposition and difficulty and the author chose to use short sentences and repetition to highlight this important part of the story.

Language Arts: Literature - Vocabulary

In addition to the word "perseverance" mentioned in the above lessons, any of the vocabulary words below could be introduced as they relate to *The Tree Lady*. These words are not found in the text, but fit with the subject of this book. For younger children you might just choose one or two to discuss.

Arbor Day A holiday celebrated on the last Friday in April in which individuals and groups are encouraged to plant trees.

arboretum A collection or botanical garden composed of trees and sometimes woody plants.

arborist One who studies and cares for trees as a profession.

horticulture The art or practice of garden cultivation as well as managing a garden.

horticulturist A professional gardener.

Language Arts: Literary Theme - Perseverance

Many Five in a Row book selections highlight the character trait of perseverance. If your student used *Before Five in a Row* in her preschool years, she may remember reading *The Carrot Seed* by Ruth Krauss.

The young boy in *The Carrot Seed* planted a seed. One at a time, everyone that came by told him, "It won't come up." Each time the boy simply watered or weeded or waited. Eventually, after a *long* time, the carrot came up! This boy demonstrated perseverance when no one around him, young or old, thought he could succeed. Talk with your student about how the scenario from *The Carrot Seed* is like the theme of *The Tree Lady*. Then discuss how to respectfully and kindly continue trying things that one thinks are important. How can discouragement be overcome? It might be fun to revisit this book and the *Before Five in a Row* character lesson now that your student is much older!

Language Arts: Greek and Latin Word Roots

Kate used a microscope to study science in school. The word microscope comes from the Greek words mikrós which means *small*, and skopeîn which means *to see*. Microscope therefore means to see something that is small.

It's never too early to start a list of Greek or Latin word roots for your student to remember and review (You can start a list with the activity sheet at the end of this unit.) Greek and Latin roots of words are often found in the English language and knowing their meanings can help your student make meaningful connections between the English word and its meaning. As you come across words with Greek or Latin roots in books you read together, add them to your list and occasionally review any words you've learned with your student.

Language Arts: Literature - Go-Along Books

A Gardener's Alphabet by Mary Azarian. This unique alphabet book has many beautifully illustrated gardening words, including such words as topiary and xeriscape.

Grandpa Green by Lane Smith. A most imaginative and glorious look into a man and his life via topiary. This Caldecott Honor book is also available as a digital Mini Unit study on the Five in a Row website!

Art: Point of View

The image on the dust jacket cover as well as the double page of the same image in the book are illustrated using an aerial viewpoint, overhead view or bird's eye view. This point of view technique is used in art to show something from an elevated viewpoint; one directly overhead, as if a bird was flying over an object and you were seeing it from the bird's eye. This is also the perspective that is used to create maps.

Discuss with your student why the illustrator might have used a bird's eye view to show Kate and the forest? There could be many correct answers, but the text also gives us a clue to the point of view choice the illustrator made. The story says, "Kate felt the trees were her friends. She loved the way they reached toward the sky...". Perhaps the illustrator was showing the trees reaching toward the sky, or maybe she wanted to represent how tall the trees were. With Kate looking tiny on the floor of the forest you can begin to see how big the trees might have been. They look huge!

Have your student try drawing something from a bird's eye view. Maybe she can even try looking at something that way. Place an object on the floor and then climb a ladder above it and look directly down onto the object. What does she see? Is the whole object visible or is she only seeing the top of the object? Then have her try to draw what she sees.

Art: Focal Point

The focal point is something that draws your attention to the most important part of a piece of artwork. There are things that an artist can do to help create a successful focal point in their piece. The use of contrast, structure, color and shapes can all help to define an area as a focal point.

In the bird's eye view illustration of Kate lying on the ground in the forest, the artist used three of those components to create a dramatic focal point. There is contrast between the dark trees and bushes and the light grass area where Kate is lying. The structure of a piece tells our eyes where to look; in this image the lines of the trees draw your eyes down to the circle. Lastly, the illustrator used a clean circle shape in the midst of all the other lines and shapes on the page to define the focal point of her illustration.

Look through magazines, other books or artwork with your student and see if together you can find other images or illustrations with a strong focal point. See if the artist used contrast, structure, color or shape to draw your eyes to the focal point. Now have your student draw, paint or collage a piece of art using some of these tools to create a strong focal point.

Art: Dust Jacket and Book Cover

If you're able to look under or remove the dust jacket of *The Tree Lady*, notice that the illustrator or book designer chose to place a different illustration on the cover of the dust jacket than she did on the cover of the actual book. Often the dust jacket image is the same as image on the book cover.

Discuss with your student why someone might have chosen to use two different illustrations. Maybe the illustrator had an illustration that she loved which didn't make it into the book but she wanted a way to include it? Perhaps she thought it would be a surprise for the reader to discover a different image under the dust jacket?

This brings up another interesting discussion point, which is covered in the next lesson ... the differences between an illustrator and a graphic designer.

Art: Illustration and Graphic Design

Your student probably knows all about book illustrators. An illustrator creates the art/images that appear in the books your child reads. An illustrator usually has fine art training including painting and drawing. They create a single element, an image or a set of images that can stand alone (fine art paintings or drawings) or can be combined with other elements (like text) by a graphic designer. When an illustration or illustrations are combined by a graphic designer with text, the combination can become a book, a menu, a poster, a greeting card or many other things.

Sometimes an illustrator creates their images first and then writes or has someone else write a story to go with their images. Other times, someone will write a story and then find an illustrator to create images that represent or illustrate the written story.

A graphic designer may have some fine art training but their education is heavier in layout design (the use of space to balance several elements working together), color theory (how colors work together) and typography (how letters/words look on the page). They mainly use computer design programs to bring artistic elements together into a new piece of art that is designed to convey a message or an idea. You could compare a graphic designer to someone putting a puzzle together; they take many different pieces (color, type/words, art) and put them together in a way to create a complete image.

Let your student try out being an illustrator and a graphic designer. First, have her draw or paint something—this is how most illustrators do their job. Then have her try her hand at graphic design. Collage is a great way to work like a graphic designer (without having to use a computer) by bringing multiple elements together into a new piece of art. Using her drawing or painting and adding words or letters printed or cut from or newspapers, along with other images or colors, have your student make a new design with all of these pieces together. This is similar to how graphic designers do their job (they just use a computer to bring the elements together). After experimenting with these two types of art, ask your student if she enjoys being an illustrator or a graphic designer more and why?

Art: Design a Dream Garden

If there is interest, and if your student has favorite plants, trees, shrubs, flowers, etc., or even using imaginary ones, she could design a "dream" garden. Your older student can design her dream garden on graph paper using an aerial view, while younger students can draw with colored pencils, or use paint to illustrate their wonder garden. You could even find gardening magazines or catalogs and have your student cut and paste a "dream" garden collage.

Art: Prints, Chains, and Decorative Arrangements

Inspired by the hand prints at the beginning of *The Tree Lady*, your student could make some handprints of her own. Or you can use potato carving techniques to make prints of your student's own design. It is easy to make a leaf print with tempera by pressing the painted leaf onto paper, or your student can do a rubbing of an interesting leaf she's found while on a nature walk.

Kate O. Sessions made beautiful necklaces with the bits of nature she found around her. Has your student ever made a dandelion necklace in the spring, or a daisy chain or clover blossom necklace in the summer? She could try one, just like Kate! Even if you don't have flowers available, a small shell or a little stone with a hole in it could go on a cord, for a nature souvenir.

While most people think of arrangements as "floral" arrangements, there are many pretty grasses, pine cones and other bits of nature that make lovely arrangements on a table and bring back good memories of being outdoors.

And for another project, begin with a salad-sized plate and put a white paper doily on it. Next, scatter some pretty ferns and perhaps a violet blossom or two (in spring) or petals from seasonal flowers. Finally place a clear plastic or glass plate on top and use the plates for a lunch or dessert. Voilà! Beautiful decorations from nature!

Math: Time in Days, Months and Years

The Panama-California Exposition was announced in 1909 and was held in 1915. How long did Kate have to plant the thousands of trees that she wanted for the fair?

For a younger student you can simply talk about how many years Kate had to get ready. Using addition, count up from 1909 until 1915 (six years). Older students can use multiplication to figure out how many months or even how many days the six years gave Kate and her friends to plant all those trees.

Math: Fractions

Read the author's note on the final page of the book and you'll learn some wonderful facts about Katherine Sessions and her life's work that weren't covered in the story. One interesting thing that's mentioned in the second paragraph is that by the early 1900s, one in four trees growing in San Diego came from Kate's nursery.

To illustrate this point, have your student draw a picture of four trees. Then have them circle one of the four. You can discuss fractions and how "one in four" can be shown as a picture (like theirs) or in fraction form as 1/4 (one over four) or as 25%. You can mention that we can call it one-fourth or one-quarter (quarter meaning 25%, or 25/100). This is a great introduction to basic fractions and the different ways we can say and show them.

Science: Tree Nursery

When Kate became a gardener she had a tree nursery where she planted seeds and tended the trees until they became large enough to plant around the city. A nursery is a place where gardeners can plant and take care of seeds and seedlings (small trees), giving them what they need to grow big and strong until they are ready to be transplanted. Some nurseries are outdoors and some are inside greenhouses.

Greenhouses or glass houses have a glass or plastic roof and walls. They absorb the sunlight which creates warm air inside that can't easily escape. They are often used in colder climates or during winter months to create a warm environment to start growing seeds and seedlings before they would be able to be planted outside.

Your student may know the term nursery as it relates to a room or place for babies. Comparing the two and discussing that seeds and seedlings are like babies and need special care might help your student remember that places for growing and caring for young plants and trees is called a nursery.

Visit a nearby plant nursery and notice if it's in a greenhouse or outdoors. What kinds of plants or trees are growing there? You could even have your student pick a small plant from the nursery to bring home and grow. Succulent plants are often found in greenhouse nurseries and can make a great starter plant for your student to grow at home. Succulent plants retain more water in their thicker, fleshier leaves than other plants and can live in dry and arid climates (desert areas) similar to San Diego. They don't need to be watered very often and can grow in gravel with a small amout of soil. You can find small succulents that aren't spiny (not a cactus) that can be planted in a small pot or bowl. Talk with the nursery workers and find a small succulent that would brighten your kitchen or school room and allow your student to flex her green thumb.

Science: Gardening

There are many types of gardens, and many methods of gardening. Katherine Sessions researched and developed gardens in areas that were hot and dry. Other gardeners grow their works in other climates. Also, besides shrubs and trees, some gardeners grow vegetables, roses, perennial and annual flowers, or specialize in things like cacti or prairie grasses. If your student has a "love of growing things" there are many fields, topics and methods for her to explore.

There is an illustration by Jill McElmurry just a few pages from the end of the *The Tree Lady* that shows four gardening implements (tools). Pictured from left to right are a hoe, a pitchfork, a shovel, and a rake. Does your student know what each of these gardening tools are used for? Can she name any other common outdoor tools?

Glance through seed or gardening catalogs which you can gather from gardening stores for students to enjoy seeing all the different variety of plants that can be grown in a garden.

Science: Latin Names for Trees - Genus, Species

While in school as a young girl, Kate loved studying science and especially trees! On the third page of our book (opposite the page with all the school desks) we see tree names written out in Latin. Why are there Latin names for plants and trees? Well, we usually call plants and trees by common names ... such as maple tree or rose. Latin names are needed because they are very specific, whereas common names for the same flower or tree might vary from one area of the country (or the world) to another. Several different plants could even be called the same common name.

Giving a plant or tree a Latin name will keep it from being confused with a different plant or tree. Latin names also give clues about the plant or tree if you pay attention and learn the Latin meanings. For example, they can tell you where a plant is from, or the color and the shape of the plant.

A Latin name for a plant or animal contains two parts, the **genus** and the **species**. For example, the Latin name for the common red maple tree is *Acer rubrum*. The genus is the first of the two words, Acer, which refers to the family or group of maple trees. The species is the second word, rubrum, which defines the tree as one specific tree out of the bigger group, a *red* maple. The Latin word rubrum means red, so in this case it's telling us the color of the maple tree.

Have your student look online to find the common names for the three Latin tree names in *The Tree Lady*. (From left to right, they are: coast live oak, American elm and giant sequoia.)

Science: Microscope

We can see in the illustrations that Kate used a microscope to study science in school. As mentioned in the Language Arts: Greek and Latin Word Roots lesson, the word microscope comes from the Greek words mikrós which means *small*, and skopeîn which means *to see*. Microscope therefore means to see something that is small.

Scientists use microscopes to see things that can't be seen by looking at them with the naked eye and to study those things in detail. If you have access to a microscope you can gather leaves or other things from nature or from around the house (salt, sugar, etc.) and study them under the microscope.

You can also purchase small handheld microscopes online or at science or teaching stores. These take up less space and are not too expensive but will allow your student to see things up close.

If you don't have access to a microscope of any kind, check some books out from your library about microscopes and things seen through a microscope. Some libraries even have microscopes you can check out to use at home.

Science: Photosynthesis

When Kate studied science in college she learned how plants ate and drank. A plant drinks by drawing water up from the soil through its root system. **Photosynthesis** is the process by which plants make food. Water, sunlight, minerals and carbon dioxide are all absorbed by the plant either through the roots or into the leaves. The plant is then able to turn those things into glucose/sugar which is the energy or food that supports the plant and helps it grow.

That is why plants need sunlight and water to grow. Plants also give off oxygen which they create during the photosynthesis process. This oxygen helps keep our air clean and pure so that we have good air to breathe.

Try an experiment with your students: use three cups from a cardboard egg carton (or plastic cups, or whatever you have available). Place a little potting soil in each cup and plant a sunflower or daisy seed (follow planting instructions for depth). Label the cups A, B and C. Water cups A and B but not C. Place cup A in a place with no natural light (a closet or a bathroom). Place cup B and C in a naturally sunny location (kitchen counter near a window).

Be sure to keep the soil moist on cups A and B. See which cups seed grows most successfully. Cup B should be the only seed to grow successfully, because it was given light, minerals (from the soil), carbon dioxide and water ... all the ingredients a plant needs to grow.

Discuss with your student why the seeds in cup A and C didn't grow or didn't grow as well as the seed in cup B.

Science: Landscaping - Xeriscape

When Kate O. Sessions first observed San Diego's lack of trees and gardens, she might have said, "What is needed here is xeriscaping!" This is one of those big words that younger students do not have to memorize. But they might enjoy saying the word and just listening to what it means. Your older students will be interested in how it is spelled. It's an interesting word isn't it?

Kate Sessions didn't say that word (in 1881) because that word would not come into use for almost seventy years.

Xeriscape is a type of gardening that utilizes plants that can tolerate dry conditions, the spreading of proper mulches, and using minimal efficient irrigation.

Rather than create gardens with species of plants that need to be carefully tended, especially that require lots of water, xeriscape gardening is accomplished with plants, trees and shrubs that can thrive in arid, warm climates.

So even though Kate Sessions pioneered the idea of xeriscaping through researching plants, trees, etc., that grow in dry, warm climates, and though she made a great success of using those plantings to make amazing gardens, the word "xeriscape" to describe her ideas would not come into use and common practice until many years later.

Look online at the landscaping/gardening companies in your area and see if any of them are experts in xeriscape gardening. You could see if they would host a small field trip for your students and talk to them about xeriscaping—which would be the kind of gardening that Kate O. Sessions did so long ago in Southern California!

If your student is keeping a science or nature notebook, have her draw and label some species of plants, shrubs and trees that would do well in a xeriscape garden.

Also, if your student is interested in words and meanings, here are three *words* (they are **not** a prefix or suffix) that she will likely find interesting:

xeric Not needing an abundance of moisture; able to thrive in arid conditions.

hydric Needing an abundance of moisture.

xeriscape Garden with plants that can thrive without much moisture.

Science: Critical Exposure to Nature

What would most probably have happened in Kate's life if she had never been able to spend time outside? She wouldn't have fallen in love with trees. She probably would not have wanted to be a scientist, and the beautiful plantings of Balboa Gardens that came from all her careful research would not have been ready for the Exposition of 1915!

Compared to the early 1900s, many students in the United States today have very little knowledge of their natural surroundings. An emphasis on safety has become a factor preventing children from just wandering about, exploring the creeks, fields, and woods on their own as they used to do. Teachers need to make time for this important aspect of life, and plan walking trips in safe places or with a group, or even guided tours.

In addition to today's perceived dangers curtailing personal nature time, computers, iPads, video games and other electronic entertainments are competing for much of students' free time. The unfortunate result however, is that today's students often have a neglected understanding of the nature that directly surrounds them, or the varieties of nature found in their own countries, or even across the globe.

The failure to understand how the natural elements of the world work robs students of the "peace and joy of soul" nature has been created to give. In this story, Kate Sessions deeply enjoyed the benefits of time spent in natural surroundings. Find pages that show her in nature and how it affected her. In addition, indifference to nature may cause many to see conservation measures as unnecessary. Even simple things like picking up and disposing of trash isn't terribly important to a person who never spends enough time in the outdoors to know and have a passion for pristine beauty.

Check your county wildlife society or association and see if they have programs you and your students could attend to learn more about the nature in your area. Your state may have a conservation department or department of natural resources that teaches and publishes information about the flora and fauna in your particular part of the state.

You may also want to try the *Five in a Row Nature Studies*, one for each season, and available digitally at the Five in a Row website. These beautiful guides have information on a great many topics of nature, as well as tips on things such as microscopes and binoculars, along with titles of great nature books and guides. As the teacher, you'll want to read through the unit on the season to come, getting ready to explain the changes that will take place in that next season. Each of these units have enough information, activities, and sheets to be used for your entire teaching journey as you encourage and inspire your students to fall in love with the world of nature!

Science: Research - Scientific Methods

A simple definition of research is: gathering data, information, or facts to further knowledge.

When Kate became a gardener her passion was trees! She wanted San Diego to be full of trees. The story says, "She knew she must plant trees that could live in dry soil with lots and lots of sunshine."

Kate didn't know what kind of trees would grow well in the hot, dry, desert area of San Diego. Discuss with your student what she would do if she needed to find out information about something. There are certainly different ways to acquire information, and we have easy online access to more answers then we could possibly need. Kate didn't have easy access to find the answers to her questions.

She was a scientist though, and she knew that she could use *scientific methods* to find answers to her questions. She could *observe* (notice) what trees grew in similar climates around the country. She could also *experiment* with growing trees and see if they would grow well in San Diego. She also *asked questions* of people who knew more than she did. She talked with people that lived in different places but had the same kind of weather and soil to see what grew in those areas.

Talk with your student and pick a subject she'd like to learn more about. Discuss how she can observe her subject, how she might find answers to her questions or how she'll gather data, information or facts to further her knowledge. Research is a lifelong skill that takes practice but will be beneficial to your child throughout her education, her career and her life.

Teacher's Notes

The *Five in a Row* lesson options for each unit in the manual are all you need to teach your child. The additional resource area provided below is simply a place to jot down relevant info you've found that you might want to reference.

THE TREE LADY

Date:

Student:

Five in a Row Lesson Topics Chosen:

Social Studies:

Language Arts:

Art:

Math:

Science:

Relevant Library Resources: Books, DVDs, Audio Books

Websites or Video Links:

Related Field Trip Opportunities:

Favorite Quote or Memory During Study:

Name:

Date:

Geography: **California Flag**

The flag of California features the California grizzly bear (once common, now extinct) as a sign of strength; the bear faces left and is standing on a patch of grass. The lone red star is a symbol of sovereignty; the red color of the star and the stripe across the bottom of the flag stand for courage and the white background represents purity. *For more information, see Parts of a Flag on page 266.*

Color in the California flag below.

Name:

Date:

Language Arts: **Greek and Latin Word Roots**

It's never too early to start a list of Greek or Latin word roots for your student to remember and review. Look up the following roots and their meanings, and add some of your own! Have fun seeing how many modern words have been created from Greek and Latin roots.

Greek or Latin Root	Meaning	Example
micro	small	microscope, microchip
scope	to see	telescope, periscope
ped	foot	pedestrian, pedal
naut, nav	relating to the sea	nautical, Navy
therm	heat, temperature	thermometer, thermos
graph		
mal		
bio		
astro		
geo		
ology		
auto		

Name:

Date:

Social Studies: **History - Timeline of Katherine Sessions' Life**

Using the timeline below record important dates in Katherine's life and the story. Research and find other important events and people that were influencing the world during the same time period. If your student researches other female contemporaries of Sessions they can plot their lives out along the same timeline. Add printed pictures if desired and use hash marks along the timeline to represent specific dates and mark accordingly.

1857 **1940**

The Pumpkin Runner

Title:	*The Pumpkin Runner*
Author:	Marsha Diane Arnold
Illustrator:	Brad Sneed
Copyright:	1998
Summary:	Joshua, a man who loves to eat pumpkins, runs a race in Australia that has everyone noticing.

Social Studies: Geography - Australia

Marsha Diane Arnold's idea for the *The Pumpkin Runner* came from a true incident which happened in Australia. Your student has probably heard of Australia, but does he know that it is a **continent** as well as a country? In fact, Australia is the only country that is also a continent. This country is vast in its scope of land types (a great deal of Australia is desert), unusual animals, peoples, history, art, etc. There is far too much of this interesting country to tackle all at once, especially for your younger FIAR student. Find a few interesting facts about Australia to share with him and then have one or two picture books from the library on hand that your student may dip into at his leisure. That way he can be running to *you* with exciting bits of information to share. Remember that there are many years in which you can build on the beginning information about this country. Begin a folder or notebook section for Australia and continue to add to it throughout your student's school career. Now, find Australia on your world map and place your pumpkin story disk somewhere between its cities of Melbourne and Sydney.

For your older student, have him print out or draw a blank map of Australia including its main states and territories, as well as principal cities and the nation's

capital, Canberra. Note, too, such interesting points as the Great Barrier Reef, the central deserts area, Ayers Rock (Uluru), etc.

Social Studies: Geography - Hemispheres

Studying Australia from the story *The Pumpkin Runner* gives you an opportunity to begin or build on your student's knowledge of terms like **hemisphere** and the seasonal changes which exist in the **Southern Hemisphere**. One way to begin a lesson on hemispheres is to mention that the prefix "hemi" means "half" and the root word "sphere" means "round object." (Your student might have heard of a Hemi engine, an engine with a hemispherical combustion chamber.) Then take two apples, each of which can represent earth (and each of which are spheres) and cut one in half from the top stem down through to the bottom. Talk about the apple being cut "in half" or in two. You will have two hemi (or half) spheres. Then cut the other apple in half through the middle (the equator-like place). You will still have two pieces of apple. They will still be in two halves but they have not been cut the same way.

Now, make the analogy to a globe of the earth and show how cartographers (mapmakers) have created an imaginary line to divide the earth in half east from west (called the **prime meridian**) and another line that divides the earth in half north from south (called the **equator**). Ask your student why he thinks that people would want to make such dividing lines. You could mention that just as we name streets so that we know where to go, lines like the prime meridian, the equator and others help us pinpoint where we are on this large earth. The lines are helpful in giving directions and explaining where different areas are.

For your young student, just mentioning prime meridian and equator will be enough. For your older student you may want to include information on the additional lines called the **Tropic of Cancer**, **Tropic of Capricorn** and continue with the concepts of the lines of **latitude** and **longitude**.

Students living in the **Northern Hemisphere** will be interested to know that the seasons there are opposite from the seasons experienced in the Southern Hemisphere. For older students, find a good book at the library or a video online that explains this phenomenon. However, for young students they will just like to know that when it is summer where they live in the Northern Hemisphere (perhaps the United States or Canada) it is winter in the Southern Hemisphere (like in Australia where the pumpkin runner lived).

Even for your oldest students remember that there are years to build upon these topics. Keep your subject information as interesting and relevant as possible, for instance by reminding them that you are studying the subject of continents or hemispheres because Australia is where the pumpkin runner lived. You could ask your student, "If in this story the Koala-K Race was run in May, what kind of seasonable weather might they be having?" (It would be autumn in May in the Southern Hemisphere.) Then talk about the seasonal differences "down under." ("Down Under" is a sort of nickname for Australia since it lies completely beneath, or south of, the equator.)

Social Studies: Geography - From Paris to Hong Kong

In our story it says that the news wire told the world about Joshua and the race, "from Paris to Hong Kong." Can your student find these famous cities on a world map? If not help him discover the location of these places and how far apart they are. Where are they in relation to Melbourne and Sydney, Australia? If you can, find a globe and go from Paris around to the west (or east) till you reach Hong Kong and see how much of the world that would encompass.

Social Studies: Australian Sheep Ranches

Just like Joshua's, there are many sheep ranches (or stations) in Australia. You can easily find maps and pictures online of sheep ranching on the Australian continent. Australia produces much wool and sheep are exported, as well as used locally, as a meat supply in the form of lamb and mutton.

If you have studied the *Five in a Row* story lessons for *Warm as Wool* (Vol. 3) you may have already covered a lot of information on sheep. Briefly review the information with your student and remind him that *Warm as Wool* took place in the United States. In studying *The Pumpkin Runner*, he sees that here is another country that raises sheep—Australia. However, Australia does it on a much larger scale.

Social Studies: Sports - Running and Rowing

Most of this story centers on the sport of running a race. There are many different kinds of races in which runners participate. Some are lengthy such as a marathon, or the 900K race that Joshua ran. Others are short, called sprints, and there are many lengths of races in between. Races are timed and records are set. Runners train extensively, and generally wear certain attire to help run less encumbered and help them cut their time.

On the page with the city lampposts, you can find a picture of another sport in *The Pumpkin Runner*: rowing. In places where there are long stretches of river often there are groups of people who enjoy being part of a rowing crew. Your student may know what a simple rowboat is, but is he familiar with team rowing? In the United States there are many rowing clubs and races, some affiliated with colleges, in the eastern states. Team rowing is also an Olympic event for both men and women.

Social Studies: History of the Jeep

In *The Pumpkin Runner*, Joshua does not use a Jeep to keep up with his 10,000 acre ranch; however he does borrow one to get to the race. Does your student know what a Jeep is? Can he point to one in traffic? If you have a student who is interested, here is some information on the history of the Jeep: The name Jeep derives from the military term GP, which stands for General Purpose vehicles. The first Jeep came off the assembly line in 1941, built to government specifications and used extensively in World War II.

For students who sometimes think history is a lot of dry facts, finding out how a common vehicle like the Jeep had its origins in World War II can be very exciting! An older student may want to explore further exactly how these vehicles were used in the wartime effort.

After WWII was over, the first civilian Jeep was produced in 1945 and it was marketed to farmers and construction workers as a "workhorse" vehicle. Eventually customers who wanted an open air, rugged vehicle with off-road capabilities sought the Jeep for their vehicle. Today many people enjoy owning a Jeep. Jeeps are now used for an infinite variety of work and play activities as well some military applications.

Social Studies: Character Relationships - Disagreeable People, Cheating, Reactions

Dodgerelle must have been afraid that it was possible for Joshua to win the race. What did Damien do? (He paid a balloonist to carry him over part of the racecourse so he could win.) Damien's bragging was one thing, but to deliberately try to fix the race in his favor is what we call cheating. Cheating means to take unfair steps to win and it isn't limited to running a race, but is pertinent to all sports, games and competitions, business dealings and many other areas of life. Discuss with your student that to become people of integrity and honest, good citizens, we must make a firm decision that whether we win or lose at something, we will try our best and not give in to the temptation to cheat.

Probably your student will be able to understand and talk about the subject of cheating. See how many aspects of this topic you can discuss together, i.e., the effects it has on the perpetrator and the victims; the ideas of integrity and honor; the practice or work needed to be first or best; losing gracefully without resorting to cheating, etc.

Then, or perhaps later, you might discuss how Damien's stunt affected Joshua (no pumpkin for him at the last checkpoint) and how Joshua faces that situation. Many times people are disappointed in their plans—some get angry and quit, and some are flexible, being willing to do things a different way than they had planned. In *The Pumpkin Runner*, Joshua doesn't despair! He decides to keep running without his pumpkin energy food, and just do the best he can.

Social Studies: Character Relationships - Motivation for Participation in Sports

Ask your student why he thinks that Damien Dodgerelle wants to run in this race. Does your student think Joshua Summerhayes wants to run for the same reasons? (Your student may say that Dodgerelle seems more interested in the money and Joshua in just running for pleasure.) People enter sports for many different reasons. Some want to stay physically fit, while others want fame or prizes. But, there are some people who become involved in sports because they just feel good when they participate! In this case, Joshua loves to run. He even shuns driving on his ranch because he prefers to run from place to place—it just gives him pleasure. It will be interesting for your student as he watches Little League, college and professional sports in his life to discern what motivates the athletes and how their characters are shaped by their motivations.

Social Studies: Character Relationships - Disagreeable People, Bragging

The Pumpkin Runner gives wonderful opportunity to discuss the subject of bragging. After reading this story for a few days, ask your student about the verbal exchange between Damien and Joshua at the beginning of the story.

When Joshua wants to be friendly and introduces himself to the rest of the runners, Damien begins to tell Joshua how much he has practiced. Damien does this in a way that we call bragging. Bragging is being overly proud of what you've done and telling people (who don't ask) about it in such a way as to make the other people feel less adequate. Damien continues his bragging with information on how many weights he's lifted while performing a difficult exercise in front of Joshua.

How does Joshua react to such bragging? Joshua reacts with what is known as humility. He doesn't try to make himself look great by telling all he's done. He quietly says he's just checked his herds. (He humbly leaves out the information that his sheep ranch is ten thousand acres!) When Damien tells how many weights he's lifted, Joshua humbly says he carried in a few sheep. Even the clothes he wears show no excessive pride or desire to make himself look like a great racer.

Can you think of any personal anecdotes to share with your student about times when someone has bragged incessantly in front of you? How did it make you feel? How did you react? What did you think of them? Does your student have any incidents to share?

It is good to remember Joshua's reaction to the bragging—he rather ignores it and even when Yellow Dog growls, Joshua says, "Never mind."

Teacher's Note: If you have used previous *Five in a Row* volumes, you may have noticed that there have been many lessons on disagreeable people. Remember Mr. Sneep in *Lentil*? Or Henry B. Swap in *Mike Mulligan*? There are many others. It is interesting that in the scope of these stories the main characters usually don't react in emotional ways or with irritation, but rather quietly ignore these difficult characteristics in others while trying to do what is right themselves. *The Pumpkin Runner* continues to demonstrate for your student that he doesn't have to be blown off course by every disagreeable person who comes his way!

Language Arts and Drama: Latest News On the Wire!

When the news of the big race came out, the story says it was the "latest news on the wire." Does your student know what that means? Wire services (also called news agencies) are news gathering services (like the Associated Press and United Press International) that collect stories which have general national or international interest. These wire services send the news stories to subscribing news outlets (print, online, and television/radio) so that they can print, post or broadcast them. This service allows the local news sources to work on local stories but still have good access to stories of greater importance nationally. Your student can look at a news story and often see at the beginning of the article an **AP** or **UPI** designation which shows that these stories came from the **Associated Press** or **United Press International** news wire services.

Have your student pretend to be a reporter. Use a microphone and recorder to tape his own version of the news story of Joshua's big race. If your student is more comfortable you can be a co-anchor with him and talk back and forth about the race as announcers do.

If your student has another news incident, real or imaginary, that he would like to report, let him write the story, and announce that one as well!

Language Arts: Vocabulary

annual Occurring once a year.

anticipation Eagerly awaiting something.

attire The clothes that you wear (running attire consisted of shirt, shorts and shoes).

bearings Figuring out where you are, finding your location.

camera-shy Not wanting to have your picture taken.

clapboard Thin boards used to cover the outside walls of a house.

ewe Adult female sheep.

flex To make a muscle tight by contracting it, especially to demonstrate its size.

formulated To express in precise terms (in this case by a precise formula or recipe.)

kilometers Metric unit of length which equals 1000 meters.

lanky Exceptionally tall and thin.

mate Australian term for friend or acquaintance (pronounced more like mite).

precisely Exactly.

push-up An exercise done to strengthen upper body muscles.

registration To sign up, as for a competition, etc.

shoo-in Term used in competitions meaning "should win easily."

spectators Those who come to watch an event.

swerved Turned sharply away from an object.

winks A slang term for sleep: "I need a few more winks."

Language Arts: Tall Tale

If you and your student have read about Paul Bunyan or Pecos Bill, you are familiar with the literture genre called **tall tale**. A story that is written humorously and with an obvious fictional exaggeration is called a tall tale. Fish stories about "the big one that got away" can be a tall tale, as well as stories about historical figures such as Davy Crockett, who was said to have "killed him a bar (bear) when he was only three!"

Reading the last pages of *The Pumpkin Runner* you will find that this tale stems from a true incident! Marsha Diane Arnold used this information and built a fanciful tale around the main character. Find the parts of the story that are actually true and then list all the extra incidents that have been built around these actual facts! There are some outlandish, exaggerated incidents that certainly help brand this story is a tall tale. With your student think about the newspaper that blew smack into Joshua's face and just happened to have the race news on it or the idea that a ten-year old could run 24 miles in a day. There is also the pumpkin filling Jeep, as well as the balloon crash!

Remind your student that he can find an interesting article or hear an interesting story on the news and build a story around what he's found, just like Marsha Diane Arnold!

Language Arts: Fable

The Pumpkin Runner is also reminiscent of a famous **fable** called "The Tortoise and the Hare." Fables are short stories that teach some kind of moral. Often these stories have animals as the characters. As your student becomes acquainted with some of the more famous fables, he will notice how writers borrow basic plot lines from these old stories and make new stories from them. Marsha Diane Arnold had only a few facts to begin her story but the way she stages the race reminds us of the old story of the tortoise and hare.

After a few days of reading *The Pumpkin Runner*, read the fable of the tortoise race and see if your student picks up on the similar plot line. If not, open up a discussion about it. You could begin by saying, "It seems to me that this fable and *The Pumpkin Runner* story are a bit alike. Can you see any similarity?" Then go on to explain if necessary. One of the story actions that can remind us of the old fable is the beginning of the race. At the gun, the other eight runners sprinted by. How did Joshua take off? The story says he shuffled by. And even when Damien tried to cheat, the slow, steady pace of Joshua won the race. Indeed that is the moral of "The Tortoise and the Hare:" Slow and steady wins the race. Many people begin a project or competition with great enthusiasm but only proceed in spurts. It is often the slow, steady plodders that reach the finish line or finish their projects in good time. (In all fairness to some personality types, be sure to recognize that some people can start a project in a flurry and still finish first! Many others though, having begun with great enthusiasm might have been better off to start more slowly and be diligent to finish.) How would your student describe himself when it comes to projects that take a lot of effort?

Learning to make connections between themes and plot lines of books, poems, essays, etc., is a vital skill for work in the upper grades and college. In an enjoyable way, with these kinds of lessons, you can gently begin to train your student to "see" such connections.

Language Arts: Comprehending the Concepts and Illustrations

Here are a few questions that you might talk over with your student. Near the beginning of the story, why did the race official Mr. Manning think Joshua probably wasn't in the right place? Why didn't Joshua tell Damien that his herds covered a 10,000 acre ranch? Why did reporters push Joshua aside to interview Damien? Does your student actually think Yellow Dog looks camera shy, as Joshua tells the photographers, "Not too many pictures ... "? It seems as if Yellow Dog is enjoying the notoriety immensely.

Language Arts: Using True Incidents to Create a Good Story

Through the time you have used your *Five in a Row* curriculum you have studied stories which were birthed from true incidents. Can your student remember some of them? Volume 1, *The Glorious Flight* by Provensen; Volume 2, *The Giraffe That Walked to Paris* by Milton; Volume 3 *Paul Revere's Ride* by Longfellow and *Warm as Wool* by Sanders.

The story of *The Pumpkin Runner* is based on true incidents of a man named Cliff Young. Read the author's note at the bottom of the last page for the details. Again, remind your student to watch for interesting articles or news stories that would inspire a good children's story!

Language Arts: Story Ending

The delightful ending of *The Pumpkin Runner* leaves us believing that Joshua and his dog are still running somewhere in Australia! As the story text says, "But Joshua Summerhayes still likes to run ... with Yellow Dog trailing behind him." This is an "off into the sunset"* type of ending that makes the story seem even more real and continuing! It makes the reader feel it is possible that someday he, himself, might actually run into Joshua Summerhayes! Remind your student that when he writes a story he also can use this type of ending to create that sense of timeless continuation.

*Notice how the illustration shows Joshua running off "into the sunset," an example of the illustrator faithfully portraying the subtle meanings of the story.

Language Arts: Literary Device - Alliteration

Marsha Diane Arnold chose many character names for her story *The Pumpkin Runner*. Make a list of these names with your student. (Joshua Summerhayes, Yellow Dog, Aunt Millie, Damien Dodgerelle, Rancher Waudley, Mr. Manning, Katerina Volta) Does one name sort of stand out—sounding (to your ears) more interesting? Is there one name, which is rather fun to say over and over? You may have picked the name that has the same letter beginning the first and last name: Damien Dodgerelle. Using the same letter to begin a series of words is called alliteration. It makes the words sound more interesting, such as: Susie's galoshes make splishes and sploshes. Authors make use of this literary device called alliteration to make their work sound melodic and interesting. Technically, the character Mr. Manning would also be alliterative. The author could have chosen a last name not beginning with the letter "m." There are also some place names in this story that have the same alliterative quality. See if you can find them. (Cockatoo Canyon, Platypus Pond)

Remind your student that in his writing he can make use of this device, too. Notice, though, that Arnold did not use this device for every character. Too much alliteration is wearing on the listener's ears and lessens the impact of the word sounds.

Language Arts: Common Sayings and Their Meanings

As you have read through *The Pumpkin Runner* with your student have you noticed such sayings as "he's a shoo-in" (which means it seems as if he'll be the easy winner), or "looking down his nose"(which means feeling superior)? Talk about what these phrases mean and look for similar sayings and phrases in other stories that you read together. If your student enjoys list making, he could even begin a list of common sayings he finds in the stories he reads. He can keep this list in the Language Arts section of his notebook.

Art: Identifying Places Through Famous Architecture

If you used previous volumes of *Five in a Row,* you will remember that your student learned to identify such famous landmarks as the Eiffel Tower (*Madeline*), the skyline of Moscow (*Another Celebrated Dancing Bear*), the canals of Venice and the Rialto Bridge (*Papa Piccolo*), Egyptian pyramids (*Giraffe That Walked to Paris*), Jefferson's home in Monticello, Virginia (*Paul Revere's Ride*), and Islamic style architecture (*Miss Rumphius*).

The Pumpkin Runner offers the opportunity for your student to become familiar with another famous landmark. In the illustration opposite the last page of the story is a picture of Joshua running his final steps of the race. In the background you can see the city where the race ended—Sydney, Australia. Sydney is on the coast in a bay area and you can see not only the Sydney Harbor Bridge but also the famous **Sydney Opera House** in Sydney Harbor. It is the building that looks like it has two petal-shaped towers that appear to be unfolding. Actually these structures represent the billowing sails of the boats of the harbor. The Sydney Opera House, completed in 1973, has become internationally famous for its original and beautiful architecture.

Your student will enjoy knowing about the Sydney Opera House because, like the Eiffel Tower visually represents Paris, the Sydney Opera House has come to visually represent Australia in the worldwide media.

If your older upper grade level student has a passion for architecture you can find a library book or look online for more information about the design, building and use of the Sydney Opera House.

Art: Variety

Teacher's Note: Many of these art lessons are simply to enable your student to notice and enjoy more of the illustrator's wonderful artwork. The lesson's activities are just observing and discussing what the artist has done. Perhaps someday your student will remember some of this artist's choices and use them as he draws or paints his own works of art.

Discuss with your student the fact that Brad Sneed could have painted all the illustrations for *The Pumpkin Runner* in the same daylight as the cover picture. Did your student notice that instead Mr. Sneed alternates some daylight pictures with some that are very dark? Page quickly through the story and notice this artistic effect. The variety and contrast in these pictures helps hold the viewer's interest and creates an energy and excitement for the race as the pictures move from light to dark and back to light again.

Art: Tying Illustrations to the Story

Brad Sneed, using oil paint on canvas, prepared these engaging pictures in *The Pumpkin Runner*. This illustrator is known for his paintings that have exaggerated proportions. So, it is most fitting for this tall tale to also have illustrations of exaggerated proportions! Enjoy looking over the illustrations again thinking about how well they express the story's *tall* tale and *stretched* truths!

As a story, *The Pumpkin Runner* has a great deal of humor and the illustrator has marvelously captured this humor in his paintings, along with wonderful scenes full of action. With your student, glance through the illustrations pointing out to each other the pictures you each find humorous. (Don't miss Aunt Millie sleeping on top of the pumpkins!) Look, too, for those illustrations that display action!

Also, have you noticed how many pages of the story have illustrations that are painted with orange—like a pumpkin? Here is another way an illustrator can thematically tie his artwork to the story line.

Art: Viewpoint

Look at the picture next to the text where Katerina talks about her secret power punch. It is as if we are looking into the picture from further away than the dog yet at Yellow Dog's own eye level! This is what the world actually looks like to Yellow Dog—giant feet and low-level views. (Just for fun, also notice Yellow Dog's expression as he looks at the purple power drink.)

Art: Elements of Perspective

Teacher's Note: This is a long lesson. You may want to break it up into parts for different days or take only one element to discuss. If you have an older student, he might enjoy the entire lesson.

Look with your student at the picture of the runners warming up and stretching while Joshua is eating a piece of pumpkin. Brad Sneed has used several different elements of perspective to create a sense of depth in this picture. If your student does not understand the preceding statement, try this exercise to heighten his awareness. Clear a book shelf or counter at your student's eye level. Place several objects on the shelf—some in front, some in the middle and some at the back. It helps if the objects are all the same: small play-people figures, miniature small cars, etc. Have your student notice where the feet of the figures (or the car's tires) appear on the shelf. It looks as if the middle figure's feet (or tires) are above the foremost figure's, and that the back figure's feet (or tires) are even higher than those of the middle figures'. It is easy to see with such a model and figures that there is depth to the arrangement. Let your student put his hand up to the shelf and push it to the back of the shelf. Now explain that an artist begins with a flat piece of paper. How do you show that the figures or cars go back in space when you have a flat piece of paper? In order to paint scenes that look three-dimensional, the artist uses certain elements of drawing called perspective. Several of these elements of perspective are clear in the pictures Brad Sneed painted for *The Pumpkin Runner*.

As an exercise in drawing perspective, first take a piece of tracing paper and place it on top of the illustration of the stretching runners and Joshua eating the pumpkin. Using a ruler, have your student draw a line across the paper at approximately the level of the spectators feet (in the background of the picture). Also, notice how tall these spectators are. (Make a small vertical mark to show their height as they stand on the street.) Then draw another parallel line across the paper at the bottom of the feet of the nearest runner warming up. Notice that the runners are larger and taller than the spectators are, but smaller than Joshua. Make a vertical mark over the standing runner to show height. Now look at Joshua and Yellow Dog. Their feet are so low on the picture that they have disappeared! The bottom of the paper will be the base line or line where the foreground begins. Make a vertical line to represent Joshua's height. This is a simple exercise in observation, demonstrating that an artist can choose to show depth by varying the **size** of his figures as well as where the feet are **spaced** on the paper. In the placement of the foreground (or even falling off the foreground) the size of figures are large and the feet are low. In the middle ground the size of the figures are medium and the feet are higher, and the background the size of the figures are quite small and the feet are higher still. Now go back and find the illustration where Yellow Dog is looking up at the runners and glaring at the purple power punch. See Joshua's feet and notice the same element of space used to show the mid-ground runners (their feet are higher up on the page) and background spectators who appear to be the deepest in the picture. If your student enjoys it, let him look for other examples of this element of perspective in Brad Sneed's illustrations.

Second, draw your student's attention to Joshua as he's enjoying his slice of pumpkin. Point out the bright color in Joshua's clothes. Now look at the runners that are stretching and warming up for the big race. Notice the colors of their clothes. (The clothes of the runners have some color but they are far less colorful than Joshua's and they appear slightly gray.) Last, look at the spectators behind the blockades. Their clothes are all grayed. This is another technique called intensity that an artist may employ to give the effect of depth in a painting. The element of **intensity** (or density) is in use when the background figures' colors are grayed (in other pictures it could be trees or buildings, etc.) and they have much less detail or appear blurry. (Your student may remember a similar lesson in *Five in a Row* Volume 1 when he studied Allen Say's paintings. If you still have or can obtain a copy of *Grandfather's Journey*, look with your student through the illustrations and see if you can find pictures that use this element of perspective.)

Then, mention to your student that Joshua is at the front of this picture. Your student can tell Joshua is in front because he is hiding parts of the runners behind him. In other words Joshua overlaps the runners that are behind him. Joshua and the stretching runners are both **overlapping** the tiny spectators in the background.

These are some of the ways that an artist can choose to create depth in his paintings and drawings. Your student can begin to notice that many artists use these techniques as he examines drawings and paintings he sees at galleries, in books and online. Learning to see objects clearly is a large part of learning how to draw. From these studies your student will begin to see objects around him more clearly and will understand that he can use these same **elements of perspective** in his own drawings whenever he wants.

For more information and instruction on this topic, see the Perspective: Principles of Drawing for Depth section at the end of this manual.

Math: Metric System

This story, based in Australia, provides a wonderful opportunity to introduce or re-examine the metric system or to explore a new facet of it. The race in which Joshua wants to compete is 900 kilometers. You may wish to explore millimeters, meters and kilometers at this time. There are wonderful simple books on introducing the metric system to your children at your library, as well as books which go into more depth for those older students who are ready for more detailed information.

In *The Pumpkin Runner*, author Marsha Diane Arnold also writes on page two that Joshua, "... ran forty kilometers, all the way to Cockatoo Canyon, just to check on a newborn lamb." With your student, do the conversions to find out how many miles it would be to the canyon? The approximate conversion factor for kilometers to miles is 0.6. Multiply the kilometers times 0.6 to know approximately how many miles it is. (40 kilometers is approximately 24 miles)

Math: Unit Measure of Land - Acre

Joshua Summerhayes worked on a 10,000 acre ranch. How big would that be? With a bit of figuring it seems that the ranch could be about four miles square. You may be able to find an area that you could drive around in the car that was four miles by four miles just to give your student an idea of how big a ranch like that would be. If you have any vacant or farm acreage around you, you could point out for sale signs that tell how many acres each land parcel includes.

Math: Division

The text of our story says, "The crowd squeezed around as Mr. Manning presented Joshua the check for $10,000." Then it goes on to say that Joshua split the winnings with his fellow runners.

Your older student may or may not be ready for actual division, but for any student not ready and for the younger student you could proceed in this way.

(**Note:** Including Joshua, there are actually nine runners, but for the sake of simplicity and even numbers, use eight runners for this lesson.) Problem: If there were eight runners, how much of the prize money did each runner receive? ($1250.00)

Set up eight objects to represent the runners (if you have toy people from various games and toy sets these would be great). Make ten pieces of paper and mark one thousand dollars on each of these. (See the dollar bill templates activity sheet at the end of this unit.) Have your child take these bills and distribute them one to each runner figure until there are not enough to give each an equal number. He will have two left over—not enough to go around. Ask him if he can think of how this problem might be solved. Have ready twenty bills marked one hundred dollars each. Your student can turn in the leftover two thousand-dollar bills and receive the **equivalent** amount of twenty one hundred dollar bills. Let your student distribute these equally among the eight figures. He will end up with four left over. What does your student think should happen with this leftover money? Have him trade in the four hundred dollar bills for eight fifty dollar bills. Explain that this is an equivalent amount. Now let your student distribute the money again and this time he should come out even. The ten thousand dollars has been divided equally between eight runners. Help your student add up the amounts listed on the three pieces of paper at one of the figure's place. Adding one thousand, then two hundred and another fifty he should get the answer $1250.00 that each runner received.

Now on a whiteboard or piece of paper set up the same problem as a typical division problem. You do the math and let your student see you come up with the same answer as he did without all the paper distribution. Tell him that there may be a few more things that he needs to learn but soon he will be able to work the "how much money did each runner receive" problem with more efficient skills of long division.

Math: Catching the Clues for Figures

How old, according to the story, is Joshua? How can you tell? Read that part of the story again and listen. Can you figure it out? The author says that Joshua has been running for 50 years since he was 10 years old. That would make Joshua Summerhayes 60 years old. You can figure this out, even though the story never says *specifically* that Joshua is 60, if you pay attention to the clues.

This would just be a guess, but how old do you suppose Aunt Millie is? There is no real clue but if you think of ages by generation, then Aunt Millie (being the sibling of either Joshua's mother or father) could be as much as twenty years older than Joshua. So Aunt Millie could possibly be in her 80s!

Science: Flora of Australia

Teacher's Note: Flora is a special scientific word to describe the trees and plants of a specific region or period. Mention this word to your student but it is not necessary that he memorize it. In years to come, he will quickly recognize it in his science lessons.

In *The Pumpkin Runner* there are some specific plants and trees mentioned. Let your student list these and help him with ones he might miss. His list could include: Gum trees, eucalyptus trees*, wattle grove, etc. They must have pumpkins in Australia, too! Find a simple book on Australia and add some additional common examples of the flora found there. Have your student list and draw some of these Australian plants and place the work into his science notebook. (There is a Flora and Fauna activity sheet at the end of this unit.)

Teacher's Note: You could find some eucalyptus so your student can smell its pungent smell. Florist shops and hobby stores are good places to look!

Science: Botany - Pumpkins

Has your student ever wondered about the fact that there are so many different kinds of plants? All the kinds that he has seen himself are only a small fraction of the total number of plants in the world. Of those known plants can he think of any plant that is called by several different names? (The Monarda is a flower that grows by the roadside and is also called bee balm and Oswego tea. Maybe you know of an example that is more relevant to your particular student.)

So how do scientists find a specific name for all these plants so that when a person talks about a certain plant every scientist in the world knows exactly which one he is talking about? Scientists have solved this problem of a plant's multiple common labels with a classification (or naming) system developed by a Swedish scientist named Linnaeus. The system of scientific classification of plants which Linnaeus began in the eighteenth century (1700s) is still used (with a few changes) and allows scientists to know exactly which particular plant is being discussed.

Therefore, the Monarda flower, having several common names, mentioned above would be called *Monarda didyma* by scientists. Monarda didyma is the brilliant red Monarda. In gardening catalogs the other colors (purple, rose, etc.) would have different species names.

While pumpkins are related to the squash family, they actually belong to the gourd family whose family name is Cururbitacea, genus name *Cururbita,* and then there are several different species of pumpkins. Your student might enjoy looking online or in a gardening book or seed catalog for some of these different types of pumpkins. The name for the large October orange pumpkin is *Cururbita pepo.* (In many gardening catalogs plants are listed by a common name, and often in the back of the catalog they will re-list the plants with their scientific names. If you want your student to examine such a magazine or catalog just search for one that has the scientific names listed either by the plants for sale, or in some type of extra index.)

Pumpkins are rich in vitamin A and potassium. People enjoy making pies, quick breads, cookies, cakes and soups from the delicious pumpkin. It certainly seems that Joshua Summerhayes loved pumpkins—almost more than anything!

Perhaps you have the room to let your student grow some pumpkins. Whether you grow the mini-type or the sugar pie type (sweeter and richer than the large October ones) or the large fall decorating pumpkin, it would be fun to see the progress of your own pumpkin patch. There are so many lessons to be learned with such a project: flowers and pollination, soil conditions, water needs, insect pests, etc. If you grow a larger pumpkin, try carving your student's name in the outer skin (not too deep) and see if the name grows along with the pumpkin!

Science: Physics - Buoyancy and Density

While Joshua Summerhayes ran in a contest to see who was the fastest, your student can also conduct a contest, with pumpkins, to see which ones float the best! Gather together as many different sizes of pumpkins as you can find. (Have one or two of the mini-pumpkins, the ones that are about the size of an apple. Then include at least two more sizes—a small pie-type pumpkin and a regular large pumpkin.) Have your student make a chart of the pumpkin sizes with two boxes next to each size that say: "Float" or "Doesn't Float." Now fill a sink 1/2 full of water and tell your student that he is going to test each size of pumpkin and see if it floats or if it does not. First, ask your student for his hypothesis: What does he think will happen and why? Then let him test his hypothesis by setting one pumpkin in the water and seeing if it floats. Have him mark the appropriate box. Why did your student find? Did he find that the miniature pumpkins were much more difficult to float than the really large pumpkin? That seems like a sort of mystery. Why does he think that might be? While your student is watching, cut the pumpkins in half. Let him examine the center of the large pumpkin and of the small pumpkin ... does he see any difference? Usually the biggest pumpkins have proportionally a much larger hollow space in the center. This hollow space filled with air causes the larger pumpkin to be more **buoyant**. Perhaps your student will remember the hollow barrel on the little boy's back in the *Five in a Row* Volume 1 lessons for *The Story of Ping*? That hollow wooden barrel, full of air, helped the little boy float and stay safe in the water.

Older students may have already heard about buoyancy and you can review briefly and then use this same lesson to talk about density. Density is the mass per unit volume of an object.

You can continue this exploration of density of matter if you have a small rock and a larger pumice rock. The small rock will sink while the larger pumice piece will float because it is full of air holes. The holes cause the pumice to be not as dense (the materials which make up the rock are not as closely packed) as the small rock. This experiment shows that it is not just the size of an object that determines whether it will float or not—the **density** (how tightly the molecules are packed) of the object plays a significant part.

Science: Fauna of Australia

Teacher's Note: Fauna is a special scientific word to describe animals of a specific region or period. You can mention this to your student but it's not necessary that he memorize it. In later years of science lessons, he will quickly recognize the familiarity of this word.

Let your student follow throughout the story making a list of Australian animals that he hears mentioned. His list might include: sheep, wombat, cockatoo, bandicoot, koala, wallaby, platypus, etc.

Let him pick an animal or two with which he is unfamiliar and help him research these animals. Help him discover what they look like, where in Australia they live, what they eat, and special facts about how they live. Have your student put this information, along with an illustration, in his science notebook. (There is a Flora and Fauna activity sheet at the end of this unit.)

The Great Barrier Reef of Australia is famous for its corals, many beautiful fishes and other marine life. Check the lessons for *Arabella,* later in this manual, for information on coral.

Science: Physics - The Physical Science of Hot Air Ballooning and Buoyancy

Reporters rush for a view and stories of the race in *The Pumpkin Runner*. They even use hot air balloons to get an aerial view. Explain to your student what an aerial view is. Just like he may have studied in *The Glorious Flight* (Vol. 1), an aerial view is looking over something from high up in the air.

Has your student ever seen a real hot air balloon or had a ride in one? Does he understand how they work? Floating in air, a hot air balloon utilizes the principle that hot air rises. A small but powerful burner is turned on and the flame heats the air inside the balloon. As the air is heated, the molecules spread further apart and some of the air is forced out of the balloon. When the surrounding air is **more dense** than the heated **less dense** air inside the balloon, it allows the balloon to become buoyant and it rises. An object like a cloud, feather, hot air balloon, etc., will float in the air as long as its density is less than the surrounding air. In the first days of ballooning there was no control to how high a balloon could fly, how far it went or where it came down. Today, the burners can be opened to heat more air (and cause greater rising) or closed to cool the balloon's air and allow descent so there is much more control. To prevent the balloon from going higher than the operator of the balloon intends, the flyer turns the burner down or off and the balloon will drift and then begin to sink. More heat causes the balloon to rise again, etc. The operator and passengers of the hot air balloon as well as the burner unit sit in a basket that is attached to the balloon fabric by tape-like cords.

Temperature and winds play a part in how much fuel for the heating flame is used and how the balloon flies. If you see a hot air balloon in flight, listen for the roaring sound of the burner being turned off and on at intervals. This sound can be heard quite easily even when the balloon is fairly high.

Teacher's Note: For an older upper grade school level student, you may want to explain that hot air rises because as it is heated it expands or spreads out, and has less weight per cubic volume than colder dense, closely packed air molecules. Your older student may also want to check online for interesting facts about balloons, their history—such as their role in warfare, and balloons' many uses including weather monitoring.

Science: The Anatomy of Running - Bones, Muscles, Joints and Ligaments

The Pumpkin Runner gives you the opportunity to study any of the following elements of the human body: bones, muscles, joints or ligaments, or all four and how they work together. First review any information in your student's science notebook that you have already covered on bones, etc. Then using the sports theme of running, add new information and show how the parts of the body work together to allow walking, running, etc.

There are simple books with good illustrations that explain how each of these parts of the human body work and how they work together. For your young student, a very brief overview of this kind of material is sufficient. Such an overview might include the idea that inside our body are bones and muscles, each of which have different kinds of cells and which, along with parts of the body called joints, tendons and ligaments, allow us to move our bodies in a variety of directions. Show him pictures from books or online of the body skeleton and how the muscle masses are arranged over the bones.

Your student may be interested and amazed to know that there are three major bones that make up the leg (femur, fibula and tibia), a bone called the patella (kneecap) and twenty-six bones that make up the foot. Since bones by themselves cannot move, the muscles, ligaments and tendons are what enable a person to have a range of motion. There is an important tendon called the Achilles tendon* which attaches the calf muscle to the back of the ankle, along with a variety of muscles, ligaments and tendons along the front and back of the leg and foot that allow a person to move, walk, jump, skip and run!

***Teacher's Note:** As a side topic, there is, in Greek mythology, a man named Achilles and the story of his mother's attempt (and failure) to make her son immortal. If you desire you can review and mention this story to your older student to help him understand the origin of the name of this tendon in the human body.

For your older *Five in a Row* student you would want him to find information in the library books and have him make some notes on what he has learned. This is accomplished by reading the simple book together once and then going back and asking your student what he thinks the most important points of information are? What does he think he should write down? Add any you think necessary, and have him make his notes on paper and draw illustrations from the book that will help him remember the concepts. These pages he can place in the Science portion of his notebook. For those who love artistic details, pictures or drawings of runners or races could decorate the edges of the notebook pages as well.

Three wonderful resource books on the Human Body (which will be valuable for many additional topics) are: *Blood and Guts: A Working Guide to Your Own Insides* by Linda Allison, which has an excellent chapter on muscles, etc., with working models that you can make from household materials. *Blood and Guts* has some evolutionary references so it is best used as a resource book by the teacher who presents what she feels is appropriate. *Start Exploring Gray's Anatomy*, by Freddy Stark, Ph.D,, a coloring book that can be used and reviewed over again for years, is another resource that your student might enjoy. Also see *Janice VanCleave's The Human Body for Every Kid: Easy Activities That Make Learning Science Fun*.

If you cannot obtain these books there are many good books at your library and resources online that will give you the necessary information.

Science: Physical Fitness

Use *The Pumpkin Runner* as an opportunity to talk about physical fitness! Does your student think that Joshua was physically fit? What does that mean? Physical fitness includes areas such as exercise, nutrition, normal weight, blood pressure, and getting plenty of sleep. Keeping oneself physically fit is even part of being a good citizen! In this way one will be able to do his work (and play) at optimum levels of efficiency. Keeping fit physically is important for bright mental alertness as well. For many years, the President's Challenge helped children assess and work on improving their physical fitness, and now the Presidential Youth Fitness Program (PYFP) carries on this tradition. You can find these and other physical fitness programs onine or in library books. Use them to begin a workout or exercise schedule and chart daily what your student does and let him notice the progress that he makes.

You can continue learning about physical fitness by discussing any of the following:

The importance of stretching before sports or walking, like the runners flexed and stretched in the illustrations. Muscle fibers are long and stretchy like a rubber band. But like a rubber band that breaks, if muscles are stretched too far, too fast they can be injured. With a thick rubber band try pulling it to the breaking point and note how many inches that is. Now pull and release the rubber band as if you were warming up a muscle by stretching it. After six or seven pulls and releases can you more easily—with less danger of breaking the band—stretch it even more inches than you could at the first try? This a simple demonstration of why muscles need to be warmed up and stretched out before strenuous exercise.

The importance of good nutrition. Cells make up bones, muscles and ligaments as well as all parts of our bodies. Find a book or website on the human body that shows what muscle cells, nerve cells, bone cells, etc., look like, because each type of cell is different. Let your student draw illustrations of these types of cells and label them for his Science notebook. These cells need certain elements of nutrition to stay healthy. A diet rich in vitamins, minerals, and other nutrients will help a person perform at higher levels than a body where the cells are starved by poor nutrition. When one does strenuous exercise (like running a marathon) the body needs good nutrition and lots of water! Find a good simple book on nutrition and enjoy exploring how sound nutrition helps us stay physically fit in so many different ways.

The importance of proper attire while exercising—especially shoes and clothing. The fact that Joshua wears his overalls and gum boots and still wins is part of what makes this true story still have the aspects of a tall tale!

Teacher's Notes

The *Five in a Row* lesson options for each unit in the manual are all you need to teach your child. The additional resource area provided below is simply a place to jot down relevant info you've found that you might want to reference.

THE PUMPKIN RUNNER

Date:

Student:

Five in a Row Lesson Topics Chosen:

Social Studies:

Language Arts:

Art:

Math:

Science:

Relevant Library Resources: Books, DVDs, Audio Books

Websites or Video Links:

Related Field Trip Opportunities:

Favorite Quote or Memory During Study:

Name:
Date:
Geography: **Flag of Australia**

The flag of Australia has a dark blue field with the United Kingdom flag in the upper left quarter – above a large white seven-pointed star and next to the Southern Cross constellation. *For more information, see Parts of a Flag on page 266.*

Color in the Australian flag below.

Math: **Division**

Copy the dollar bill templates below for the math lesson on division.

10 - $1,000 bills
20 - $100 bills
8 - $50 bills

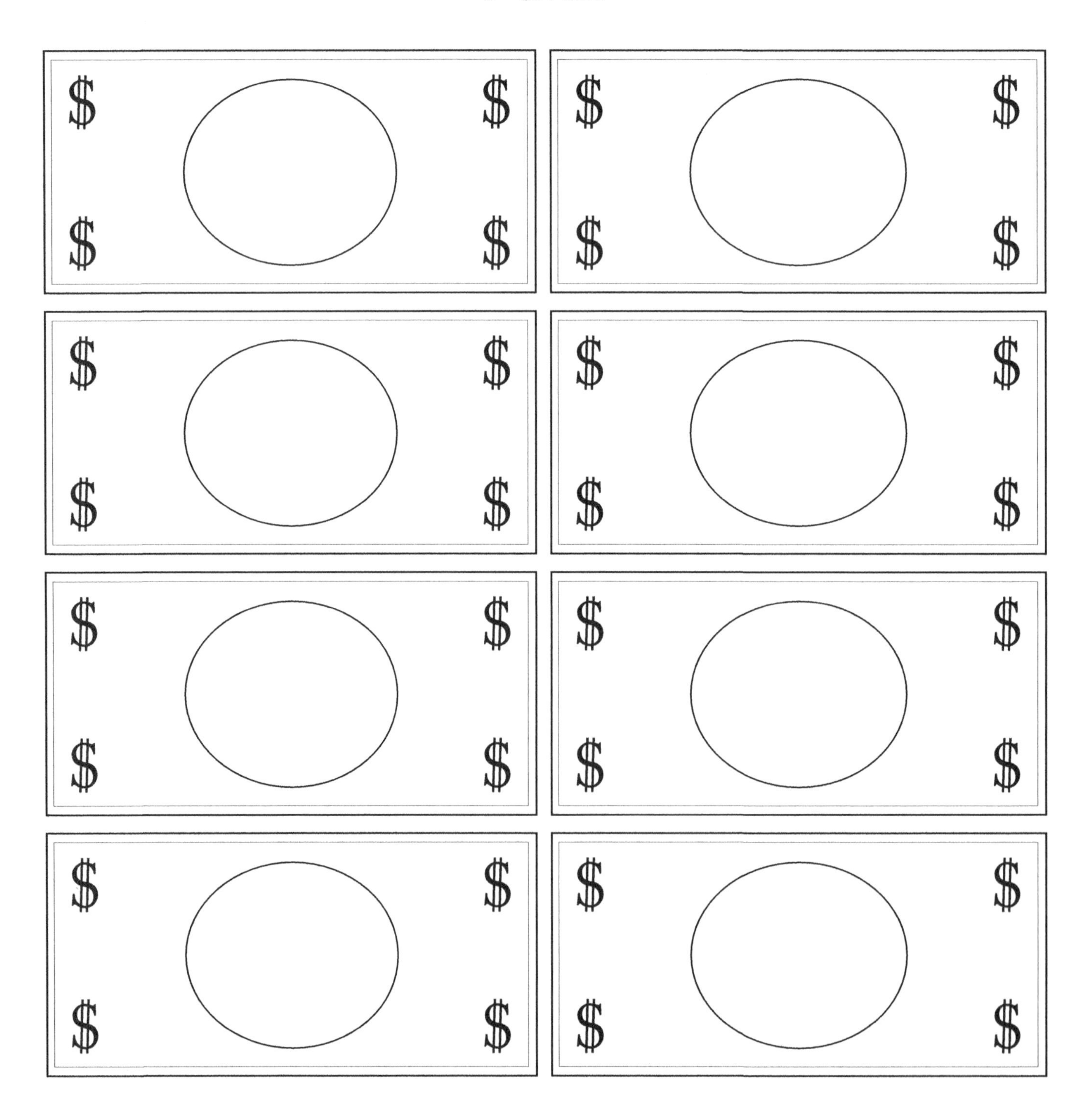

Name:

Date:

Language Arts: **Inspired by a True Incident**

The Pumpkin Runner is based on facts about a man named Cliff Young. Read the author's note at the bottom of the last page for the details. Have your student research Cliff Young and find articles that tell more about him. Then using that research and the *Pumpkin Runner* story, compare the events of the story and find which events were the same and which were different. Use the Venn diagram below to mark down the events.

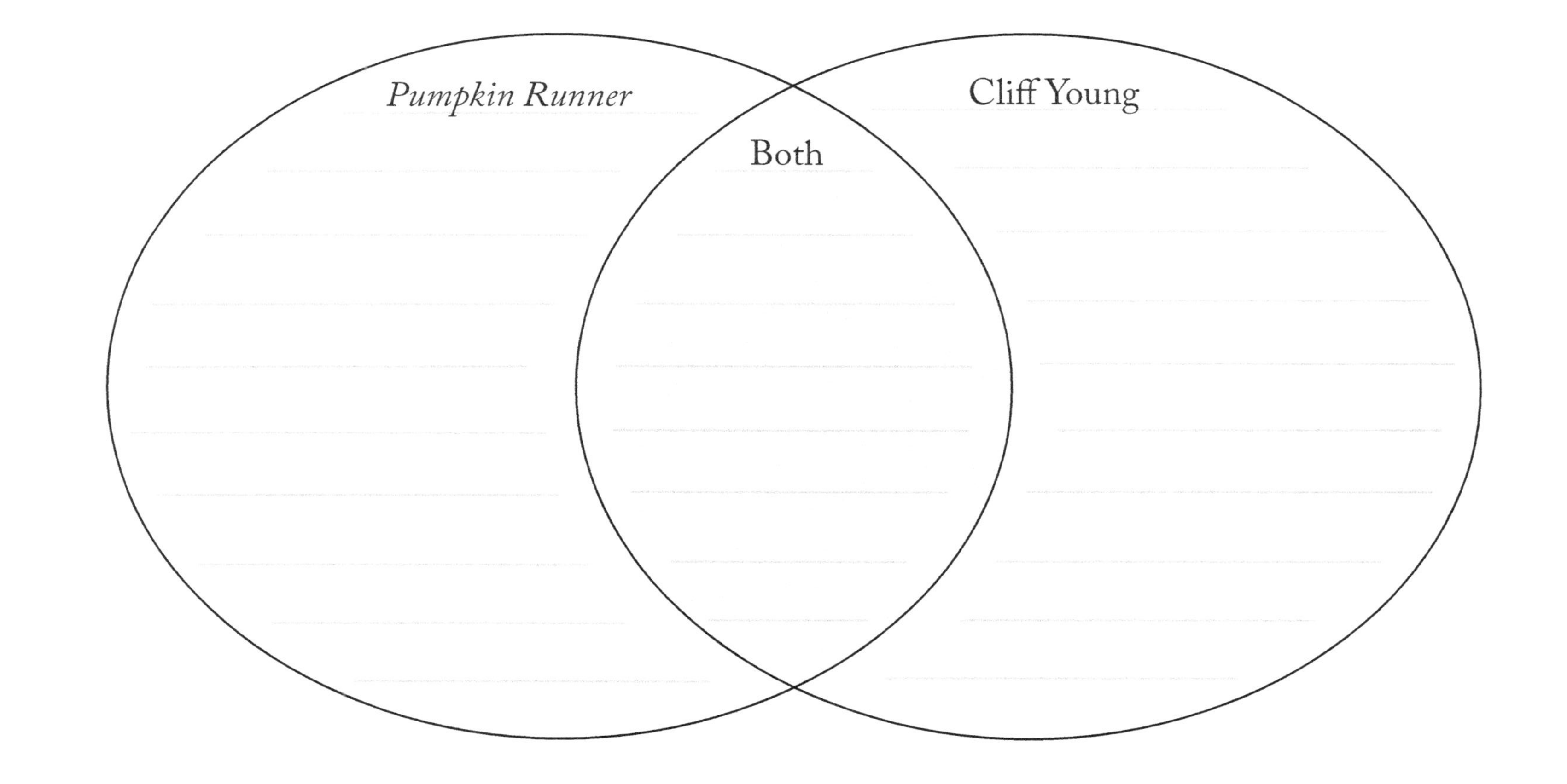

Name:

Date:

Science: **Flora and Fauna of Australia**

Using the research recommended in the lessons on Flora and Fauna, print or cut out examples of plants and animals of Australia and paste them below.

Flora	Fauna

Hanna's Cold Winter

Title: *Hanna's Cold Winter*
Author: Trish Marx
Illustrator: Barbara Knutson
Copyright: 1993
Summary: A cold winter, starving animals and a town with a heart weaves a story based on a true incident that will intrigue all of its readers.

Teacher's Note: For the name of the character actually telling this story (Tibor) preview the Language Arts lesson on first-person point of view in this unit section.

Social Studies: Geography - Budapest, Hungary

Hanna's Cold Winter takes place in the country of Hungary and in a city called Budapest. The story says the city was actually the twin cities of Buda and Pest, divided by the Danube River. Place your story disk on Hungary or on Budapest if your map shows it.

The second-longest river in Europe, the Danube River has its source (beginning) in West Germany and flows through 10 countries on its way to its mouth (end point) at the Black Sea.

Did you know that you can still see the giant lion statues on the Lanchid Bridge at the Danube River? The famous Gellert warm mineral baths in Budapest still draw crowds of tourists. (In Europe the word *bathing* means swimming. See the girl's swimsuit in the pictures of the Gellert baths?) There is also still a zoo in Budapest and they still have hippopotamuses! Use the Virtual Field Trip activity sheet at the end of this unit to visit the Budapest Zoo online and plan a virtual visit.

The monetary unit (money) used in Hungary is the forint. Tibor's papa has forints jingling in his pocket! It was kind of the children not to beg Papa to go to the zoo. It cost money and they knew he would take them if he could. Waiting for things you enjoy is part of growing up. It was an enjoyable tradition that Papa created, too, to stand and jingle the forints in his pocket when it was a zoo Sunday. Traditions like this are remembered for a lifetime!

Look also at the market where Tibor's brother disappears to do his shopping. The text talks about eggs, tomatoes, chickens, cheese, spices and candy being sold in the market. Ask your student what else she can see in the pictures. In the illustrations there are cabbages, flowers and possibly green beans. And, are those red paprika peppers hanging at the back of the stalls? (Remember Tibor's papa loads peppers at the factory?) The next page says that the family has to purchase sugar, butter, cloth for pants and shoes, though we don't know if all of those items come from the same market.

Social Studies: History - Through the Illustrations and Text

In Budapest, during the fighting of WWII, Tibor's family stays indoors and sits in front of the fire listening to the radio. Their family does not have television for news but rather a radio. (Television, invented in 1930s, was not marketed to most homes until after WWII.) Just as in this story, people throughout the world sat by their radios to hear the news of the day and wait for word that the war had ended.

Look at the unusual fireplace in Tibor's home. It is a tall with tiles covering the inside chimney portion. You can see similar fireplaces in stories set in Europe and in pictures of European homes. When you see this type of fireplace in a story illustration, stop and remember you are probably reading a story set somewhere in Europe!

Tibor's family rides a cog train when returning from visiting the zoo. What is a cog railway (rack railway) and how is it different from the kinds of trains that are more familiar? Cog railways were built and used for areas with extremely steep grades. A traditional railroad (the kind most of us know) have smooth wheels which run upon smooth tracks. This works well for most settings. However, for an extremely steep grade the smooth wheel and track does not provide enough friction and the wheel slips, causing the train to slide backwards. In order to combat this problem rack railways have tracks which are built with a jagged surface (just like cog gears) that mesh with a wheel that also has a jagged gear-like surface.

The meshing of the wheel and rail surface eliminates the friction problem and allows an engine to pull a train up a steep grade with no danger of slipping backwards. Look up cog railway or rack railway online to see images and videos of this historical mode of transportation that is sometimes still used today.

Teacher's Note: The architecture of the walls in the picture with the cog train actually duplicates the gear like pattern of the tracks and wheels!

Social Studies: History - World War II

Does your student remember what the **conflict of the plot** is in a story? A conflict is the problem for which the characters seek a solution. The conflict of the plot in *Hanna's Cold Winter* stems from the fact that the Budapest Zoo animals can't get enough food that winter due to the war. World War II (1939-1945) included fighting in many countries. In *Five in a Row* Volume 1, you may have studied lessons from the book *Grandfather's Journey* by Allen Say and discussed lessons about WWII concerning Japan. In *Five in a Row* Volume 2 perhaps you read *A New Coat for Anna* by Harriet Ziefert and learned about countries of Europe with bombing damage from WWII. You could also now tie in the lessons of Mrs. Katz (*Mrs. Katz and Tush*, by Patricia Polacco, Volume 2) as she leaves her home in Poland and how WWII affected Poland. FIAR Volume 2 also has the story lessons for *All Those Secrets of the World* by Jane Yolen showing American soldiers leaving the United States for areas of action in Europe and the Pacific Basin during WWII. Gently, through these picture books, your student is beginning to see the wide scope of WWII. *Hanna's Cold Winter* continues the picture.

These kinds of lessons are often not introduced until the junior high level, but they will give your student a strong foundation for history lessons in the later years! Your student will remember via the story characters some of the feelings of that historic time including feelings of fear, sadness, loneliness, frustration, loss, flexibility and the creativity of having to "make do."

At this time, if you have an older grade level student, you may want to take the opportunity and find a very simple book on WWII. Begin to tie together all the story pieces your student already knows and give her a *very simple* framework of how WWII began and developed.

Social Studies: Relationships and Problem Solving

The Budapest zoo has a problem. The city is experiencing one of the coldest winters ever and with the war going on, food cannot be brought into the zoo. Tibor's papa is concerned. Discuss with your student that sometimes people become concerned over an issue and they don't even attempt to think of solutions. They just worry and hope the problem is quickly resolved. However, Tibor's father thinks about his concerns and tries to find a way to help. He comes up with a solution and the family makes a trip to the zoo to share it with the zookeeper. When the zookeeper agrees that the solution might work, Tibor's family (and others) begin to band together to save their beloved hippos. With the help of the entire city and their donations of straw the animals are saved. *Hanna's Cold Winter* showcases people of compassion who are also people willing to go into action! Can your student think of some situations that she has witnessed where someone has seen a problem, thought of a solution and then implemented that solution?

The story doesn't tell us how Tibor's papa comes up with his wonderful solution. It might be that he is trying to think of the all the things hippos eat and just happens to look down at his own slippers! However, the idea comes to Papa, just as ideas can come to each of us. Encourage your student to be looking for problems and creative ways to solve them just like in *Hanna's Cold Winter*! If your student shares such a problem and solution of her own, write it down and include it in your social studies notebook.

Social Studies: History - Six-Day Work Week

Talk about the different methods of scheduling a work week. Many jobs today are 8:00 A.M. to 5:00 P.M. jobs. There are also jobs that have three or four shifts including night shifts. There are jobs like firefighting where the employees work a day on, day off, day on and then they are off for a few days because each of their shifts is twenty-four hours long.

It was more common during the time of WWII in Europe and in North America for people to work six days a week, having only Sunday off. Can you help your student make a list of people she knows—family and adult friends that work? Help her chart what type of work schedules they each have.

This is not a critical academic lesson, however it is a lesson to widen your student's knowledge base about the working world, both past and present. If you choose to do it you will be helping her realize the great diversity of work schedules.

Social Studies: Famous Features of Your Area or State

If your student previously studied the lessons for *The Giraffe That Walked to Paris*, *Five in a Row* Volume 2, you might enjoy reminiscing and discussing how much the people of Paris loved La Giraffe. They had signs, decorations, clothing, etc., with pictures of La Giraffe. The people of Hungary loved the hippos, too. That is why many of the people in the town worked together to help save them. Discuss with your student anything that is famous or revered about your town or state. It may not be a particular animal. Perhaps your area has well known types of trees or forest such as the Hartwick Pines area of Michigan, or beloved light houses, a national landmark, etc.

Language Arts: First Person Point of View

Does your student know from what point of view *Hanna's Cold Winter* is written? Does she remember stories like *Night of the Moonjellies* (Vol. 1), or *Owl Moon* and *All Those Secrets of the World* (Vol. 2), or *The Wild Horses of Sweetbriar* (Vol. 3)? All of these stories were written in first person point of view in which the pronoun "I" is used for the person telling the story.

Now, here is a bit of detective work. There are three children in the family of the story *Hanna's Cold Winter*. Two of these are boys and one is a girl. Ask your student if she knows which of the three children is telling the story. You can find out which one of the three is actually telling the story by making some observations. On the page where the lions are first visible on the Lanchid bridge (across from the Gellert baths) you can read the lines, "My sister ... " From this you can then assume that the storyteller is one of the two boys. But, which one? The next page of text says, "My older brother, Gabor, ... " so now you know it is the younger boy who is telling the story. Where do you first read the name of this boy? When Papa is asking his younger son about the riddle of the lions at the Lanchid bridge he says, "Little Tibor ... " So the younger son is named Tibor and it is Tibor who is remembering his childhood and telling the story!

Language Arts: Story Writing - Introduction and Plot

Author Trish Marx begins the story of Hanna with the line, "When I was a child ..." and proceeds to reminisce about Tibor and this imaginary character's childhood years. Let your student try to pattern a story after this type of introduction. She can begin her story with "When I was a child" and reminisce about her own childhood or she can make up a fictional story using the same beginning as Trish Marx. You may need to remind your student of the elements of plot: conflict, rising action, climax, falling action (or denouement). Can she find these plot elements in *Hanna's Cold Winter*?

Another idea for your student is to do a reminiscent story of her own life based on photographs and incidents she obtains from her parents. This type of story might begin, "When I was two years old ..." or "When I was four years old ..." and be documented by copies of photographs. In this type of writing, plot would not be as important because the story could just be a running commentary of life incidents. This assignment might be easier and more enjoyable for your younger student.

Language Arts: Literature Genre - Riddles

Riddles are a language genre that has a long history. People love riddles and they have always used the playful art of riddles to encourage creative thinking and humor. Find a good riddle book and enjoy some riddles together just like Papa and little Tibor. If your student desires, she may begin to think of some original riddles to share!

Language Arts: Comparing and Contrasting Themes in Literature

There is a slight **comparative** connection between the story of *Hanna's Cold Winter* and the folk tale *Stone Soup*. Find a copy of *Stone Soup* at your library. Search by title for there may be several different renditions of this old tale. In *Hanna* it says that during the war, their meat runs out, then their potatoes and with only a few vegetables and sometimes a thin chicken Mama stretches the soup pot. Then read the tale of *Stone Soup* and of the story of a man who also wants to stretch his pot of soup. So, both stories have the theme of stretching the soup pot.

Yet, a **contrast** in another theme of these two stories is in the actual implementing of the project. In both stories the community needs to band together to produce the desired benefit. However, the man in *Stone Soup* tricks the townspeople into sharing their vegetables to make his soup, while in *Hanna* the people of the town are willingly persuaded to consolidate their items of straw and give them to help the hippos.

This is not a lesson to labor over but to just suggest that comparing and contrasting themes in literature is helpful in understanding the richness of our literary heritage as well as stimulating critical thinking. As children begin to think in terms of "this reminds me of something in one way, but it is opposite to it in other ways" they are beginning to form thinking skills that will be invaluable in the high school and college years.

Language Arts: Poetry

Here is a poem that your student might find humorous regarding the subject of the hippopotamus.

The Hippopotamus

Behold the hippopotamus!
We laugh at how he looks to us,
And yet, in moments dank and grim,
I wonder how we look to him.

Peace, peace, thou hippopotamus!
We really look all right to us,
As you no doubt delight the eye
Of other hippopotami.

Anonymous

Teacher's Note: You might take this opportunity to explain to your student what the term **Anonymous** means at the end of a poem, quote or writing. It means that there is no one who is given credit for that writing. It *does not* mean that whoever used the quote didn't do research to find attribution, but rather that the words, themselves, have never been credited to a particular person.

Art: Watercolor Illustrations

Barbara Knutson uses beautiful colors and gentle strokes to produce lovely illustrations for *Hanna's Cold Winter*. Look at the double page picture of the hippo house right after the picture of the family arriving at the zoo. The blues and greens are quiet and peaceful as the hippos peek out from the hot springs. Notice the dappled patterns of gray on the hippos. The varied light coming through the leaves of the trees causes a pattern on the hippo standing by the water.

Don't forget to look at this lovely summer picture and contrast it to the view of the hippo house in winter, eight pages later. In the winter scene the trees are bare and the pond is frozen. If you add the view from the cover picture you see icicles and snow. What a difference in the feelings conveyed from the summer season to the winter season pictures!

This is a lovely lesson in simple artistic appreciation. If however, you have an artist student, perhaps this variety of seasonal illustrations might inspire her to draw or paint several scenes of a particular place, each with different seasonal aspects.

Art: Comparing Photographs of Architecture with Illustrations

Look for books at your library on Hungary, or do a search online. Try to match photographs that you find with the buildings, bridges, etc., of the story illustrations. Many of the buildings and places from *Hanna's Cold Winter* still exist in Hungary today.

Also, look at the title page with the sketched drawings of Budapest. Find some of the buildings and sites there. (You can see the zoo, Lanchid Bridge, Gellert Hotel, and the cog train.) There are many ways to portray the sights of a city. List some of the different ways such as painting, modeling, photographing, needle working (as in tapestries), etc.

Art: Drawing Villages

On the title page of *Hanna's Cold Winter*, Barbara Knutson has sketched the city of Budapest. In the drawing she has included signs which name some of the buildings and sights seen in the story. If you have a copy of Bruce McIntyre's *The Drawing Textbook*, find the picture of his sketched fantasy city and drawing techniques. If your student is interested in learning to draw and is inspired by these pictures from McIntyre and Knutson, she can begin to practice the techniques and work on drawing her own towns.

Art: Architecture - Lions Bridge and Cover Building

Just for enjoyment, notice the architecture in the Lions Bridge, and the beautiful building for the hippos on the cover of the story. These structures have their own beauty, color, lines and amazing sculpture—a world of art for us to enjoy.

Art: Bath Scene - Focal Point Off-Center

In *Five in a Row* Volume 1, you may have studied composition in drawings and paintings, where there is a lesson on composition in *The Story of Ping* by Marjorie Flack. If so you may want to review that lesson and the pictures in *Ping*.

In the Gellert Bath scene in *Hanna's Cold Winter* you can see a beautiful room with tiles on the floor, huge columns that flow upward to an arched ceiling, upper hanging terraces and sculptured figures. Isn't it interesting that the little girl (maybe Eva) in her red suit is not in the center of the picture? Often artists will avoid having a main object in the center of their artistic composition. Rather, they will set the main object (people, plants, animals, buildings, etc.) just off-center. They feel it makes a more pleasing composition. Your student is welcome to try drawing, painting or even making a collage where the main object in the picture is off-center. However, if this is not an enjoyable project, then just be aware of this element of composition when you look together at books, artwork, etc., and point out examples to your student.

Art: Balance and Curves

Look at the last peaceful picture of three hippos together. The view is cut off by a half circle of sky at the top. This half circle curve is repeated in the hind quarters of the lower left hippo and the shoulder of the hippo lying on the ground facing the viewer. The curve is also repeated in the fence.

How do you take three hippos, each in a different position, and bring balance to the painting? Knutson does achieve a **balance**. The mass weight of the right-side standing hippo head plus the entire mass of the facing hippo body manages to balance the length and mass of the two left-side bodies. Art takes thought. Art takes manipulation to achieve a desired effect.

Have your student take some plastic animals, set them up and look at them from different angles. Have her think of how a picture of these animals would look. Now have her think about balance and let her try to place three animals in such a way that a balance is achieved. (Since hard plastic animals cannot be bent—claymation animals would be even better for this—your student will have to imagine how an animal's head turned a different way could help create a balance, etc.) If she enjoys this kind of thought process she might want to try with five animals, then seven. The animals do not have to be in a bunch. Two small animals on one side could balance a larger animal further away.

Art: Music - Classical Music

You can explore some musical classics along with your study of *Hanna's Cold Winter*. Franz Liszt (1811-1886) was born in Raiding, Hungary. He eventually went to Paris to study and developed several important musical forms such as the **rhapsody** and the **symphonic poem**. He used a **leitmotif** (LITE-moat-eef) which is a recurring theme (representing a person, idea or event) in his musical work. If you would like, find some musical compositions by Liszt. You might begin with *Hungarian Rhapsodies*. In this musical piece you will hear the influence of the Hungarian folk music.

Also, you can tie music to *Hanna's Cold Winter* through a famous piece of music called "The Blue Danube Waltz" ("On the Beautiful Blue Danube") by Johann Strauss, Jr. (1825-1899). Strauss lived in Vienna, Austria, one of the countries through which the Danube River flows. So while Strauss wrote of the Danube in Austria, you can still tie the river itself to this story as the river also flows through Hungary. Listen to this beautiful **waltz** and think of the Danube flowing from Germany through Austria, Hungary and other countries as well. Isn't it interesting all the variety of subjects that inspire works of music, poetry, writing, painting, etc.? In this case, Strauss must have loved the Danube and this river formed the inspiration for his famous waltz.

If your student is interested she may want to use crayon, colored pencil or watercolors to make a picture. Let the music from the "Hungarian Rhapsodies" or "The Blue Danube Waltz" influence her to fashion a work however she is inspired (even as just flowing lines) as she listens.

Science: Peppers, Paprika

Teacher's Note: In this lesson we are not talking about the small berry that makes the spice called black pepper or white pepper, but rather the family of capsicum plants which produce the green and red peppers we use cut up in salads and for chile powders and paprika.

Purchase several different colors and/or shapes of peppers and begin your lesson on this plant by letting your student see the variety. Or take your student to a market where a good variety of peppers are sold. (If there are no markets near you, a good seed catalog will have pictures of peppers of different kinds.)

Paprika is prepared by grinding up the dried pods of a capsicum pepper. The resulting seasoning is not as hot as cayenne pepper. It retains a beautiful red color and is used for seasoning and coloring in many recipes as well as for garnishing foods. Show your student a bottle of paprika or point out this seasoning at the store.

Science: More Friction or Less Friction and Ways to Solve the Problem

Friction is a force that acts to oppose two objects rubbing together or over each other. If you try to rub two pieces of large-grained sandpaper against each other it will be difficult. In contrast if you try to rub two pieces of copy paper together it is less difficult because the smoother paper creates less friction than the rough sandpaper.

In the same way, the wheels of a traditional train are smooth and the rails are also smooth. Most of the time the massive weight of a locomotive bearing down provides enough friction and allows the train to move quickly and effectively even though the wheels and rails are smooth. However, in the cases where engines have to pull a train up a very steep grade (incline) the smooth wheels can begin to slip and the train may be in danger of beginning to roll backwards. To overcome this problem of **lack of friction**, the cog railway has toothed, gear-like wheels that mesh with the toothed rails and provide the engine with the ability to pull a train up a steep hill without the chance of slipping back. (See the History - Through the Illustrations and Text lesson earlier in this unit for more information on cog railways.)

Friction is an interesting phenomenon. Sometimes you need it and sometimes you want to alleviate it. In the story of *Mr. Gumpy's Motor Car* (FIAR Vol. 2), more friction is needed. Ask your student if he remembers that Mr. Gumpy's car is stuck in the mud. The slippery mud does not offer enough friction (or traction) to move the car forward. How do the story characters solve their problem? (All the riders have to push the car, but if they had found some, they could also have sprinkled sand or gravel under the tires to increase the friction.)

In *Hanna's Cold Winter* the railroad has a similar problem. More friction or traction was needed. But in this case builders overcame the problem with a special set of tracks and wheels to help the train move uphill safely.

Talk about other times where instead of increasing friction you want to alleviate it to reduce noise, reduce wear and tear on metal parts, make an object easier to move, etc. (Like the squeaky hinges on a door, moving parts in a car's motor, a competition swimmer.) How do you cause two items to have less friction between them? There are two simple ways. One way that your student can remember easily is to use a lubricant like oil or water. She can feel the difference that a lubricant makes as she notices the difference between rubbing her hands back and forth quickly before and after she uses hand lotion. Many different types of oil are used to reduce friction in a variety of applications. Another way to reduce friction is to make the surfaces moving against each other smoother. In ice skating, the ice is scraped to reduce bumps and pits till it is as smooth as possible and the skater's skates are kept ground and smooth. Also, the weight of the skates on the ice causes a thin film of water to form between the rink and the skates. With these things together, friction is reduced and the skater glides smoothly. In swimming competitions, friction is reduced when swimmers wear tight-fitting swim caps and suits and even special types of goggles. Male swimmers even shave their chest, arms and legs to reduce the friction caused by thousands of hairs passing through water.

Teacher's Note: Friction also produces heat. If you desire you can incorporate this fact into the lesson above.

Science: Geology - Hot Springs

The hippos in *Hanna's Cold Winter* are able to make use of the hot springs area at the Budapest Zoo. The warm waters of these springs are thought to be helpful in creating an environment that encourages hippos to bring up offspring (something not usual to these animals in captivity).

But, you might ask your student, how do waters become hot (or warm)? Hot springs occur when underground water is heated by areas of hot rock or lava deep in the ground. There are many areas of hot springs in the United States. Search "hot springs" online and see what you can find. Look especially at entries for Arkansas and Yellowstone National Park.

Science: Zoology - Hippopotamuses

The name "hippopotamus" comes from two Greek words that mean "river horse." (The Greek word for horse—hippos, and the Greek word for river—potomos). If you could see a cutaway view of a river, you would be able to understand how this name might have come about. Hippos run, just like horses, on the floor of the river, underwater. They actually look like horses galloping along the river bottoms, but of course they do have to come up for air. Hippos can stay underwater for as long as six minutes.

Even though the name and actions are reminiscent of horses, and they can run up to twenty miles per hour on land, hippopotamuses are more closely related to the pig! Adult hippos reach lengths of fourteen feet and up to five feet in height, weighing as much as eight thousand pounds. (An average four-door car weighs approximately three thousand pounds.)

Hippos use a variety of grunts, growls and screams underwater in order to communicate with each other. They are plant-eating (**herbivore**) animals, with mouths that can open nearly four feet wide. Baby hippos called calves are born underwater. Hippos can live up to forty years.

The scientific name for the largest hippopotamus is Hippopotamus amphibious. Why does your student think the last part of the name is applicable? (A hippo is *not* an amphibian, but it is **amphibious** in that it can *travel* on both land and in the water. Perhaps your student knows this word in regard to military vehicles that can travel over land and also across water. During WWII, amphibious boat-trucks known as DUKW operated on both water and land, and soldiers eventually shortened their name to "Ducks."

Remember from your studies of the story *The Giraffe That Walked to Paris* (Vol. 2), how much the people loved La Giraffe? The people of Buda and Pest loved their hippos as well!

Science: Discovering Zoo History

Since ancient times people have kept wild animals. Rulers of Egypt, China and others displayed their wealth and power through personal collections.* The first public zoos were begun in Greece, and the oldest public zoo still in existence is in Vienna, Austria. It opened in the mid-1700s. The zoo from *Hanna's Cold Winter* opened in 1866 and is still in operation.

The study of zoo history is interesting. Throughout history some zoos were not run with efficiency, nor with compassion for the animals, while others were

were run quite well. Even today there are some zoos that are better than others, especially from the animals' points of view. How and why zoos began, the first children's zoos, when animal care discoveries were made (such as the invention of the moat-type environments rather than metal cages), feeding and care of animals, breeding and caring for animals that risk extinction and many more topics are waiting for an interested student who desires to do some zoo investigation.

Remind your student that the word **zoology** is the study of animals. Zoology and **botany** (the study of plants) together form the branch of science called **biology**. It is easy to remember what zoology means when your student thinks of zoo!

*Remember in the *Five in a Row* lessons for *The Giraffe That Walked to Paris*, that the ruler of Egypt sent the giraffe to the King of France who kept her in a zoo, or in French, a **menagerie**? This zoo in Paris is the third oldest public zoo in the world that is still in existence.

Teacher's Notes

The *Five in a Row* lesson options for each unit in the manual are all you need to teach your child. The additional resource area provided below is simply a place to jot down relevant info you've found that you might want to reference.

HANNA'S COLD WINTER

Date:

Student:

Five in a Row Lesson Topics Chosen:

Social Studies:

Language Arts:

Art:

Math:

Science:

Relevant Library Resources: Books, DVDs, Audio Books

Websites or Video Links:

Related Field Trip Opportunities:

Favorite Quote or Memory During Study:

Name:
Date:
Geography: **Flag of Hungary**

The Hungarian flag has three colored, horizontal stripes (red, white, green from top to bottom). This design is based upon the French flag, as a reflection of the ideas of the French revolution. The red, white, and green colors are taken from the historical Hungarian coat of arms. *For more information, see Parts of a Flag on page 266.*

Color in the Hungarian flag below.

Name:

Date:

Art: **Architecture - Bridges**

After doing the **Art: Architecture - Lions Bridge and Cover Building** lesson, have your student research famous bridges and choose one to highlight. Paste a picture of the bridge on the blank area and fill in the answers they may have found to the questions below.

Name of bridge: ________________________________

Type of bridge: ________________________________

Location: ________________________________

Length: ________________________________

How long did it take to build? ________________________

Name:
Date:
Science: **Discovering Zoo History**

Search online for the "Budapest Zoo." Using their website, plan a virtual itenerary for an imaginary visit. Print off the zoo map, search their exhibits and species list, and using the itenerary below have your student create their ideal day trip to the Budapest Zoo.

FIELD TRIP

HOUR	Food / Exhibit / Gift Shop
__ : __	________________
__ : __	________________
__ : __	________________
__ : __	________________
__ : __	________________
__ : __	________________
__ : __	________________
__ : __	________________

Albert

Title: *Albert*
Author: Donna Jo Napoli
Illustrator: Jim LaMarche
Copyright: 2001
Summary: Albert finds himself out on a limb, but ends up enjoying the ride.

Social Studies: City Living

This story doesn't have a specific geographic locality. It takes place in a city. We know that it must be a fairly large city with sidewalk vendors like those found in New York City, as well as tall apartment buildings. This story also takes place in a location within the bird range of cardinals. Put your story disk on a large city in an area where cardinals live. (Check a bird guide and a map of their territory to discover where this might be. From this exercise your student will become familiar with yet another resource book, a bird field guide, in which he can find answers to questions he has.)

Talk about apartment living with your student. Many families share a single building and you can sometimes hear people and noises above or below you or in the hallways. There may be bars on windows for safety. Apartments may also have large awnings, fire escapes, staircases or elevators, central laundry units, inside garages, etc.

If you can, visit an apartment complex. See how many of these things your student can find, and write down other observations you make as you visit.

Make an apartment building out of a large shoebox. Put in floors, halls and rooms and let your student decorate the building any way he wishes. Talk together and imagine what it would be like to live in an apartment if he has never had this experience before.

The story *Albert* mentions a lady selling flowers (like a sidewalk vendor) and someone selling golden bean cakes, again probably a sidewalk vendor. If your student has never seen such vendors explain that like a man standing on the corner with a pushcart of ice cream cones to sell to anyone who passes by, vendors sell all sorts of things on city sidewalks. They probably have to have permits from the city to be at the locations where they sell. They may also have to meet other requirements (especially city health requirements if there is food involved). Look for examples of sidewalk vendors in stories that you read and point them out to your students. There is a very interesting book for your older grade level student called *The Pushcart War* by Jean Merrill.

Through this introduction, your student will recognize many other types of "vendor" characters and scenes in books, movies and plays.

Social Studies: Discovering the Truth

Discuss with your student what kept Albert from going outside. Your student may say it was the weather and you can agree with him, but gently probe a bit deeper. Reread each section that talks about the weather being too damp, or too hot, etc. Now, notice what occurs just before each test of the weather. Each time Albert decides the weather is not right, he has just heard a noise that he considers "not a good noise." Now ask again. What *really* kept Albert indoors? Albert didn't like anything (especially noise) that wasn't "good." The weather was just sort of a—what? An excuse! It is good to be able to see through our excuses and know what it is that really bothers us. That way we can deal directly with the situation.

Can your student think of a time when he has not wanted to do something or has been afraid to do something and rather than say so, he offered an excuse? Do you have any of your own examples to share with him?

Now reread the part of the story where Albert protects the baby birds from the cat. What kind of a noise does Albert make to scare the cat away? (Screech!) If Albert had heard someone else make that same noise as he was looking through his window, would he have considered it a good noise or a bad noise? You see, in this case it was good because it protected the birds. In the same way, many noises can be considered either bad or good depending on the circumstances. In either case, all these noises are a part of the world we live in.

Social Studies: Character Relationships - Fears That Rob Us

Albert was afraid to go outside and for a long time he allowed his fears to control his actions. All the time that Albert stayed closed up indoors he was missing the wonderful life that was going on right outside on his own sidewalk! Talk with your student about fears. There are some fears that are legitimate and help us steer clear of truly dangerous situations—as a normal fear of (or respect for) fire. However, so many times the fears we have are actually groundless and these are the fears that rob us of so much of life's joy. Work together to come up with a system to help your student evaluate his fears and help him find out which ones need to be addressed and which ones are groundless. Fears are often best dealt with by finding out the truth just like Albert did!

Social Studies: Character Relationship - Compassion

Once your student has passed his amazement at the somewhat tall tale of a man holding a nest in his hand for several weeks, you might talk about the fact that many people don't pay much attention to wildlife. Perhaps it is because so much of the wonder of life is missing, or maybe that people are too busy with their own pursuits to enjoy and care for wildlife. A person who has learned to be in awe of creatures from tiny ants to soaring eagles is usually a happier person. This kind of person is one who often will sacrifice in some way—spending money for birdseed or a bird bath, or caring enough to make the call to a nature center on behalf of an injured wild animal. Albert shows the reader, in an admittedly stretched (if not tall) tale scenario, the character of someone who really does care about wild creatures.

Language Arts: The Comics

Did your student enjoy the fact that Albert reads the comics? Comics are a series of cartoon boxes that tell a story. They may tell this story entirely in one comic strip or the story may be ongoing with many adventures over weeks, months or even years. Some may even end each week in a cliff-hanger. The first comic strips appeared in newspapers in the early 1900s and they are still featured in newspapers, magazines, comic books, and graphic novels today. Many of the original comic strips were humorous, thus they became known also as "the funnies."

As a genre, comic strips include both writing and art. Most often one person both writes and draws the work.

Have your student try making a box comic strip with one or more squares and then writing and illustrating his own comics, or you can work on one together. Obviously the number of boxes will be determined by how many your student needs to complete his idea. See the activity sheet at the end of this unit.

Language Arts: List Making

What kinds of things did Albert do to keep busy? Make a list. What kinds of things does your student like to do to keep himself busy? Make another list. As the teacher, you could also make a list of the things you like to do and then compare your list with your student's.

Language Arts: Postcard

If your student does not know what a postcard is, purchase some and show them to him. You can often find postcards at grocery stores, big box stores, or the post office. Explain that you can send a quick note on a post card for less money than it takes to mail a letter. Find out the difference in the two prices.

Have your student write a postcard to a friend or relative. Show him where the message goes and where the address should be placed. Then, unlike Albert, who never sent his cards, your student can actually take joy in going outside and posting it!

Language Arts: Imagination

At first, when Albert heard the airplane roar he was afraid of the loud noise. But because he had to stay at the window, he began to think of the places an airplane might go. Where does your student think the airplane might be going? If he has lots of ideas let him make a list. Now ask him where he would like to go. Many times the answer will be different because your student wasn't thinking specifically of what he would like. If he has lots of answers let him make another list. Again, if you care to, you could make a list of where *you* would like to go and compare your list with that of your student.

Language Arts: Subtle Symbolism

Your student may be too young to make much of this lesson, however, you can mention it in passing and see if the concepts are understood.

Discuss with your student the fact that Albert was afraid to go outside. He was afraid of the "not good" noises that he heard and of what they might mean. When a person is afraid in this way, it is like they put themselves in a little jail. Symbolically these fearful people seem to look out from between the bars (just like Albert actually did at his window) and they cannot seem to get out. With your student, look at all the illustrations of Albert and his window. Choose the one you think looks most like he is in a jail cell.

After being forced to spend enough time at the window to understand that all the noises were part of his wonderful world, Albert became freed from his fears and was happy to go outside of his self-imposed jail. The illustration of him flying in the swing like a bird is symbolic of this new-found freedom. We often talk about flying "free like a bird" and Albert was happy doing so!

Language Arts: Suspension of Reality

Teacher's Note: This is a lesson to discuss with your student ONLY if the subject comes up in questions and conversation. Children are quite able to happily suspend reality to enjoy a good story and it would be something of an insult to this happy childhood ability if in the name of academics this became an intrusive lesson. However, some students have an extremely practical nature and they insist on answers. If your student is one of these, this lesson could be useful.

Albert puts his hand out the window and a bird begins to build her nest on his palm. The bird parents raise their bird family over a three-week period. Eventually the birds begin to feed Albert. During all this time Albert stands at the window.

Your student may wonder about Albert's ability to stand up for so long, to sleep standing up, and about other functions that would not be possible with his arm permanently stuck out the window. Discuss with your student how sometimes authors set aside "how things would *really* work" for an imaginative story line that could not actually happen otherwise. This type of imaginative event can sometimes be used for the background of a special story.

Countless childhood stories are written in this manner. In some, animals are dressed like people and talk or have emotions. In others, like *Cloudy with a Chance of Meatballs* by Judi Barrett, the grandfather who is fixing pancakes tells a story that completely suspends reality, where there is a land that rains down various types of food. Wonderful stories are written with parts that are real mixed with parts that are not believable. In these stories it is always fun to pretend that just possibly the unbelievable parts could happen. *Albert* is one of these stories.

In Napoli's story *Albert*, the author, in the interest of making her point, suspends reality. The point of the story is not Albert's ability to perform this super-human feat of standing with his arm out the window for weeks. Rather the point of the story is the fact that being forced to stand at the window *changes* Albert's view of the world. Standing at the window takes Albert out of his comfort zone—and he is changed!

An older student might enjoy writing a similar type story where reality is suspended for the good of the story's message.

Art: Music

Albert's birds make their nest in the spring. This is a wonderful opportunity to play Antonio Vivaldi's famous composition *The Four Seasons*. Particularly the "Spring" portion of this work would tie in to the story of *Albert*.

Also, Albert whistles at the fledgling. You might want to try whistling and have your student try. If you can both whistle try a duet! There is a song, made famous by the Disney movie *Snow White*, called "Whistle While You Work." If your student doesn't know this song, he might enjoy learning the words and music and thinking about Albert whistling as he encouraged the young bird.

Art: Artist's Medium and Watercolor Papers

Jim LaMarche's beautiful illustrations for the story *Albert* are executed in colored pencils on watercolor paper. If your student is showing interest in illustrating his own work, drawing in a nature journal, or pursuing other artistic efforts, it might be time to visit an art store or hobby store that carries art supplies. With your student look at the different types of colored pencils and buy the best set you can afford. Prismacolor™ makes an excellent pencil and comes in sets of many sizes. Since colored pencils are not as easy to mix as paints (you can blend, but not exactly mix), the larger the set the more variety the student has for his work. Perhaps he could receive a good set of pencils for a birthday, etc. There are also excellent sets of colored pencils that you can use with some water to make a blend of colored pencil technique and watercolor technique. You might want to try a small set of those as well. When you have finished looking over the colored pencils, let your student see the variety of watercolor papers on the market. There are some that are smooth and some that have a great deal of texture to them. Jim LaMarche has used a watercolor paper with texture for his illustrations for *Albert*, so that in those pictures the student can see pencil marks as wells as texture marks from the paper. Perhaps you can purchase a sheet or two of textured watercolor paper for you student to experiment with.

Art: Sculpture and Painting Project

Find a nest or purchase one at the craft store and then let your student make cardinal eggs. Your student can research the size, shape, color, etc. and model them from Crayola Model Magic® which will harden in the air. When dry and hard these eggs can be painted in cardinal colors with the spots and marks added. Display your student's work (eggs in the nest) on a forked twig in a bookcase or on a tabletop. (Your student can also examine the illustration on the back dust jacket of *Albert*.)

Art: Illustrations - Progressive Details

As your student's ability to observe details grows increasingly better, he will begin to notice whether or not a book's illustrations are consistent with the story and with the other illustrations themselves. In *Albert* there are at least two good examples of these types of consistent illustrations. Look with your student at the windowsill where Albert stands for so long. There is a little vine-type plant sitting there. As the story progresses the vine grows! You can tell that it is taller in the pictures that follow the first time you see it.

In the same way, Albert's beard grows! At the beginning of the story he is clean shaven and as time goes by while he is standing at the window, each successive picture shows more beard!

These are the kinds of details that good artists think about when they do the illustrations for books. Maybe your student would like to write a short story and illustrate it with progressive details just like Jim LaMarche does in *Albert*. A story of a garden, from the first plowing to the harvesting of the crops would be a wonderful vehicle for this type of illustration. Can you think of other story lines that would be good? (A child growing up? Even a story set with a background of washing the dishes would look better if the illustrations showed a full sink of sudsy dishes and then later a picture of the water draining away, etc.) Use the activity sheet at the end of this unit for your student's short story with progressive illustrations.

Art: Cooking - Golden Bean Cakes

There are actually at least two different types of food called golden bean cakes. One is a fried bean cake with a meat filling eaten with chili sauce, and the other is a sweet dessert made with crushed beans. Search online for recipes for each. You can also inquire about golden bean cakes at an Asian food market or look for recipes in Asian cookbooks.

Art: Pantomime

Albert watched many people from his window. Sometimes he could hear noises (he knew for instance that the people were arguing but he couldn't hear the exact words). Much of what Albert witnessed was in the form of pantomime. A pantomime is when someone performs pretend actions without words. Use this story as an opportunity to introduce pantomime to your student. Explain how it relates to the story (that Albert could often see, but not hear everything) and then allow your student the time to try acting out in pantomime some of the scenarios both from the story and those which he makes up on his own.

Pantomime is a form of entertainment that consists of acting without words. The word comes from the word "mimic" and is often shortened to "mime," when speaking of the actors or of their performance. The acting usually tells a story and may or may not be accompanied by music. Because the acting does not use words or sounds, it must be exaggerated in movement and expression so the audience can understand what is going on.

Suggest that you and your student act out, in pantomime, the scene in *Albert* where he views the couple on the street arguing. Talk out the scene: You each pretend to come out of a building, yelling at each other, and eventually turning your backs on each other and walking off offended. (What would that look like in pantomime without making any actual sounds? You could use excited, erratic hand gestures, along with wide open mouths and extremely angry facial expressions. Then make a large, quick turn as you walk away and angry walk, feet stomping, etc. Feel free to add or subtract any of these ideas and create your own interpretation of the feud.)

Next, talk out the reunion of these two people: With pretend packages they meet, laugh, hug and you are free to add anything else to the story. Again, all the actions will be large and expressive. There is little subtlety in pantomime! After you have tried these scenarios, find others in the story* or make up your own and enjoy this form of entertainment and expression as much as you'd like. If you feel comfortable doing so, invite a small audience and see if they can understand what is happening in the quiet little scenes being performed.

For extra interest see if you can find some videos of famous mimes and their work. Watching these films might give your creative student some extra ideas for improving his own performances. Perhaps the most famous mime of all is Marcel Marceau. There are also great scenes of Charlie Chaplin miming in silent movies.

*Have your young student act out the scenario of being in an egg, hatching, being fed and fledging. Your older student could pretend to be the proud parent bird. Can someone who is not in on the pantomime rehearsal tell the story that is being acted out?

Teacher's Note: For your own information, pantomime is more popular in Great Britain and is often associated with seasonal performances there. In England you will hear people saying that they are practicing for an upcoming panto. This is their shortened or slang form of the word pantomime.

Math: Divisions of Time

Donna Jo Napoli, the author of *Albert*, uses the words morning, midday and night in her story. Can you find these words with your student? On a sheet of paper, list activities that your student thinks of as morning, midday and night activities. Now, assign approximate times of day for these activities. For instance: hearing Mom make breakfast 7:00 am; lunch 11:30 am; outdoor time 1:00 P.M., bedtime 9:00 P.M. This is just an exercise in using hours of the day and time on the clock to mark certain daily events. You can also discuss the term *midday* that is derived and shortened from the phrase "middle of the day."

If you have not discussed that an hour consists of sixty minutes or minutes consist of sixty seconds each, you can do this as well. With an older student you can also figure the number of hours in a day, week, month, etc.

Ask your student why he thinks people use such terms as morning, noon (midday) and night and why they bother to divide the day into hours? (It isn't just so there will be more to learn! Maybe he will come up with the idea on his own that we use such divisions to help us communicate when certain things happen. If someone says that their mail is delivered about lunch time we understand that it comes about noon, not in the morning or the evening. When we want to meet someone we can give a certain time and if each party is keeping track of the time they can meet together without a lot of guessing or waiting.)

There is also a saying that might be interesting to your student. Some people describe something as being 24/7. Can your student figure out what that means? If a person said that you could call them anytime—twenty-four/seven—they mean you could call them any hour of the day (twenty-four hours) and any time during the week (seven days a week). In other words they really do mean *any time*!

Math: Learning to Average

Teacher's Note: This lesson requires the student have a beginning knowledge of division.

Let your student tackle the adventure of figuring the **average** number of weeks in the cardinals' nesting period. Have your student look at the upcoming science lesson for the cardinal and add up the number of days to build a nest (between 2-9 days), number of days to lay the eggs (varies; 2-6 depending on how many eggs), how long till the eggs hatch (12-13 days) and how long before they fledge or leave the nest (between 10 and 20+ days). For each of these categories he will have to calculate and then add the average figure.

For instance, to figure the average number of eggs let him add 2 + 3 + 4 + 5 + 6 together because the number of eggs listed 2-6. He will add these and find the total is 21. Then have him count the number of entries he added (5) and divide 5 into 21. The average number of eggs laid is then 4. He might be able to tell just by looking that the average days until fledging 10-20, is 15. If not, let him do the computations. Also do the average for the length of time it takes to build a nest. When he has all the averages let him add them up to find the average number of days it takes a cardinal to build, lay and raise a brood. (The number should be 36 or 37. This is an average! Some birds will take a longer time and some a shorter time raising their broods.)

Remind your student once again the reason he is finding an average is because the same type of bird will behave differently under different conditions, and your student is just seeking to know what the *average* for any cardinal might be.

Math: Mathematics in Baseball

Albert listened to baseball games when he was in his apartment. Does your student know that there is a great deal of math connected with the game of baseball? There are all the dimensions of the playing field, for instance, 60 feet 6 inches from the pitcher's rubber to home plate. There are exact dimensions for the batter's box and for the distance between the coach's box to the base lines. If your student is interested, let him look up "baseball measurements" online and see for himself all the interesting measurements.

The sport of baseball itself is filled with an area of mathematics known as statistics. Many different baseball skills are categorized or averaged such as batting averages, stolen bases, strikeouts, earned run averages, slugging percentages, etc. This is a whole sub-study in itself for your student.

Outs are counted at the rate of three per inning. This is a great opportunity to work on "counting by threes." And, in baseball the number of balls and strikes are also recorded and entered into the statistical record as well. Any student interested in finding out for himself the amazing world of baseball math will be well rewarded with rich discoveries!

Math: Altitude and Speed

Albert listened to the roar of a plane when he was standing at his window. The plane was up in the sky and was moving along at a certain speed. Does your student have any curiosity about how high (at what *altitude*) most commercial airline planes fly? Obviously these planes take off from the ground and spend some time reaching their cruising altitude. Cruising altitude for most commercial jet airliners is between 30,000 and 37,000 feet. Smaller private propeller planes might fly anywhere from 1000 to 15,000 feet above the earth's surface. How fast does a jet airliner travel? Cruising speeds range from 400 to 600 mph. Small private propeller driven planes fly at anywhere from 75 to 200 mph.

Speeds are also measured in "knots." Ask your student if he knows what a knot is. A knot is equal to one nautical mile, or about 1.15 statue miles. So a plane traveling at 100 knots would be flying at about 115 mph. How fast would a plane flying 350 knots be traveling? How many knots is a plane traveling when it's flying at 450 mph?

Science: Tomatoes and Tomato Juice

Teacher's Note: This is another long lesson. Use only as much information as will intrigue your student. Some of the technical facts were added as a point of observation, not for memorization. For instance, the details about botanists vs. horticulturists are included just so your student can see that there are various ways to group objects. Just as your student could group small model cars in more than one way—by color, then number of doors, or even by the use of vehicles. In the same way, tomatoes can also be a part of different groups or categories!

Remind your student that Albert sits at the table and drinks tomato juice as he listens to the morning noises. Has your student ever had tomato juice? If possible have a tomato handy to examine as you present a few facts about this common food.

A tomato is a highly nutritious food that contains vitamins (A, C, E, etc.) and minerals, as well as other important nutrients. Your older student may enjoy looking up "tomato nutrition" online and listing vitamins, carbohydrates, sugar, fat content, etc. Most tomatoes are also a highly acidic food, though some varieties have been cultivated to have less acid content.

Tomatoes are grown commercially on large farms as well as avidly by home gardeners. They come in multitudes of sizes (from grape size to those weighing well over two pounds) and in various colors: orange, red, yellow, etc. Take your student to a farmer's market or a grocery store with a large produce section and let him find all the varieties of tomatoes he can. Often there will be grape, cherry, plum, and cluster tomatoes as well as the more common garden varieties. If your student can look through a good seed catalog he will be surprised at the large variety of tomato seeds which are available.

Tomatoes are considered both a fruit and a vegetable. It just depends on whether one is speaking with a botanist (definitely a fruit) or a horticulturist (definitely a vegetable). Botanists are concerned with grouping plants by how a plant is formed—plant parts, and how they grow—their life cycle. A horticulturist is concerned with how plants are propagated and raised or farmed. When speaking of tomatoes, a botanist will say that a tomato is a fruit because the flesh of the tomato encloses the seeds. (In the same way, cucumbers, squash, pumpkins, green peppers would also be considered fruits.) However, the horticulturist would say that a fruit grows on woody stemmed plants or plants that are *not* replanted each year, like strawberry plants. To a horticultural scientist, fruit would be that which grows on trees or shrubs, like blueberries, cherries, pears, apples, etc., and strawberries which are perennial plants.

Isn't it interesting that different areas of science will group the same plant differently? Probably if one spoke to a chef he would say that certain foods such as fruits are used primarily for desserts while others are always eaten with the meal—vegetables! That would put the tomato back into the vegetable category. Tomatoes provide a main ingredient to many of the condiments that we use in cooking. Your student may not realize that tomatoes form the base of catsup, salsas, tomato sauce, tomato paste, pizza sauce, spaghetti sauces, and some salad dressings. And there is always tomato soup!

Teacher's Note: Just for your own information: A further interesting fact about tomatoes is that the United States government in the late 1800s officially declared the tomato a vegetable for the purpose of tariffs on imports. However, it doesn't change at all the minds of botanists who still maintain that a tomato is a fruit! If you have upper grade level students they might enjoy researching the two sides of the "*tomato—fruit or vegetable*?" question and having a debate over the proper category of a tomato.

Perhaps now is the time to try some tomato juice. If you have never tried homemade tomato juice, it is a delight compared to any canned or store bottled product. Sometimes, too, when a student helps with the project, he is more likely to enjoy the results. So, here is a recipe for you and your student to make your own tomato juice. Be sure to serve it well chilled:

Crockpot Tomato Juice

10 large tomatoes
1 teaspoon salt
1 teaspoon seasoned salt
1/4 teaspoon pepper
1 tablespoon sugar

Wash and drain tomatoes. Remove the core and the blossom ends. Place the tomatoes in a slow cooker. Cover and cook on low 4 to 6 hours or until tomatoes are done. Press through a sieve or food mill. Add seasonings; chill well and stir before serving. Keep refrigerated for up to three days. Think of Albert as you enjoy your tomato juice.

Science: Noise

Remind your student of the plane that roared, the one Albert thinks is not a good noise. Ask your student for his own definition of noise.

Noise is actually a sound where you don't want it to be. (It's sort of like the definition of a weed, which is a plant that is where you don't want it to be. An apple tree in a wheat field might be considered a weed!) So, a sound that is irritating might be considered by some to be a noise and by others to be pleasant. Some people enjoy the droning sound of a fan while they go to sleep while others think it noisy and prefer the quiet.

On the other hand there are sounds which have such a high pitch or loud volume that it actually hurts the ear. Most people would consider these sounds noise. So there is both an aspect of personally irritating sounds as well as those sounds which actually cause pain to the ear. Both are considered noise.

Sound pressure is measured in decibels designated by the symbol dB, with 10 dB being sounds that the human ear can hardly hear and 70 or 80 dB being what most people would consider noisy. A loud live rock concert might be in excess of 140dB! This kind of noise (because it is in the form of music generally considered enjoyable) is not as easily noticeable in causing hearing loss. The range of 85+ dB is great enough to cause hearing loss if there is long enough exposure. The reduction in hearing often comes slowly and after long periods of exposure and is caused by the hearing nerves being damaged. Concert goers and people who listen to loud music on a regular basis, as well as those who use loud equipment or work in noisy factories can take precautions by wearing protective hearing devices. Aging also has an effect in the reduction of hearing, as do disease and injury.

With housing developments built near airports, apartments situated near crowded city traffic, and louder industrial and construction types of equipment being used, noise pollution has become a problem to be dealt with in cities. Your student might enjoy researching this topic and finding out the latest solutions to helping this problem.

Your student will be interested in looking at these decibel levels for common sounds listed by the Canadian Hearing Society:

120 dB Thunderclap or ambulance siren

117 dB Football game at a stadium or a movie in a theatre

110 dB Leaf blower, live rock music

95 dB Motorcycle, jet boats/personal water craft

85 dB Lawnmower, many industrial workplaces, noisy restaurant

80 dB Average city traffic noise

70 dB Vacuum cleaner, sewing machine, hairdryer

60 dB Normal conversation

30 dB Whisper

Now list the words for the kinds of noises that Albert heard: Clatter, bark, giggle, rumble, sing, shout, laugh, argue, a radio, whistle, chatter, chirp, plane's roar, yell, screech, chuckle, peep, and a siren, and talk about the decibel level you think each might be.

Then listen carefully and list all the sounds your student can hear in three or four minutes' time. He'll really have to concentrate to hear the tiny sounds around him. Think about the difference in this list if he is outdoors or indoors, and the differences at different times of the day or night.

Science: Weather and the Spring Season

The weather mentioned in the story *Albert* includes cold weather, damp weather and breezy weather. Ask your student when birds build their nests and lay their eggs. In what season of the year does this usually happen? (This happens mostly in the spring, and sometimes on into summer.) Ask your student what he knows about springtime weather? (He may say that it is sometimes warm and sometimes cold. He may also say that the spring season can be a very breezy or windy season and that it is often rainy or damp.) It sounds as though Albert's birds built their nest in the spring and that whether Albert liked it or not, the weather was most typical for that season of the year!

Since there are many different areas of climate, sit down with your student and make a chart of the four seasons (or whatever seasons you experience) and write down the typical weather patterns for each season in the area where your student lives.

Science: Berries

Since the birds fed Albert berries, take this opportunity to explore these delicious small fruits.

Make a list of as many kinds of berries as you know. (Remember *The Duchess Bakes a Cake* in Vol. 2? There were many berries listed in that story! Are they all real? "Bilberries, gooseberries, cranberries, bogberries, blackberries, mulberries, burberries, dogberries" ... and then don't forget to add raspberries, blueberries, loganberries and there are surely more! Ah, your student remembered! Strawberries!)

Since the birds feed Albert blackberries, find some fresh or frozen berries to examine. Let your student look at the small fruit under a magnifying glass, feel it and even dissect it to see how the parts fit together and what it looks like inside. Because blackberries can stain fingers and clothing you could have aprons or smocks ready to protect garments, and even thin flexible plastic gloves might be helpful.

After your student has examined the fruit, written about it and drawn its shape, let him taste it. You may want to provide a bowl of berries and a dollop of whipped cream or yogurt for a treat after the lesson. While he is enjoying the berries (or some blackberry jam on bread) explain to him how a blackberry grows on a bush. Birds often eat berries and drop the digested seeds over the ground. Some of these seeds germinate and grow where there are favorable conditions. Blackberries grow where they can enjoy a light soil with humus that holds the moisture, protection from fierce summer afternoon sun, and while they need good amounts of moisture they do not tolerate standing water or swampy areas. The berries grow on bushes or on canes (or brambles) which have thorns, and they have an oval serrated leaf. In many areas of the United States and Canada you can take your student for a walk in the country along wooded areas and find wild blackberries growing. There are also small fruit farms where you may go to pick your own blackberries.

Teacher's Note: Albert eventually ate some insects as well. There are many countries of the world where insects are commonly eaten and enjoyed. Insects provide protein and nutrients. Some insects that are most popular for food include grasshoppers, ants, crickets, beetles and grubs.

Science: Zoology - Cardinal

Cardinalis cardinalis is the scientific name for the familiar red bird from the story *Albert*. In this lesson, your student may find information online or in library books. By consulting differnet sources, he will learn that good research means reading the observations and opinions of many sources and synthesizing that information into usable facts for his particular project. Based on locality and other factors, there are numerous conflicting facts for almost every single aspect of the life of a cardinal. The same species of bird in different climate areas may nest more or fewer times in a season. These birds may build nests in different kinds of trees or shrubs based on what is available in that locality and they may eat different kinds of foods, or build their nest with different kinds of materials—again based on what is available, etc. The important lesson here is to learn that the information in bird field guides is **approximate** and when watching birds, to be ready for slight variations in the information based on these different factors. (An exception might be state-specific bird guides such as those by Stan Tekiela.)

For instance, in researching the number of days a female cardinal takes to build her nest, there are sources that say 2 to 5 days or 4 to 6 days, while other sources lengthen the time span and say 3 to 9 days. These nests are built from 3 to 20 feet above the ground (most are 3 to 8 feet above ground) in shrubs or bushes or trees. The female building the nest makes a cup-shaped impression in the center with her body and lines the nest in hair, grasses, bark, etc.

Some books say that eggs are laid in a **clutch** of 2 to 4 eggs, while others say 2 to 5 oval eggs are laid. (These eggs are laid one per day until the clutch is complete and then **incubation** begins.) Incubation lasts 12 or 13 days.

Your student may find information that says cardinals raise 2-4 families a year, while you can also find that the young **fledge** (or leave the nest and begin to fly) in 9 to 10 days, 11 days, or 21 to 28 days! In most cases both parents feed the young until they fledge unless the female is sitting on a new clutch of eggs at a new nest, in which case the male does all the hunting and feeding.

One of the most interesting differences in the cardinals' life cycle is the color of the eggs! Statistics from different cardinals' nest observations indicate that egg color may range from white or gray spotted with brown, gray or purple specks, to buff or pale green eggs, speckled with brown or lilac; to glossy light green with reddish brown specks or blotches, or, in some cases, grayish, blue-ish or greenish white eggs with markings of brown, gray or purple. (The markings are deposited on the egg as the egg passes through the oviduct—in other words, as it is being laid.)

Science: Observing Birds

Mention that Albert was able to learn a great deal about cardinals from his personal observations. There are many facts to know about this perky red bird.

Cardinals eat seeds, insects and fruit in the summer months, but are able to winter in areas that have no fruit or insects. This is because they have such strong beaks that they can still eat many hard-coated seeds even when other food is scarce. Their strong beaks act like nutcrackers and allow them to get to the edible part of covered seeds. For this reason they are easily attracted to backyard bird feeders where they enjoy black oil sunflower seeds, safflower seeds, peanut hearts and dried berries. Other types of birds that lack such a strong seed-cracking bill as the cardinal often have to migrate to more southerly climates where insects and fruit are found even during winter months.

Perhaps there is an area where you can set up a backyard bird feeder for your student's observation. There are many books and websites on feeding wild birds that would provide you with helpful and interesting information. Your student will begin make obserations such as, "The cardinals in my backyard seem to come to the feeder for one last meal about 30 minutes before the sun sets." There is no substitute for being able to watch and observe personally. In time add a pair of good binoculars to the viewing area for even better observation.

Another facet of observing birds is discovering and discussing how birds differ. Why do some birds have extremely long legs such as herons, or sandpipers, or cranes? (These would belong to birds that frequent watery places. The long legs are usually for wading! A few species of birds have long legs that are used for running, like an ostrich or a roadrunner.) Birds' legs, long and short, and even the way the feet are formed, help show whether a bird is a wader (herons, cranes, etc.), a bird that perches (robins, cardinals, blue jays, etc.), or a **raptor** with talons (such as an owl, hawk, eagle, etc.). Woodpeckers even have feet fashioned to help them cling to a tree without falling backwards!

Birds also have different **beaks**. Have your student think of the difference between a cardinal, a woodpecker, a hummingbird, a duck or goose, and an eagle (with his powerful curved beak). Each of these birds has a different lifestyle and each eats different foods. The next time your student sees a bird in the wild, remind him to think about looking at the bird's beak and legs to see if he can guess the foods and habitats of the bird he is watching.

Other easily observable differences in birds are their size, body shape and color, their songs, their flight patterns, their nests, etc. For instance, learning to gauge the size of a bird accurately is a big help when your student consults a bird book to identify it. Was the bird he saw as big as a robin or bigger? As small as a sparrow or smaller? When he notices the color, was there yet another color at the throat or on top of the head or around the eyes? All these points will help identify the bird that was observed.

Finally, does your student know what the word **preen** means? What is a bird doing when it is preening its feathers? When a bird preens its feathers it is straightening them and often distributing body oil along the length of the feather as well. Find or buy a feather to have on hand for this lesson. Show your student how a feather can become split apart and separated. Carefully smooth the feather between your fingers so that the feather fits neatly together again. This movement is something like preening which a bird accomplishes mostly with its beak, and now and then, with a foot.

Teacher's Note: If you have a small hand-held viewing microscope, have your student examine the feather and see how it fits together. It is also interesting to note that *people* are sometimes accused of preening if they are spending a great deal of time fixing their hair, make-up, clothes or in general trying to "look good."

Science: Radio

Remind your student that the story says Albert listened to the radio. He listened to baseball games. Does your student know how a radio works?

A radio works by means of transmitted radio waves that are measured by their frequency. There are many types of radio signals in use all around us, but the two we most commonly hear are "AM" and "FM." Other broadcast signals include garage door openers, baby monitors, cell phones, cordless phones, radio-controlled toys, television, ham radio, police and fire department radios, etc.

Radio stations on an FM radio (**F**requency **M**odulation) broadcast their signal at frequencies between 88 and 108 Megahertz. (Mega equals one million.) So an FM radio station listed as 89.3 broadcasts its signal by oscillating (vibrating) 89,300,000 times per second.

Stations found on an AM radio (**A**mplitude **M**odulation) broadcast their signals between 535 and 1,700 kilohertz. (Kilo means one thousand.) So an AM radio station listed as 980 broadcasts its signal by oscillating (vibrating) 980,000 times per second. It's amazing that Albert can hear the games because of all that oscillating!

Science: Plants with Vines

Albert had a plant growing on the windowsill near where he stood for such a long time. This plant was growing taller by winding itself around the bars outside Albert's window.

There are two kinds of plants that produce vines: those with woody stems and those with herbaceous stems. The little plant in the pot is an example of the kind with soft herbaceous (her BAY shus) stem while the kind that is growing up the wall outside Albert's home is the kind with thick, woody stems.

Help your student begin a project of growing a member of the morning glory family: morning glory, moonflower, or sweet potato. These plants from the same family all have a soft, herbaceous (not woody) vine stem and tendrils that wrap around supports, which have to be provided, and allow the plant to grow upward. As the plant grows, have your student watch its progress and note interesting observations.

The following is just a touch of higher science, which may be interesting if you are making many observations of actual growing vines. If you pose the question and your student is interested, let him observe and research the direction of the growth of a plant's tendrils. Do they always grow in the same direction? What might influence this growth? Below are some categories for research. Which one of these might influence the growth direction of the vine and its tendrils?

Tropism is the **orientation of an organism toward or away from a stimulus**. Below are some various categories.

Hydrotropism (hydro = water): how a plant's roots grow toward water

Phototropism (photo = light): how a plant grows toward or moves toward light or the sun (Do experiments to prove this concept or observe the behavior of plants in a garden; during the day a plant will rotate its face toward the sun, etc.)

Geotropism (geo = earth): how a plant grows influenced by the turning of the earth (this may affect the direction the tendrils of a vine grow)

Teacher's Note: There will be some additional facts added to the information in this lesson when you study *Grass Sandals*. All of the above information needs to be presented in a creative, exploratory, interesting way, and shortened, amended or skipped altogether, if need be, depending on the age and interest of your student. These are not required ideas and concepts, but they sometimes prove interesting as a short introduction when the topics arise from your student's *own* observations, such as, "I noticed the sunflowers this morning were facing the sun to the east and now they are facing the sun to the south? Why is that?"

Science: Natural Enemies

While Albert is caring for his birds, he has to make scary noises to chase off a predatory cat. Cats are a bird's natural enemy. If your student is not familiar with that term, help him understand that in the animal kingdom there is what is called the food chain. While some animals eat plants, there are many which kill and eat other animals. Different birds, for instance, eat insects and worms, as well as fruits and grains. Cats often kill and eat birds as well as rodents of all shapes and sizes. The cat has the ability to stealthily creep up on a bird and the ability to pounce quickly, sometimes catching the bird unaware. These abilities in the cat along with its sharp claws and teeth, enable it to catch and kill a bird, while a frog for instance could not—therefore a frog would not be a bird's natural enemy, but a cat would. This is a short introduction to the concept of natural enemies and it does not have to be presented in greater depth. However, an interesting fact is, that among the animals, the polar bear is so big and powerful it is said to have no natural enemies except man! Let your student ponder on this as he is beginning to process information on natural enemies. Watch for observations he may make in the year to come as he witnesses life in the animal kingdom all around him. The activity sheet at the end of this unit provides a visual for this discussion-based lesson.

An entire old TV cartoon series was devoted to the idea that the cat, Sylvester, was always after the bird, named Tweety. The cartoon's adventures centered on this natural enmity between cat and bird.

Science: Human Body - Joints

"Albert rotated his shoulders to get the kinks out." Show your student some exercises with shoulder rotations. (Just swinging your arms around in circles will rotate the shoulder.) Have him imagine how good this might have felt to Albert after the birds have flown away!

What are joints? Joints occur at the place where two or more bones meet together with cartilage between and tendons to connect the bones. Can your student name some of the joints of the human body? The shoulder, hip, elbow, knee, jaw, fingers and toes all have joints. Some of these joints do rotate, such as the shoulder and hips (called ball and socket joints), and some move only in one direction like a hinge. The knee joint and the lower jawbone would be examples of a hinge joint. Pivot-joints are like those found in the elbow. There are other amazing types of joints with other functions as well. If your student is fascinated with the study of bones, joints, and muscles let him choose a topic or two and do some additional research.

If your student is a sports fan, he may have heard of baseball pitchers or other players, with rotator cuff injuries. The rotator cuff is comprised of four muscles which work together to allow overhand movement from the shoulder. This kind of injury (which is a strain or tear of this muscle/tendon group) can be serious. For milder injuries, rest is often indicated and more serious injuries may require surgery.

Your student might also have heard of tennis elbow, which is an inflammation of the tendon at the elbow joint. Again, like the rotator cuff injury, tennis elbow is usually the result of extended repetitive movements, all of which involve the joints as well as the tendons and ligaments.

Science: Trees - Maple

Near Albert's apartment, outside the window is a maple tree. It was to this tree that the father cardinal flew to "sing his joy." Can your student identify a maple tree? Ask him if he thinks he could find a maple tree in his neighborhood. How would it be different from an oak tree or a spruce tree? (It would have different bark and leaves than an oak tree, and a spruce tree would have needles instead of leaves because it is an evergreen tree.) Perhaps you have a good tree book that shows the trunk, leaves, seeds, etc., of a maple. There are many varieties of maple trees. Some will have yellow, orange or red leaves in the fall. Some have silvery green leaves in the summer rather than green ones. But maple leaves are similar in that they have five divisional sections or lobes that are usually pointed at the ends. You can see these leaves in the illustrations as Albert stands at the window with the father bird looking down at him.

If at all possible, find actual specimens from nature to show your student and let him make (or guide him gently into making) the discoveries below:

Maple leaves are shaped something like a human hand, with the main veins which run up each lobe starting together at the joining of the stem (or petiole). While looking at a maple leaf, ask your student if the edges of the lobes are smooth or toothed (serrated)? How is this leaf different from an elm leaf, for instance? An elm leaf does not have indentions or lobes but is a single oval leaf shape with serrated edges. The veins of an elm leaf are branching with opposite pairs of veins coming out from a central vein (midrib) which runs the length of the leaf (from stem—or petiole, to leaf tip). Both the elm and the maple leaves are called simple leaves. If you are able to study *The Hickory Chair* later in this volume, you will have a chance to review this lesson and then move on to compound leaf structures, because a hickory leaf is a compound leaf.

Have your student identify a maple tree, draw its leafless trunk and branch outline and one of its leaves. Then have him put this page in his science notebook. If he desires, he can decorate the page with cardinals, nests or eggs to remind him of the story. Or he can add these types of pages to his nature journal if he is keeping one.

You may not be in the season to find maple seeds (spring) but if you mention them, your student may remember seeing these helicopter-like seeds that spin round as they fall from the tree. If you can, examine the real thing and let your student write and illustrate everything he observes in this amazing seed. Then take a knife and cut the seed in half and let your student examine the inside of the seed. He can even place a seed or two in a pot of soil and see if it germinates and begins to grow.

Maple trees are also the source of delicious maple syrup. Trees are tapped (a hole made, and spigot placed into the trunk) in the spring. As the sap begins to run into the trees, after the long winter, some of the sugar liquid is tapped off and gathered in buckets. The liquid is cooked for a time and pure maple syrup is the result.

Teacher's Note: Does your student know that the maple leaf is Canadian national symbol? The beautiful red and white flag of Canada features a red maple leaf. Your student may remember this from *Very Last First Time* in FIAR Vol. 1.

Teacher's Notes

The *Five in a Row* lesson options for each unit in the manual are all you need to teach your child. The additional resource area provided below is simply a place to jot down relevant info you've found that you might want to reference.

ALBERT

Date:

Student:

Five in a Row Lesson Topics Chosen:

Social Studies:

Language Arts:

Art:

Math:

Science:

Relevant Library Resources: Books, DVDs, Audio Books

Websites or Video Links:

Related Field Trip Opportunities:

Favorite Quote or Memory During Study:

Name:

Date:

Art: **Short Story with Progressive Illustrations**

Have your student try writing and illustrating his own story with progressive illustrations. The space provided will accommodate a three-paragraph short story and a progressive illustration for each paragraph.

Name:
Date:
Math: **Altitude**

Cruising altitudes for most commercial jet airplanes is 30,000-37,000 ft. Small propellar planes fly at 1,000-1,500 ft. Hang gliders typically fly at 5,000-10,000 ft. During migration the Canada goose flies at 2,000-8,000 ft.

Copy and cut out the commercial jet, propeller plane, hang glider, and the Canada goose and paste them onto the graph at their typical flying altitudes.

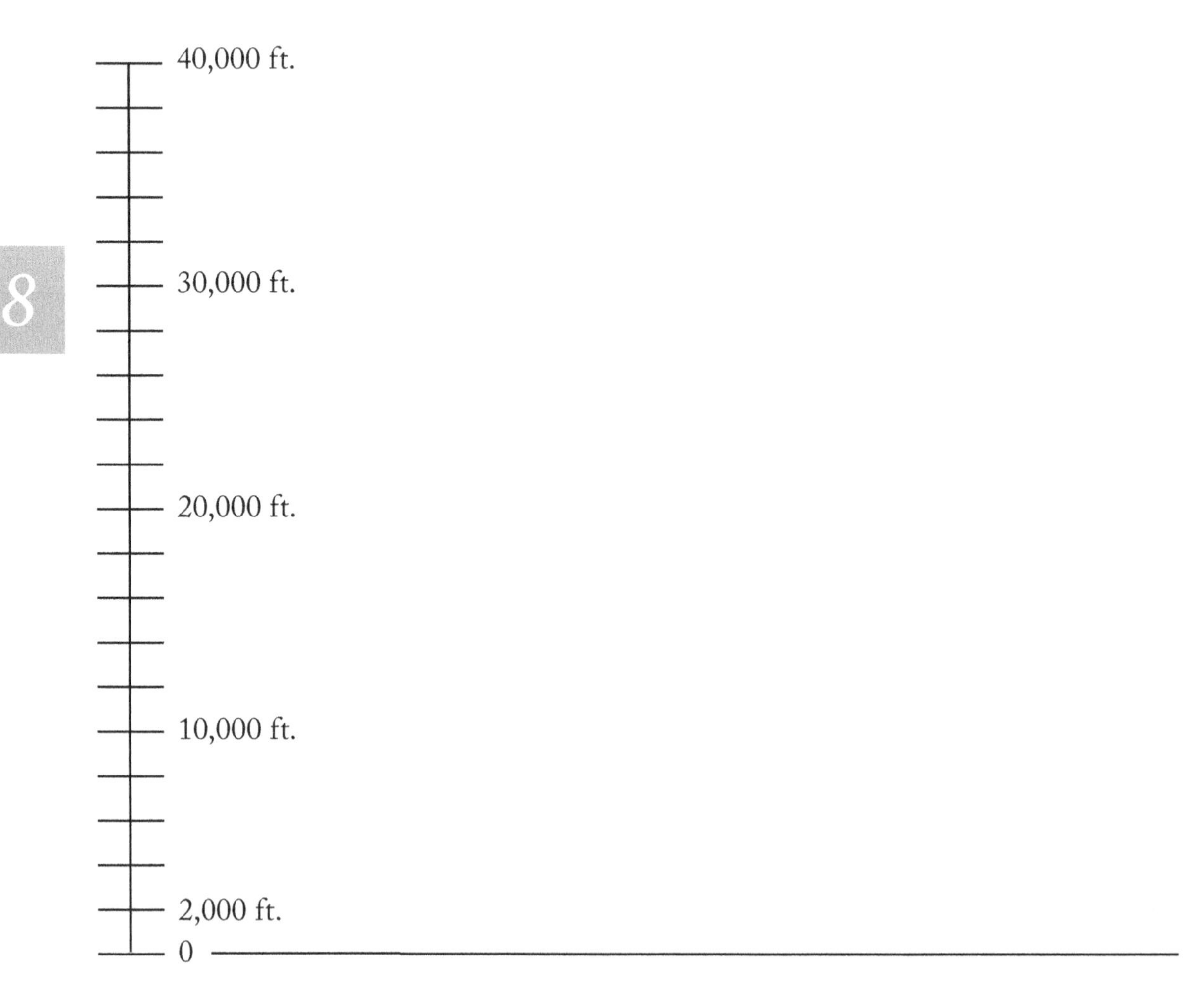

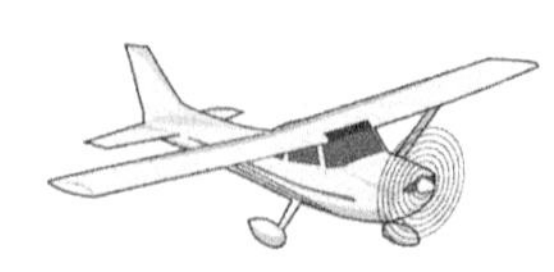

Name:

Date:

Language Arts: **The Comics**

Have your student try writing and illustrating his own comic strip, or you can work on one together. Obviously the number of boxes will be determined by how many your student needs to complete his idea.

Name:

Date:

Science: **Natural Enemies - Food Chain**

The food pyramid below provides your student a visual example of the discussion-based learning from the Science: Natural Enemies lesson.

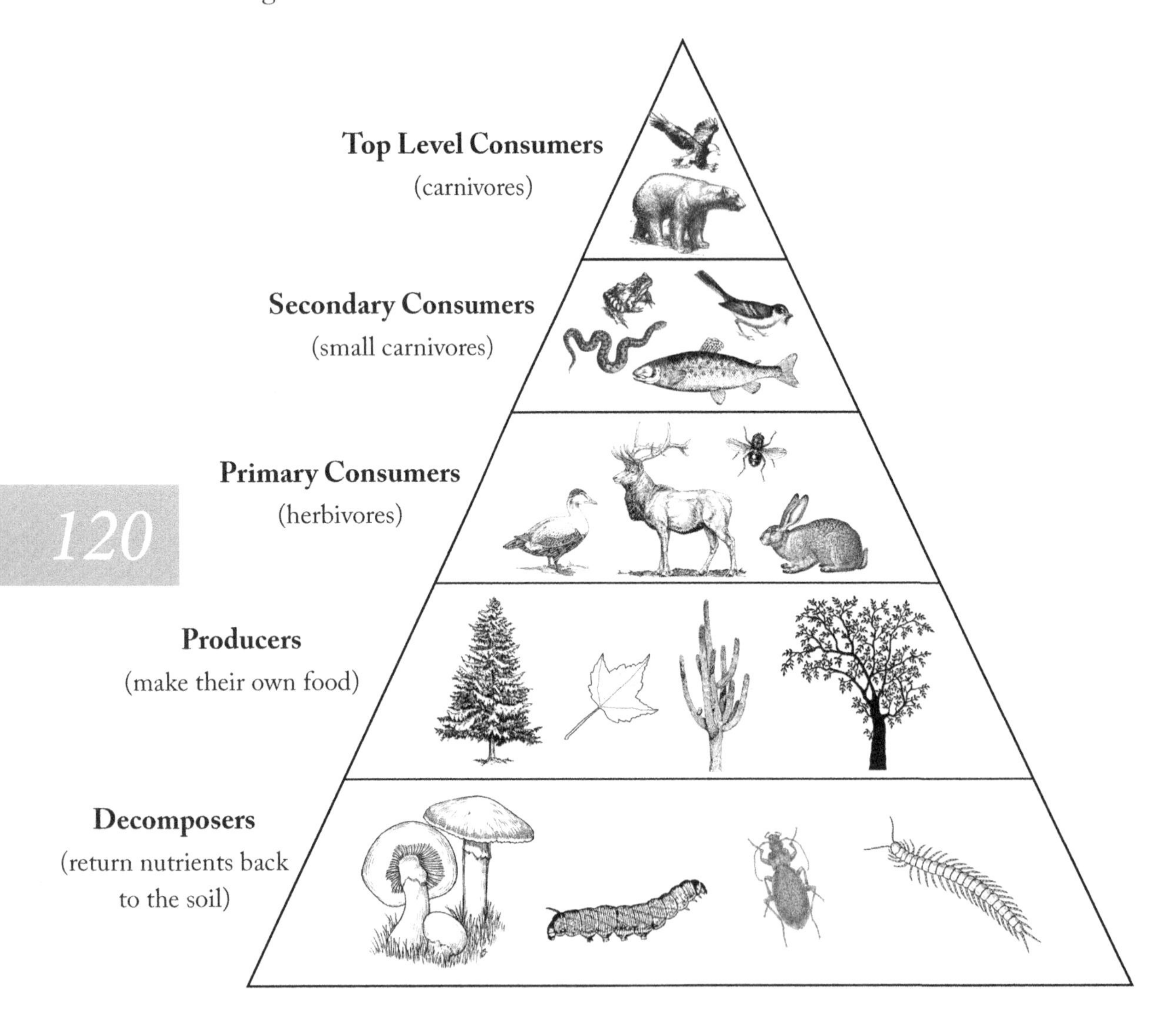

Help your older student research the categories above and list additional plants and animals below.

Top Level Consumers	Secondary Consumers	Primary Consumers	Producers	Decomposers

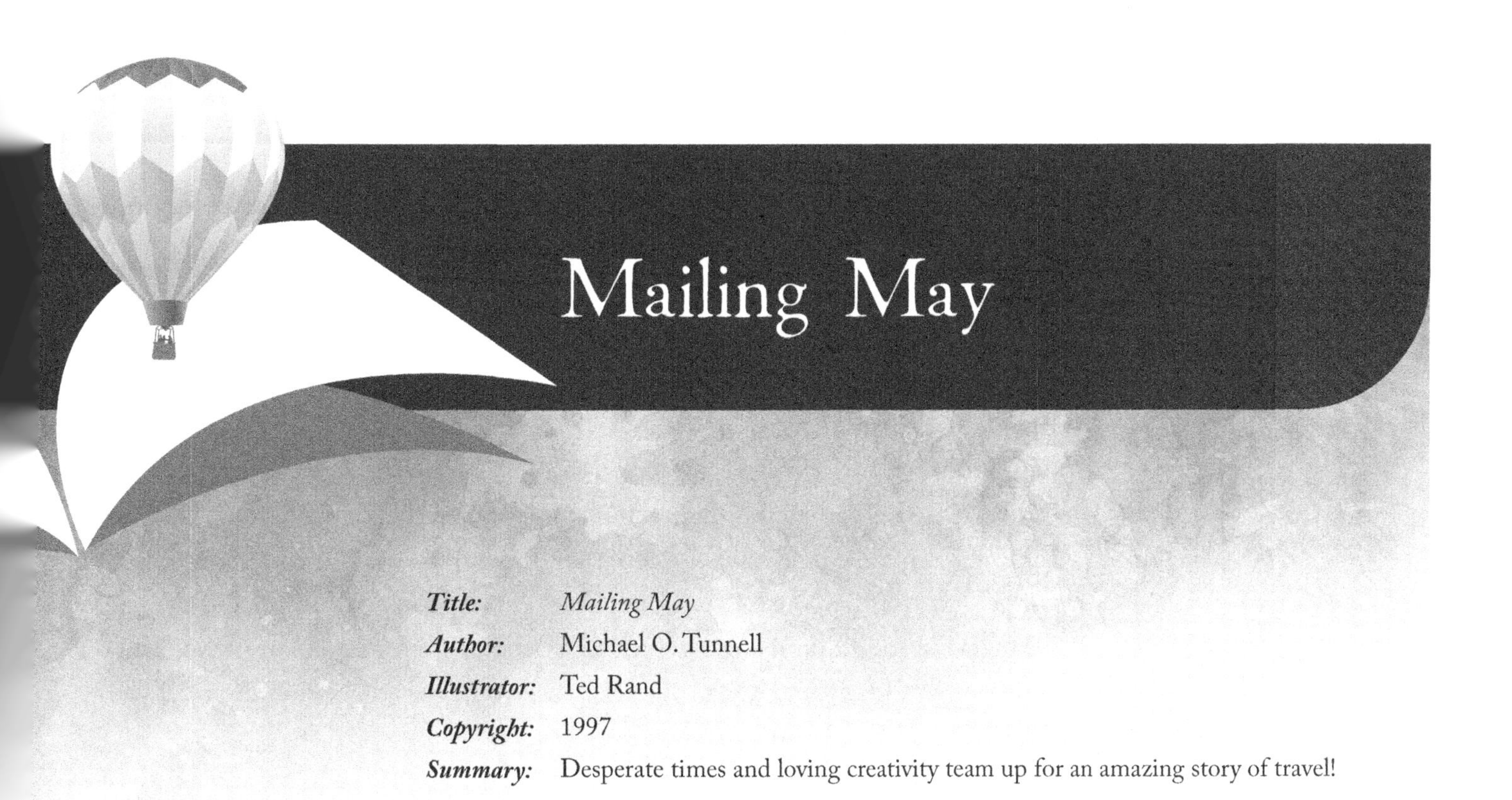

Mailing May

Title: *Mailing May*
Author: Michael O. Tunnell
Illustrator: Ted Rand
Copyright: 1997
Summary: Desperate times and loving creativity team up for an amazing story of travel!

Teacher's Note: There is a short discussion lesson called "Cover and Story" in the Art lessons for this book. If you want to do the lesson, you need to do it before you read the story. If your student has already read *Mailing May*, just skip this lesson.

Social Studies: Geography

Mailing May allows your student to make discoveries about the state of Idaho. If you are studying this state for the first time, you may want to start by asking, "In our story today, May traveled to Grandma Mary's across the state of Idaho. Do you know anything special about this state? Can you find it on a map?" Or try going to the map and saying, "Idaho, let me see ... where is it?" As you are looking over the map your excited older student might surprise you and say, "It's on this side!"—or even point to it. In these ways you are modeling respect for your student by gently asking about new topics and discovering what she already knows. Be sure to compliment her for information if appropriate. But, remember to be careful not to put your student on the spot, so to speak, and when you share information try to do it without a "superior attitude." You could say something like, "You know there was a time when I had never even heard of Idaho. Even now there is so much about that state I don't know. Let's explore it together!" One of your goals, as teacher, is to create a safe, comfortable atmosphere in which your student can wonder and learn.

Idaho was the 43rd state to join the Union in the United States of America in 1890. The capital of Idaho is Boise (BOY zee). Lewis and Clark passed through Idaho on their way to the Pacific in 1805 and made their camp near what is now the town of Lewiston. Lewiston is the same town where May visits her Grandma! Also included in the text of this story are the names Grangeville and Lapwai Canyon. Grangeville is a town southeast of Lewiston. The Lapwai Canyon is a part of the Nez Perce Indian Reservation. You can easily see Lewiston, Grangeville and Lapwai Reservation on a detailed political map of Idaho. Enjoy your study of Idaho and don't forget to place your story disk on Idaho or, if your map is large enough, on Grangeville or Lewiston!

One thing your student may be able to associate with this state is the potato. That is because in addition to wheat and sugar beet production, Idaho grows more potatoes than any other state. See if the potatoes you buy from the grocery store mention Idaho or have an outline of the state on the bag. People throughout the United States love hot baked potatoes that have been grown in Idaho!

Idaho also has incredible natural resources of forests (much of which is milled and made into paper) and minerals (silver, copper, gold, zinc and lead). Have your student watch the highways for semi-trucks carrying paper from Idaho to other states across the country. You will be able to tell the shipment is from Idaho by the logos on these trucks. In addition, Idaho is included in the Rocky Mountain States, with scenic vistas from magnificent waterfalls and beautiful rivers to majestic mountains and breathtaking valleys.

Social Studies: Relationships - Being Willing to Be Part of the Solution

May is deeply disappointed when her parents tell her she has to wait to visit her grandma. May's willingness to seek a job to pay for her train ticket is highly commendable. May is ready to cheerfully get a job herself, and save for the ticket!

Discuss disagreeable people who always seem to want everything done for them. Some of these people would never consider trying to help themselves. Some would never think about trying to be part of the solution to their own problem. The next time such a situation presents itself, encourage your student to remember May and her heart of integrity. Maybe your student will think about ways she can help be a part of the solutions to her own problems!

Remember *Down, Down the Mountain* (Vol. 2) and *Andy and the Circus* (Vol. 3)? In each of these stories the children have to be cheerful, hardworking and resourceful to solve their problems. In *Mailing May*, May tries unsuccessfully to help with the ticket, but her heart is certainly willing, just like the characters in *Down, Down the Mountain* and *Andy and the Circus*.

Social Studies: Problem Solving

The story of *Mailing May* offers an opportunity to talk about problem solving. May's parents have a problem. May wants to visit her Grandma Mary and May's parents don't want to disappoint her. Life presents many problems and situations that can be baffling and seemingly without solutions. Learning to think beyond the obvious, creatively and resourcefully is an important life skill. Can you think of a time you solved a hard problem in a creative way? If you can, think of some difficult problems you have faced and let your student try to think of creative ways those problems could have been solved. A good way to encourage your student to think creatively is to play brainteaser games, and to read books of riddles and mysteries. Trying to solve the riddles and mysteries and brainteasers helps expand your student's solution thinking. The next time your student has a problem to solve, remind her of *Mailing May* and work together to find a creative solution.

Social Studies: History - The American Flag of 1914

If the flags shown in the illustrations of the post office were current, how many stars would be on each one? You can decide if you want to present this information, or have your student research and find it out for herself. (The flag in May's post office, if current to the 1914 timeframe of the story, would have had forty-eight stars. New Mexico and Arizona had entered the Union in 1912 as the forty-seventh and forty-eighth states. It would be 1959 before the additions of Alaska and Hawaii would make the fifty states currently in the Union.)

Social Studies: History - Daniel Boone

Why did May say she "felt as adventuresome as Daniel Boone?" If your student has never heard of Daniel Boone, take a moment to introduce her to this famous American frontiersman. Continue by adding facts and reading more stories about Boone if your student is already familiar with him.

Daniel Boone was born in Pennsylvania (to a Quaker family) in 1734. He is still famous for his woodsman's skills, his calm, quick thinking and his marksmanship. He explored the unsettled land now known as Kentucky and helped develop the Wilderness Road. This road made it possible for settlers to get through the mountains to the new fertile lands of Kentucky. Boone also explored in North Carolina and Missouri, etc. There is a famous poem by Arthur Guiterman called "Daniel Boone." You can find it online or in *Favorite Poems Old and New*, ed. by Helen Ferris. This poem is probably too long and difficult for your young student but the first stanza can be enjoyed and it ends with the well-known line "Elbow room! laughed Daniel Boone." Boone was a man always wanting to be out in the wilderness with lots of room, never too close to towns full of people! He died in 1820. Boone is often considered America's most famous frontiersman and simple books about him can be found at any library.

After learning some facts about Daniel Boone and his incredible life of adventure, your student can understand how extremely adventuresome May must have been feeling!

Social Studies: Trains

In *Mailing May*, illustrations show a steam train, a trestle bridge, a mail car and a depot. Point out these illustrations and identify the terms for your student. If she demonstrates a love for the subject of trains you have a nearly limitless topic to explore. There are simple books on trains past and present. Finding out about modern trains allows you the fun of visiting a switching yard or examining trains as they pass by in your own area.

The train in *Mailing May* was a steam train and you can build a train like this using chairs and a large box for the engine with a cut-out windshield and painted gauges, etc. Then act out the steps necessary to operate such a steam engine. You and your student could demonstrate shoveling coal or chopping wood and stocking the tender, stopping and filling up with water at the water tower, stopping for cows on the tracks, and seeing American Indians and buffalo, etc. You could also act out stopping for mail, passengers and various shipments of cargo, traveling over giant trestle bridges in the mountains, and stopping to clear the snow from mountain passes so you can get through.

Don't miss the opportunity to sing together or listen to such songs as, "I've Been Working On the Railroad," "The Wabash Cannonball," "Casey Jones," or "John Henry."

Your younger student will have fun making train cars (past or present) from shoeboxes and oatmeal or salt boxes, while your older student may want to investigate setting up an actual model railroad! (She can choose to model a steam railroad with mail cars, etc., as in this story or she can build a modern railroad with diesels and container cars.)

There are many other areas of rail lore to be explored. Some of these topics might be: the setting of the Golden Spike, the actual number of miles of railroad track in a country, the different names and routes of famous trains, the different kinds of train cars, how truck lines use the railroad, etc. In all of these topics, find a small area of interest and pursue it. Later, you can come back to the subject and present more information.

Teacher's Note: It is interesting to note that the dividing of the United States into **time zones** (Eastern, Central, Rocky Mountain and Pacific) was instituted because the railroads wanted a more accurate and universal method to keep time so the trains could run on schedule!

Social Studies: Department Stores

May goes to a department store to ask for a job. Gaze at the vast array of items in the department store illustration. There is food, and shelves of dishes and glassware. Customers can buy a money order there. And though we can't see from the picture, the store probably carries a line of clothes, gardening items, and possibly furniture. Discuss with your student what a **department** store is and name a few in your area. Don't forget the big box stores! One of the goals of *Five in a Row* is to introduce what life was like at a certain time in history and then help your student correlate it to today's culture.

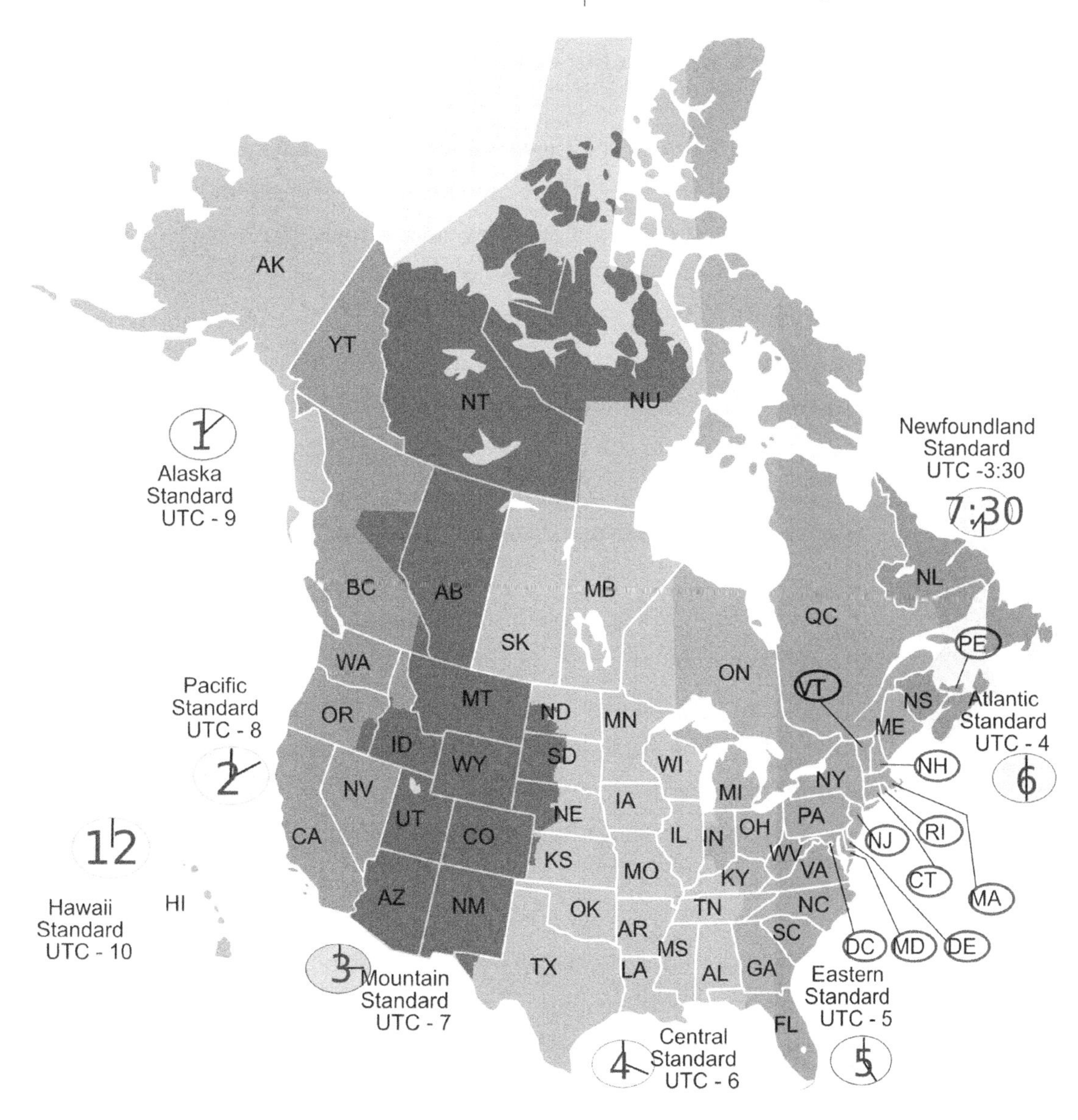

This story takes place early in the twentieth century, around 1914. (You can even tell this from the illustrations where you see horse-drawn carriages as well as cars in the picture of the depot at Lewiston!) Prior to this time, in the late 1800s, a department store might have been called a **general store** or a **mercantile** (meaning trading wares). May does not get a job at the department store. What does your student think were some of the reasons she was turned down? If your student was the manager of the store does she think she could find something for May to do?

Rachel Field wrote a poem called "The General Store." You might enjoy finding it and reading it together along with this lesson. It begins, "Someday, I'm going to have a store, with a tinkling bell hung over the door. And real glass cases and counters wide, and drawers all spill-y with things inside ..." The poem goes on to enumerate the goods found in a general store of country America.

Social Studies: Details of Life in the Early 1900s

Even in the picture of the Lewiston station the reader can see the changes beginning in the early 1900s. There are still horses to ride and to pull carriages and wagons, but in the illustrations the reader can also see a car. In the town of Lewiston, cars were beginning to be introduced and electricity was beginning to be used in homes. With your student look at the illustrations in the story and find these items: oil lamps (electricity and electric lights came to cities before the rural farms—are there electric lights in the post office?), high button shoes, formal style portraits, pot bellied stoves, and women's long dresses.

Social Studies: Stamps and Stamp Collecting

A postage stamp illustrates the title on the cover of *Mailing May*. There are also stamps under the text on the page where May is being weighed. Stamps are amazingly full of color, have fascinating pictures, exciting history, and more! Show your young student the stamp on the front cover of the book. Then show her some stamps you have purchased at the post office or grocery store. Let her look for illustrations of other stamps in the story. Explain how postage stamps are purchased and used.

For your older student, stamp collecting, or philately (phil AT uh lee) might be an enjoyable and educational topic to investigate. Simple books on this subject will help broaden knowledge and interests and give instruction on how to collect and preserve stamps. You might even know a relative or neighbor who has a fine stamp collection. They might enjoy sharing how they began and what they have learned through this interesting hobby.

Teacher's Note: For a quick stamp-related art project, have your student trace several times the perforated outline of the stamp on the front cover of *Mailing May*. Then let him think of something he would like to honor, or an issue he would like to bring attention to, or an historic event to showcase and have him design some stamps of his own.

Social Studies: Post Office and the Postal Service

May was mailed to her Grandma Mary from the Grangeville, Idaho, post office. There are many postal related topics spoken of and illustrated in *Mailing May*. The post office of the early 1900s had some things that are different from today and many things that are still the same. If you like, look through your book and make a list of the things you see in the illustrations of the post office. Some of these things might be: horse drawn delivery, wanted posters, postal workers, stamps, mail cart (May was riding on one by the steam engine), mail scales, American flag, etc. Make two rows of boxes for yes and no down the column of your list of postal items. Then visit a post office and let you student see how many of the same things she can find. She can mark no in the box if your post office doesn't have the item and yes if it does. Read the list for your non-reading student and let her mark the appropriate boxes. Feel free to add things to the list that your modern post office has.

Today mail is transported by air—airmail, and some first class mail. Mail is also carried by truck and rail. With your student talk about what happens to a letter or package after it is mailed. Find out if you can have a tour of your post office and have them explain the process.

Teacher's Note: You could briefly mention the Pony Express that operated only about a year but was an exciting postal venture in U. S. history! There is more about this subject in the lessons for *Cowboy Charlie* in this volume.

There are so many facets of the postal system. For instance, how many different classes of mail are there and why? First class mail is usually correspondence, payments, etc., and the price for first class mail is more than third class. This is because first class mail gets priority treatment and goes on the first plane available, etc. Third class mail consists of bulk mailings, advertisements, etc. It does not cost as much to mail these pieces partly because it does not receive priority and also because the sender presorts them according to zip codes into bundles, saving some work for the post office. Often specified amounts of pieces have to be mailed at the same time to receive discounts, such as 300 pieces, 500 pieces, etc.

What does the post office do with dead mail—undeliverable mail? A post office generally routes undeliverable mail that has been sent first class to the dead letter office, where it is opened to find out if there are any clues to direct the piece. Third class mail is usually destroyed if marked undeliverable and there is no forwarding address.

Parcel (package) post began in 1913 at the same time as insured mail and **CODs**. What is a COD? It is a parcel that is sent requiring the person receiving the package to pay for the item upon receipt. The mail service charges the seller for handling the transaction and then sends the payment to the person (seller) who sent the parcel. The letters stand for **C**ash **O**n **D**elivery. When did postal zones and zip codes come about? Though two number postal zone codes were used prior to 1963, it was in that year that the ZIP Code (standing for Zone Improvement Plan) or five-digit code was created and assigned to every address throughout the country. These digits represent an increasingly smaller geographical location, finally pinpointing an address to a specific post office (or postal zone for a larger city). These numbers were an attempt to help automate the sorting of mail.

Large post offices offer patrons the ability to obtain a passport. Another interesting bit of post office information is that the formation of the **Interstate Highway System** in the United States was actually created to make an easy way to get mail service efficiently across the country! No student can take in all this information at once. But keep in mind the small bits of knowledge and add them now and then as you read the story over again throughout the next year.

Language Arts: Literary Device - Alliteration and Hyperbole

Does your student remember the literary device called alliteration? Alliteration is a succession of similar sounds (not necessarily letters) which can occur at the beginning of words or internally. The title of Michael O. Tunnel's story is alliterative: *Mailing May*. Ask your student if she would have liked the title Mailing Samuel or Mailing Betty as much? The way the words sound together is one of the important factors in choosing a good title. Not every title is alliterative, but titles that are alliterative generally sound good when you say them. Remember the lessons in *Five in a Row* Volume 2 for the story *Down, Down the Mountain*? What were the names of the two children? (Hetty and Hank) With the letter H beginning both of their names, these names were both memorable and alliterative.

Mailing May also has an excellent example of hyperbole (hy PER bowl ee) which is the use of exaggeration, usually for great emphasis. In the first sentence of the story May says that Ma and Pa promised her she can visit her Grandma Mary who lives a million miles away. Obviously, Grandma Mary did not really live a million miles away. But, to a young girl, Grandma's house seemed that far. The author's note at the end of the story says it was seventy-five miles from Grangeville (where May lived) to Grandma's house in Lewiston. The sparing use of hyperbole is a writer's choice and brings interesting variety to a story.

Language Arts: Writing - Fictionalizing a True Incident

This is a lesson possibly for your older student. The story of *Mailing May*, we are told on the author's note page, is a taken from a true incident. The author, Michael O. Tunnel, took the basic facts and simply added extra details to make up a story. From his made up story we hear what Ma and Pa and May are thinking and saying, though no one knows exactly what really happened. With your student, find an incident in a book, online or in the newspaper and from just a few facts found in the article, try creating a story to go along with these facts. Think of dialogue and plot and characters with plenty of sights, smells, sounds, etc., just like Michael Tunnel did in *Mailing May*!

Language Arts: Vocabulary

boar hog Either a male hog, or a wild hog.

steel A strong alloy (mixture) of iron and carbon.

trestles Wooden or metal frames with attaching braces that hold up bridges or roads.

poultry A group of animals including chickens, ducks, geese and turkeys.

spell A country term for "awhile" as in "stay a spell."

Art: Cover and Story

Teacher's Note: Use this lesson first before any reading of the story. Have the title covered if your student is a reader. If your student is already familiar with the story of *Mailing May* just skip this lesson!

The events of this story seem so improbable. It might be fun to talk about the cover picture and try to think about what the illustrations of the little girl, the stamps, and the suitcase might mean. Ask your student what she thinks the story might be about. Your student may say, "It looks like a story of a girl traveling." You might respond (pointing to the stamps), "What are these? What might they have to do with the story?" It's hard to imagine anyone figuring out the story line, so you can say, "Well, let's read the story and find out!"

After you enjoy May's adventures, you can return to the cover illustration and discuss how the picture fit the text.

Art: Illustrator - Ted Rand

If you have progressed through the first three volumes of *Five in a Row*, you may have studied *Paul Revere's Ride*, illustrated by Ted Rand, as well as *The Wild Horses of Sweetbriar*. You might recognize *Mailing May* as another Ted Rand illustrated story. By this time your student will begin to recognize certain characteristics of Mr. Rand's paintings. Beginning to recognize similarities in a painter's work is learning to recognize his style! In all three stories there are examples of yellow light shining from lamps and candles, through windows, lighting up faces and animals in a familiar way.

There are also familiarities to the "tuck in bed scene" in *Wild Horses of Sweetbriar* and the picture where May's mother "wakes her up" in *Mailing May*. In the same way, with the books side by side, compare the faces in the families to each other. Can you tell that the same artist did these two books? Maybe he uses some of the same models for his work.

Ted Rand has a variety of art techniques in *Mailing May*. His painting of grand scope is visible in the scene where May is riding on the mail cart toward the giant steam engine and in the picture of the train on the trestle, both the on the title page and the across the double dedication page. The home scenes are warm with light and are full of color.

Mailing May is the only story in our *Five in a Row* studies where Ted Rand uses the technique of adding the "photographs" look. (The photographs are actually painted, too.) The use of the "photograph look" connects and unifies the illustrations throughout the story. This technique also gives a feeling to Tunnel's reminiscent style story of the events as being ones that actually happened. It is as if the reader shares with the family, as she hears the story while leafing through the family photographs—memories of times past. Isn't it amazing how the illustrations of a story add depth to the author's texts? The author never mentions the photographs but the illustrator's idea of using (painted) photographs helps make the story seem more real. Excellent books often result when the illustrator deepens the impact of story with his creative artwork!

Art: Learning How to Braid

On the first page of *Mailing May*, your student can see Mary standing on a braided rug. Has your student seen this type of rug before? You can see examples of this type of rug in museums in the Colonial American sections, and even today, you can find braided rugs like this for sale. You may want to use the story of *Mailing May* as an opportunity to teach the skill of braiding. Learning to braid can be useful in making rugs, placemats, lanyards, belts, bracelets, rope, and as a hair style.

If you think your student would enjoy trying a lesson in braiding, you can find tutorials on braiding a rug, hair, embroidery floss bracelets, etc.

Art: Drawing People to Show Their Character

Based only on what you can see from the pictures, what kind of girl is May? Notice the body language on the first page. (Explain that body language is the positioning of head, arms, legs, etc., that tell you, without any words, what a person is feeling.) On this first page, May has just been told that there isn't enough money for her longed-for visit to her grandma's. Look at her stance: her sweet face is raised and her arms are back (not on her hips as if she is angry, nor are her hands in a fist as if she were upset). In the illustration of May asking for a job at the department store her face is lifted, hands clasped in back. At the post office she appears a little shy, then a look of surprise covers her face as she realizes she is being mailed! At the end of the story the reader can see her happiness and relief upon arriving at Grandma Mary's. With this information about May gained from the illustrations and the texts, ask your student if she thinks that May is allowed to go on this extraordinary trip because she is respectful, well behaved and calm? If May had been a disrespectful, angry and rude child she probably would not have been allowed to travel to her Grandma's alone. She might also have put her mother's cousin's job in jeopardy or not been allowed to make the return trip in that special way. There are many rewards for children who have nice manners. They usually are allowed to do far more interesting things than those children who aren't respectful, and who don't follow instructions.

Art: Illustrations True to Text

The clock at the Lewiston Station says eleven thirty-five when May's train arrives. She is supposed to eat lunch with her Grandma Mary. Remind your student that as an illustrator it is important to make sure the details of the illustrations match the details of the text. If Ted Rand had not paid close attention to the text, he might have thought that a clock would be appropriate on the station roof and put just any old time on it. To be effective as a children's book illustrator the artist has to be observant and willing to faithfully render the words of the text in his pictures.

May yearns to visit her grandma. She even tries to get a job to help pay for her own ticket. This intense desire on May's part is faithfully painted in the scene where she is racing into her grandma's arms. In this illustration as May runs toward Grandma Mary, her hat, her hair and the mailing tag all fly backwards giving an excited sense of action and of her joyful forward movement. The look on her face seems, too, to be one of great relief (after her big adventure) as she flies into the safety of Grandma Mary's arms!

Art: Detail in Illustration

On the page where May asks for a job at the department store there are some interesting details in the illustrations. Look at the ceiling in the picture. This type of patterned ceiling was often made of pressed tin metal squares. You may know a shop or restaurant that has these old style ceilings. If so, visit with your student and help her realize that what she sees in books she can often find around her! In the same way you can point out the scrolled cash register and point out antique ones that you see from time to time in shops. Antique stores often use antique cash registers to ring up sales.

Look at the coffee grinder. It is large and red—the wheel is visible in the picture. You may be able to show your student one of these antiques at a coffee shop or antique mall.

Now, look at the picture of the Lewiston station with the horse carriage in the front. How many clues can your student find that show that the temperature at the station is very cold? (There is snow in the picture and there are icicles. You can see people's breath. You can see the horse's breath. The carriage driver has a blanket, red cheeks and nose, etc.)

At the Lewiston station notice May's suitcase carried by Leonard. Now check the book's front cover illustration. The entire cover is her suitcase! Did your student notice that before?

Art: Creative Painting

In the illustration of May visiting Mr. Alexander's Department Store, there is a photograph of May with a snowman. It is a traditional snowman, made with three balls of snow and dressed. On black paper using white tempera paint, white crayon or white chalk, have your student fashion the snowman of her dreams. It can be any shape or kind that she desires. Suggest that she might show some snow on the ground as well.

Math: Reading a Clock and Using Time

May's mother's cousin, Leonard, said May would eat lunch at Grandma Mary's. What time does the train arrive at Lewiston Station? Look at the clock on the station roof. It says eleven thirty-five, so May will be at her Grandma's before noon and just in time for lunch!

You can use this as an opportunity to introduce clock skills to your student. If she is already familiar with telling time, review or continue with more advanced lessons involving time, like knowing how to read an analog clock as well as a digital one, and understanding military time.

Math: Weights and Measures

In the illustration of May at the post office she stands up on some giant scales. Her weight is recorded and stamps are purchased according to that weight so she can be mailed to Lewiston. Use this opportunity to discuss with your student, at whatever level is appropriate for her, the subject of weights and measures. You can discuss ounces, pounds, tons, etc., used often at the post office, and also at the grocery store for weighing food items. (Well, maybe not tons!) In addition there are many lessons to be learned about liquid measure and metric measure.

Just for fun, you could make up a monetary scale of postage required, so much for a half-pound package, a two-pound, four-pound, six-pound, etc., all packages headed to the same destination. Then find a scale (a bathroom scale will do) and weigh various items (a book, a pillow, a pair of shoes, etc.) to find out how much your pretend posts would be to send them on their way. Design some stamps or mailing tags and put them on the items. Use a little wagon for the mail cart and if you have built a pretend train you could even take the parcels to their destination point!

Teacher's Note: An older student may enjoy learning more about various types of scales. There are tiny scales that scientists use to measure small amounts of chemical substances, postage scales for letters, scales to weigh food portions, balance scales. There are even giant scales at roadside weighstations designed to weigh 80,000 pounds or more as a semi-tractor trailer truck drives onto the scale. Each of these scales are used for different purposes and have different histories.

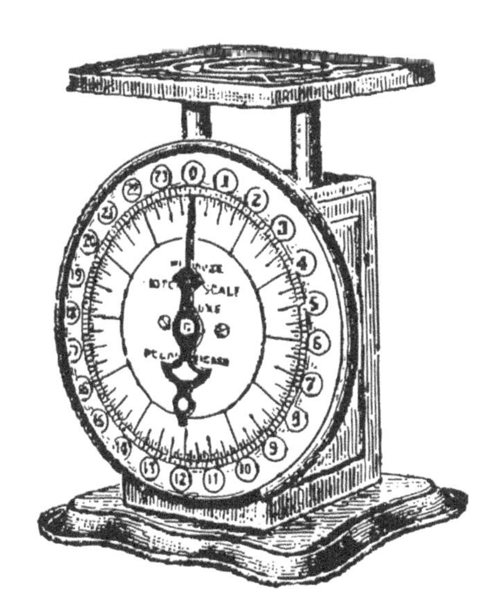

Math: Stamps and Money

When we mail a letter or a package* we use stamps, just like May's father did when he mailed her to her grandma's. Stamps cost money and they are usually purchased at the post office, sometimes at a grocery store, etc. Stamps come in specific various denominations (amounts of money). Find the common denomination of the day for mailing a letter and show your student. How much is a single stamp? How much would it cost for a book, sheet or roll of stamps? Your older student may be able to use multiplication to figure this out if she knows how many stamps are in a book or on a full sheet and she knows how much each individual stamp costs. You can also go with your student to the post office and see what other denominational amounts stamps come in and why. Some are used to mail postcards, extra postage to foreign countries, etc.

You may want to mention to your student, that people collect and save stamps. The older (or more rare) the stamp the more valuable it is. It can be worth far more than its original price.

Another name for package is parcel, hence the term parcel post. May was delivered to her grandma by way of parcel post! Service for parcel post had just begun in January of 1913. In February of 1914 May was mailed!

Math: Geometry - Shapes

When Ma and Pa make May go to bed early, they tuck her under a red, white and blue quilt. (The yellow in the picture is from the lamplight.) What are the shapes in the quilt? (triangle, square and rectangle). Have your student find all the examples of each shape, including the white shapes.

Your student might enjoy cutting out pieces of paper or cardboard and coloring them to match the shapes in May's quilt, then putting the pieces together like a puzzle using the illustration in the story for the pattern. An older student could also, with help, actually make a pillow in the same pattern as May's quilt. She could make it for herself or give it as a surprise to a younger sibling. Or possibly a relative or friend would enjoy making a pillow for your student to cuddle up with at reading time.

You can also use this opportunity to explore other geometric shapes that your student may or may not be familiar with: trapezoid, rhombus, hexagon, parallelogram, octagon, etc., as well as the different types of triangles: equilateral, isosceles and scalene.

Math: How Much Money Is Saved by Mailing May?

May's parents can't afford a train ticket. Does your student remember what the ticket cost? (The ticket cost $1.55. It is not clear whether or not this is a two-way [round trip] ticket, but we assume it is. Do tell your student about the concept of one-way and two-way tickets.) How much does it cost to mail May? (It cost fifty-three cents.) Can your student figure out how much May's parents save? (Her parents save $1.02. This does not seem like a great savings but in 1914 when this story actually happened, that would be a significant amount, twenty-five dollars or more in today's spending power. Help your student understand the concept of how buying power changes by sharing with him some common products, such as bread, milk, gasoline, etc., and what they cost when you were her age.)

Science: Railroad Mountain Engineering - Trestle and Tunnels

In the story *Mailing May* you can see an enormous **trestle**. (Look on the title page, the copyright dedication page and the mail car scene where May feels sick on the train. These structures which support bridges or roads were, in the timeframe of the story *Mailing May*, built of timber and spanned deep valleys in the mountainous regions. Trains could not take steep grades up the mountainside (inclines) and steep grades down the mountains. It was impossible for the engine to pull a heavy train up at such a steep angle and it was far too dangerous for the heavy train coming down! So, **architectural engineers** (*not* the engineers who operated the trains) solved the problem by designing a structure that could go across the valley floor and create a platform to support a railroad track crossing high above from one side of a mountain to the other. The supporting wooden frameworks that held up the bridges are called trestles. The trestle bridges made train travel possible in the mountains and cut valuable time off more indirect routes. (Today bridges and undergirdings are made of steel and concrete.)

There are also railroad **tunnels** that scare May—surely they were long and dark! Can your student think of why trains would have to go through tunnels? Again the answer is in the topography (the lay of the land). Sometimes it was easier to tunnel through a mountain than to go over it. So, by using blasting material and structural methods, tunnels were made through portions of the mountains.

Science: Human Body - Saliva

Before there were self-adhesive stamps, people had to lick the back of the stamp to activate the glue that held it to the envelope or package. After May is weighed for postage, Postmaster Sam licks a stamp. Isn't it a funny thing to think that people can lick a stamp because their mouths make a liquid called saliva? There were other ways to affix a stamp, like wetting it with a sponge, but if a person licks a stamp to put it on an envelope, she has made use of the fluid called saliva. Moistening stamps is not the reason the human body produces saliva however. Does your student know what saliva actually does? **Saliva** is produced by the body to aid in digestion. When your student eats, saliva is produced by several glands and released as she chews. Both the chewing, which breaks up food into small pieces, and the saliva which moistens food making it soft are important in the digestive process. Saliva also has an enzyme that breaks down starches into sugar. Let your student slowly chew up a saltine cracker. When she first begins to eat the cracker it will taste starchy, but if she eats slowly and allows her saliva to mix with the cracker, the starches will begin to turn to sugar and the taste will be sweeter than at the beginning. If your student is interested, you can find images of the glands that produce saliva online.

Science: Domestic and Wild Animals

In the story of *Mailing May* there are a number of animals. Look with your student and make a list of all the animals you can find. You might include: house cats, chicks (baby chickens, also described as poultry), a boar hog, a horse in harness and a caged bird. Begin a discussion on the separate categories of domestic and wild animals. Domestic (or domesticated) animals are those that live with people or are under human care. Some domesticated animals do work for people, such a herding dogs or horses. The domestic animal category distinguishes those animals that live with or are cared for by humans from wild, untamed animals. Continuing to discuss these differences, see if you can put the animals you listed before in the correct categories. You could make a chart like the one below. Can your student think of some other animals for each category that are not listed in the story?

Domestic	Wild
Cat	Boar Hog
Bird	
Horse	
Chickens (are in the animal category called **poultry**, which also includes ducks, turkeys and geese.)	

Your young student probably won't memorize this new information but from time to time you can remind her again and ask if she thinks a certain animal is wild or domestic.

Science: Animal - Boar Hog

Remind your student that in *Mailing May* the steam engine was compared, in (a simile) to a boar hog. Whereas boar could mean any male pig or hog, in this case it probably means a wild boar. Wild pigs (also called wild boars) are very vicious with big teeth and charging dispositions. Wild boars would be a good simile for a puffing great steam train!

Science: Steam Power

Mailing May is set in the early 1900s when steam trains were used to carry passengers, mail and freight. What does your student know about steam and steam power? If she completed *Five in a Row*, Volume 1, she may remember *Mike Mulligan and His Steam Shovel.* She may also remember seeing a pin wheel move by steam power. If you asked your student to make some steam, what would she need to use? Would she know that making steam takes an energy source (a fire, electric stove, etc.) and water? In which picture of our story can she see what the steam engine uses to make steam? (She cannot see the wood or coal made into a fire for the energy source. But there is a picture—one of the photographs—that shows a water tower! Trains would pull up to the water tower, take on water in a tank and when the wood or coal fire had warmed the water to boiling (in tanks called boilers), the steam would cause the pistons to turn the wheels of the train and the train would move!

Continue teaching your student about steam powered machines. Wherever she is in her knowledge, take her a step further.

Teacher's Note: There are also two pictures of teakettles with steam pouring from their spouts in the illustrations of *Mailing May*. In this case the steam only shows the water is hot enough to brew tea or coffee; it isn't actually being used to do mechanical work.

Science: Nutrition and Health - Comfort Food

When the man at the department store can't give May a job, he notices she is very sad. To help her feel better he offers her candy—which May says doesn't really do much to cheer her.

Many times people turn to food when they are bored, nervously uncomfortable, or sad. Usually this means that they eat, not because they are *hungry* but because they don't feel well in their emotions. Sometimes the food seems soothing at the moment. But, as in May's case, it doesn't solve their problem or their disappointment or really take their hurt away. While some foods really are comforting, frequent eating for emotional reasons can become a bad habit resulting in poor health.

Can you and your student think of other, healthier ways that might help provide comfort during times of stress? Answers might include talking with someone, listening to music, reading a good book, taking a walk, etc. Choosing these types of activities may not take away all the stress either, although often they can, but these activities will not do as much damage as constantly eating comfort foods! In fact, eating larger amounts of comfort foods high in sugars, fats and salt on one day, will actually cause a person to feel worse, physically, the next day.

Good, healthy nutrition dictates that a person watches the amounts of fats, sugar and salt in their diet and steers away from those foods that have excessive amounts of these ingredients. The American Heart Association has set guidelines for amount of fat intake and sodium. The suggested fat intake is 30-35% of the total calories for each day. There is also a difference in the kinds of fats a person can consume. You can find interesting information on American Heart Association dietary recommendations at www.heart.org.

Teacher's Notes

The *Five in a Row* lesson options for each unit in the manual are all you need to teach your child. The additional resource area provided below is simply a place to jot down relevant info you've found that you might want to reference.

MAILING MAY

Date:

Student:

Five in a Row Lesson Topics Chosen:

Social Studies:

Language Arts:

Art:

Math:

Science:

Relevant Library Resources: Books, DVDs, Audio Books

Websites or Video Links:

Related Field Trip Opportunities:

Favorite Quote or Memory During Study:

Name:

Date:

Social Studies: **Stamps**

Help your student "collect" four stamps that honor something or someone, or support an issue or cause. You can purchase them or find photos online and print off images. Paste them below and have your student write or dictate a brief summary of what the stamp is honoring or representing.

Name:
Date:
Geography: **Idaho Flag**

The flag of the state of Idaho has a blue field with the state seal in the middle. The words "State of Idaho" appear below the seal in gold letters on a red and gold band.

The seal depicts a miner and a woman (representing equality, liberty, and justice) as well as several symbols representing some of Idaho's natural resources: including mines, forests, farmland, and wildlife. *For more information, see Parts of a Flag on page 266.*

Color in the Idaho flag below.

Name:

Date:

Social Studies: **Trains - Time Zones**

It is interesting to note that the dividing of the United States into time zones (Eastern, Central, Rocky Mountain and Pacific) was instituted because the railroads wanted a more accurate and universal method to keep time so the trains could run on schedule!

Choose a unique color to represent each time zone. Then color in the regions that are included in the time zones with the appropriate colors.

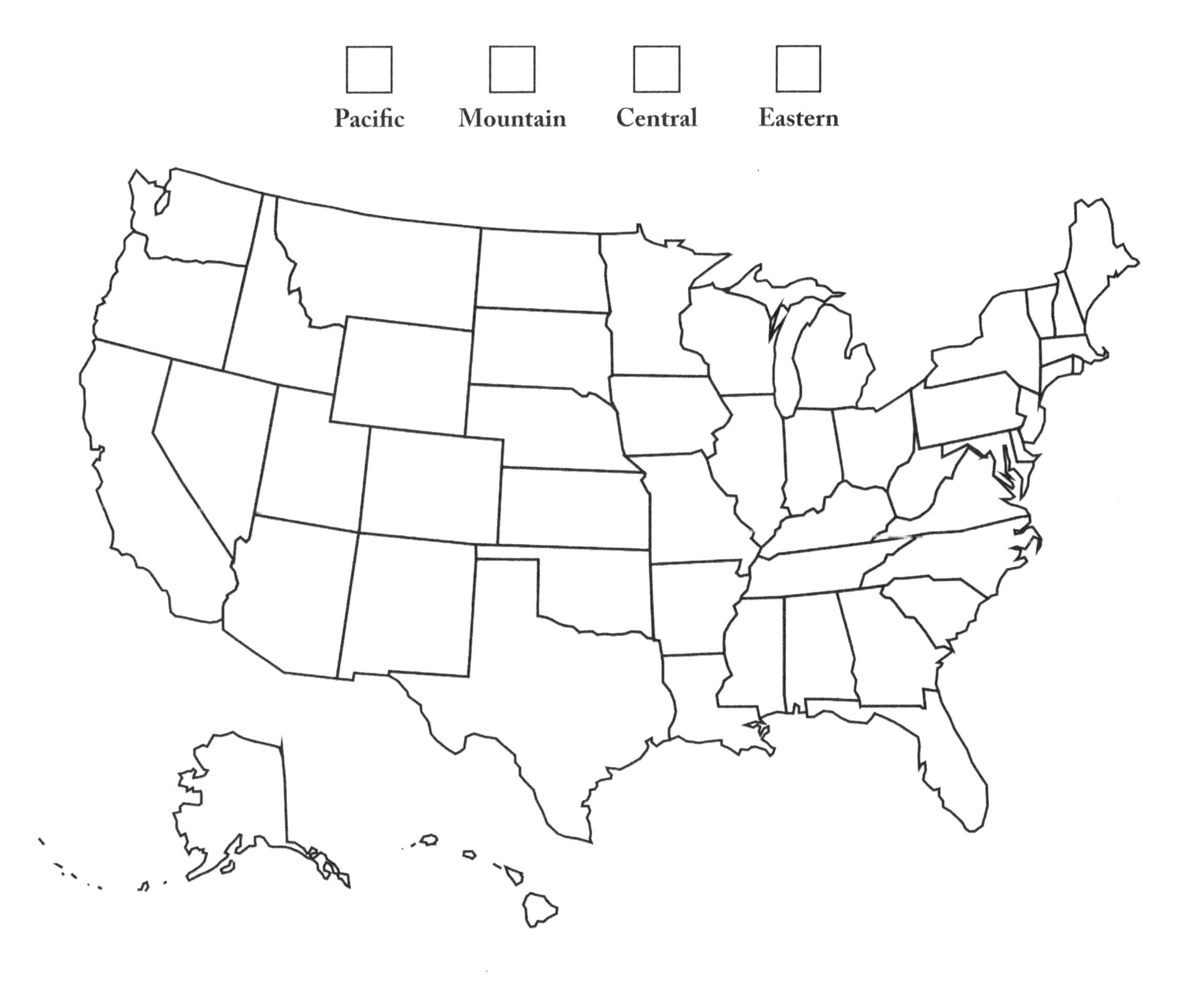

Cowboy Charlie

Title: *Cowboy Charlie*
Author: Jeanette Winter
Illustrator: Jeanette Winter
Copyright: 1995
Summary: Colorful, exciting and filled with adventure, *Cowboy Charlie* is the true story of Charles Marion Russell, artist and sculptor of the American Old West.

Social Studies: Geography - St. Louis, Missouri and Helena, Montana

At the beginning of *Cowboy Charlie*, Jeanette Winter writes that Charlie left his home in St. Louis, Missouri, to go west. You may want to take this opportunity to study just a bit about the state of Missouri before you go on to the land that was to become the state of Montana.

Search online or in library books for five interesting facts to begin a study on Missouri and Montana. Help your student also find these states on a map, as well as their capital cities.

St. Louis is home to the Gateway Arch National Park. The most famous part of this park is a 630-foot tall monument known as the Gateway Arch, a symbol of westward growth in the 1800s. Because St. Louis was often the "jumping off point" of travelers going west, it's also often referred to as the Gateway to the West!

Missouri is also associated with Mark Twain and his stories of Tom Sawyer and Huck Finn, and also the artist Thomas Hart Benton. Missouri has a diversity of agriculture and livestock interests, as well as coal, lead and other mining, but because Missouri is centrally located many national firms have corporate offices in the large cities there. Service industries make up the major percentage of Missouri's livelihood.

Montana has vast areas of forest preserves and Native American reservations. It has some farming, mining and industry, and this state frequently wrestles with the question of how much industry to encourage while trying to preserve the natural areas.

Teacher's Note: For Canadian Rowers or other international Five in a Row users, this history lesson, as well as the following lessons, can be taught in any depth you wish as you also teach lessons about your own country's exploration, expansion, settlement, etc.

Social Studies: History - Statehood and Understanding History

Missouri entered the Union in 1821 while Montana did not join the Union until 1889. There is a sixty-eight year difference in the entry date of these two states. Can your student think of a reason why Missouri might have become a state before Montana? The answer to this question requires an understanding of how the United States was explored, settled and then developed into specific states. The settlement of land moved westward with the earliest colonies on the coast becoming states in the late 1700s while the last continental states in the West (New Mexico and Arizona) entered the Union in 1912!

Therefore, there were states which made up the United States (remember the flag with thirteen stars?) long before the land which later became Missouri was explored and settled. As Missouri became a state, the land of Montana and lands further west were just beginning to be pioneered. Settlement and statehood were still sixty-eight years in the future!

"The Oregon Trail" is an educational computer game that many children have used to gain a better understanding of what it was like to move across the vast areas of the West during the 1840s and '50s. A really enjoyable family movie that shows something of the excitement of a territory which is about to enter statehood is the Disney movie, *The One and Only Genuine Original Family Band.*

Social Studies: Geography - St. Louis and the Wild West (or Old West)

Make a copy of the blank United States Map at the end of the *Mailing May* unit, or find one online. Help your student locate the city of St. Louis, Missouri. On his blank map he can place a dot for the city or draw an arch like the Gateway Arch in St. Louis, or he could draw a picture of Charlie's home.

Then, help your student find Helena, Montana (you can also look for Red Rock on a travel map of Montana, if you wish). Place a dot there and label it with the name of the city. Your student can even draw a picture of Cowboy Charlie there, if he wishes. Between St. Louis and Red Rock your student can drawn a train and train tracks, and between Red Rock and Helena, perhaps a stagecoach!

Have a discussion with your student about what geographical areas are meant when people refer to the Wild West (or the Old West). Ask him if he knows some of the land areas that are usually included. There are actually two portions of land referred to as the West. One is the land west of the Mississippi to the Rocky Mountains which encompasses the plains, and then the land west of the Rocky Mountains, which is sometimes referred to as the Far West, though both of these land areas together make up the term Wild West.

If you wish, shade these areas with different colors on your map.

Teacher's Note: Over a hundred years of history is spanned by the stories that Cowboy Charlie's father told him, the stories Charlie read for himself and the things that Cowboy Charlie saw in his own lifetime! That is why the history lessons for this book's study are so numerous. Just pick a lesson topic or two to introduce to your student and then come back to the other story lessons later for fun.

Social Studies: The Wild West

Cowboy Charlie begins with words that Charlie was born "when buffalo still roamed in the West." However, by the time Charlie traveled west at fifteen, a great number of the buffalo were gone. The intrusion of the railroads across the plains had brought an end to the giant herds that so freely roamed the land. Charlie certainly saw some buffalo, but not in the numbers that were in the West at the time he was born.

With your student, review pages 9 and 10 of *Cowboy Charlie* and have your student make a list of all the things Charlie saw:

Mule skinners Men who handled mule teams which were harnessed together to pull freight wagons. The mule skinner used a single line, called a jerk line, to guide the teams. Good mules were valuable and some of the best came from Missouri—the very state from which Charlie had come!)

Miners (Men who worked to get silver, gold, bauxite, and other minerals from the ground.)

Mountain men (Men who were hunters, trappers and explorers like Jedediah Smith and Jim Bridger. These men were often hired by large fur companies to obtain pelts and hides.)

Native Americans (Begin to do some study on basic tribes and American Indian nations and the areas of the country where each made their home.)

Bull teams (Freight outfits)

Saddle horses (Horses that were trained to be ridden)

Pack horses (Horses that were trained to carry a load)

Covered wagons (The familiar Conestoga wagons were covered wagons that traveled across the west. Built something like a boat, with the front and back swooped up higher than the middle, the wheels could be removed and the wagon floated across rivers.)

Talk about any items on the list with which your student is unfamiliar. Have him keep this list and add to it as Charlie sees more and more amazing things. Your student can list the animals he sees in the story, as well other details such as chuckwagons, campfires, scenes of bronco busting, calf roping and branding; teepees, Native American pipes, and lariats. The wooly chaps are interesting as well. Leather chaps protected the range riders against thorns and brush but the wooly chaps were also protection from the cold and were used only in the northern plains and mountain states like Montana!

Social Studies: History - Famous Cattle Drives "Up from Texas"

Discuss with your student that Cowboy Charlie is enamored with all he hears and reads about the Old West. Remind your student that many of the stories Charlie hears are about people and events that happened in the years before he was born.

Yet, the famous cattle drives from Texas to Missouri and even into Montana were in their heyday during Charlie's life and he was able to participate in them and fulfill his dream. These famous cattle drives only spanned about twenty years, from the end of the Civil War to the 1880s. If Charlie had been born any later he might have missed them altogether!

With your finger, trace the route on a U.S. map that the cattle followed north from Texas to Kansas City and St. Louis, and sometimes on north even into Montana. Now your student can see that the term "up from Texas" means moving north out of Texas.

You can make a distinction for your student between the famous large cattle drives coming up from Texas which had a short time span, and the term "round-up" which is still happening today. From the earliest times of cattle ranching in the United States until now, there have been yearly or seasonal roundups. This is the time when cattle that have been grazing on large portions of land are rounded up, nursing calves cut (separated from their mothers), the young calves branded, some cattle sold and shipped or driven to a shipping point, etc. During these roundup times you can still see cowhands, bronco busters and chuckwagon cooks!

Social Studies: History - Explorers, Pioneers and Settlers

The story *Cowboy Charlie* provides an opportunity to study how the areas west of the Mississippi were explored, pioneered and finally settled.

Explorers, Trappers and Mountain Men

Explorers of the Mississippi River included men like Jacques Marquette and Louis Joliet, while Daniel Boone, Kit Carson, Jim Bridger and others explored and trapped through the plains and Rocky Mountains. Eventually in 1804 Lewis and Clark mapped a route from near St. Louis to the mouth of the Columbia River as it emptied into the Pacific Ocean, in what is now the state of Oregon. (This is not a complete set of names of the explorers but more than enough for introductions to the topic for your student's age group.) If you can find some interesting simple books on any of these men, it would be fun for your student to read them in his free reading time.

Remind your student that Cowboy Charlie had a great-uncle Bent who was a fur trader in the Old West! The life of a fur trapper usually consisted of trapping during the fall and spring while over-wintering in a quickly built small log cabin in the remote woods areas between hunting seasons when streams and ponds were frozen. Then in the late spring the trappers would transport the furs acquired in one or more trapping seasons to forts or other pick-up points where the trapper was finally paid for his furs. Uncle Bent, as a fur trader, was the man who dealt with these various trappers, judged the quality of their furs, and bought furs from the trappers for various commercial clients and large fur companies.

Charlie's great-uncle Bent was actually an important and famous figure in early Colorado history. Born in St. Louis, he became a fur trader in the West, was friendly and fair with the American Indians, and built Fort Bent (a massive adobe structure—you can find a picture of it online). This trading post was the largest post west of St. Louis. Bent was even responsible for gathering some settlers and forming the first permanent colony in what is now the state of Colorado. Such inspiration (all the stories Charlie heard about this great-uncle) was instrumental in creating in Russell a love of the West, a heart for the Native Americans, and a desire to preserve all he saw by his paintings and sculptures!

Pioneers - Cabins, Sod, and Adobe Homes

Teacher's Note: A good reference book for the discussion on pioneers is *A Pioneer Sampler* by Barbara Greenwood.

In *Cowboy Charlie*, Charlie Russell meets a good-hearted hunter and trapper named Jake Hoover. Jake lives in a small log cabin. In the West, when a home or shelter was needed, people used materials that were nearby for construction. Transportation of distant materials would have been too costly or just impossible. So where there were forests, log cabins appeared!

On the prairies of the West, trees were often scarce or absent all together. In this case determined pioneers dug pieces of sod out of the prairie and made what is known as sod houses.

In the hot desert areas of the West, adobe homes (constructed of brick made of clay and straw, baked by the sun) were built. These homes with thick walls and small windows helped keep their occupants cooler in the warm times and warmer when it was cold. Like the timber or the sod of other areas, clay was what was readily available in these areas of the hot Southwest.

Besides refreshing your student's knowledge of log cabins, sod and adobe homes, remind him again that these various forms of housing came about because the people built with whatever materials were available for them to use. What else might a person building a house or shelter need to have near or available? Let your student think about this for a moment. (Water) Homes were built near creeks or rivers, or they had to dig wells, etc. Truly remote cabins and sod homes also need to be near enough to a fort or town to get supplies at least every six months or so.

Because pioneers were the first ones to build homes in a new area, they usually were far from neighbors. As the years went by more and more people arrived and created homes for themselves as an area became settled.

The **settlers** arrived. These people, who wanted to establish permanent homes closer to neighbors, purchased more closely adjoining land (still with land enough to raise crops) and began establishing towns with stores (rather than buying intermittently from the forts), as well as instituting town governments, schools, etc.

Social Studies: History Overview -Putting Russell in Historic Perspective

If you sense the timing is right, you can use *Cowboy Charlie* as an opportunity to do a quick overview of the early history of the United States. Just take a few minutes and discuss the list of events (highlight just the topics you think your student is ready for) leading up to the birth of Charles Marion Russell—Cowboy Charlie.

Jamestown settled on the eastern shore of what is now Virginia in 1607. Pilgrims began settlement at **Plymouth** in what is now Massachusetts in 1620. The founding of other colonies followed.

French and Indian War 1763, during which the French incited the Indians against the colonists and British. Britain defeated France in this war. **Teacher's Note:** Just for your own information, this is the historic event that prompted James Fenimore Cooper to write *The Last of the Mohicans.*

Anger is increasing in the American Colonies over arbitrary—not representative—British rule.

Battles of Lexington and Concord (technically began the American Revolution) 1775

Declaration of Independence signed and sent to England 1776

American Revolution 1776-1783

Constitution of United States ratified 1788

Bill of Rights added in 1791

Louisiana Purchase 1803 (land representing the watershed of the Mississippi bought from Napoleon, ruler of France)

1836 Remember the **Alamo**! (Seige by Santa Anna, Mexican General and place where Davy Crockett and all those at the Alamo were killed. It was this heroic incident that ignited many to rise up and fight against Santa Anna and defeat him.)

Texas Annexed in 1845

Oregon Country Cession 1846 (from Britain)

Mexican Cession 1848

Gold Rush in California 1848

The Civil War (Also called the War Between the States) 1860-1865

It was one year before the end of the Civil War that Charles Marion Russell (Cowboy Charlie) was born! Charlie was born more than 250 years *after* the founding of Jamestown, and 88 years *after* the signing of the Declaration of Independence, but *before* the end of the Civil War.

Social Studies: Native American Culture

In *Cowboy Charlie*, we read that Charlie not only meets Native Americans but he lives with them and learns about their lives. The time he spends with the Blood Indians not only enriches his life, all he learns from them helps him greatly as he pursues his career in art. Charlie (as well as his great-uncle Bent) has a respect for the people who were "there before."

The subject of Native American culture is so broad that I suggest you find the best books from your library to follow the particular areas in which you are interested.

Some ideas for topical study are:

North American Indian Tribes and Nations
Lifestyle of the North American Indian Tribes
North American Indian Art
Famous American Indians. Here are a few:
- Pocahontas
- Sitting Bull
- Sequoya
- Geronimo
- Crazy Horse
- Massasoit
- Tecumseh
- Chief Joseph (ties in to Montana study)
- Red Cloud (ties in to Montana study)
- Sacagawea (ties in to Montana study)

Your library likely carries many excellent books on cowboys and Native Americans, both historical and comtemporary. Look for good, simple books with plenty of photographs or artwork.

Social Studies: Travel

During the lifetime of Charlie Russell, people traveled across the West by various means. Many covered the distances by horseback, some in wagons, later by stagecoach and then by rail. There were even a few people who left ports on the East Coast of the United States and went by boat around the southern tip of South America and north to California. If your student would like, he could see how this type of travel by ship would work by looking at a map of North and South America and tracing the route with his finger.

Cowboy Charlie lived during the 1800s and into the early 1900s. During the 1800s rivers were the "streets" of trade and supply. Various types of boats (including steamboats) carried food and food products, building materials, furs from the fur traders—in fact most of the supplies you would find in a store of the time, to the towns along the river. From there these supplies were transported by wagon to towns further inland. Because the rivers were a major "street of commerce," cities were built on the banks of these large waterways. Indeed, the good river port played a role in deciding the location of many U. S. capital cities. Many of the capitol buildings in the United States (which were built as each state joined the Union) were constructed right on the banks of a large river. Rivers also became easy boundaries between states and it would be interesting for your student to look at a map and see how many states have rivers as the main boundary separating them from the state beside, above or below them. (Hint: look for states with jagges, uneven boarders.) Also see how many capitals are located on a major river.

After railroads were built across the country, these rivers became less important as the main means of transporting goods and products. Eventually, the interstate highway systems used by the giant semi-trailer trucks became a major transport mover. Today rivers are still used for commercial trade, though rail and trucking companies generally carry a greater percentage of the goods, products and supplies within the heart of the country. During Charlie's life however, boats, trains and wagons were the transportation system for goods and products.

Social Studies: Methods of Communication in the West

As Cowboy Charlie heard in the stories he was told, the land west of the Mississippi was rapidly opening up. People wanted to communicate with family, and especially business partners across the vast spaces of the prairies and mountains and on to the West Coast.

An adventuresome enterprise was begun in St. Joseph, Missouri called the **Pony Express**. A man riding fast on horseback would take mail and travel a certain number of miles, switch horses or riders (at designated points called stations) and keep handing off the mail to other riders until one made it to the West Coast. In this way the delivery of a letter could take less than two weeks, rather than the many months it took if an individual traveler carried the letter. The Pony Express has a colorful and exciting history and you can find out more about it through research online or from a good, simple book from your library. The amazing thing about the Pony Express is that all the rides and letter deliveries took place in a span of less than two years! As soon as the telegraph lines were strung and messages could be sent across the country by wire, the Pony Express enterprise came to an end.

While the story *Cowboy Charlie* never mentions telegraph lines, this form of communication had its working span in Cowboy Charlie's time. The telegraph began, in the United States, through the efforts of **Samuel Morse**. He built the first working telegraph (in the U.S.) in the mid 1840s and developed the **Morse Code** for quick communication. Find a good simple book on the telegraph or on Samuel Morse and enjoy it with your student.

Social Studies: The Old West Fades

Teacher's Note: Since this lesson corresponds with the end of *Cowboy Charlie*, you might want to do the lesson about opening the West early in your study and this lesson later on (along with the Math lesson). That way the history will follow the story.

On the last page of text of *Cowboy Charlie*, Jeanette Winter writes Charlie's thoughts with a poignant sadness. Charlie could see that the Old West was fading and being replaced with a different kind of lifestyle. Charlie was sad. He decided to live in a cabin and paint everything he could remember about the western way of life, cowboys, American Indians, as well as the land and animals.

In some ways, it was the building of the railroad that marked the end of the Old West. Buffalo were nearly gone and therefore Native American populations moved on, land was being fenced (no more free range cattle), towns were becoming cities, and civilization was closing in on the open prairies. And it was these changes that caused Charlie Russell to stay in his cabin studio and paint, for those generations who were to come, all he could remember of the Wild Western way of life.

His paintings were painstakingly accurate (one can identify specific Native American groups by the details of his work) and his sculpture caught the action and life of the world he saw fading around him. As Jeanette Winter has shown in her painting (the next to the last page) Russell finishes his days in his artist's studio (built to replicate Jake Hoover's cabin) and continues to wear his Western dress including the red sash!

Language Arts: Biography

Charles Marion Russell was born in 1864 and died in 1926 at the age of sixty-two. Jeanette Winter writes about Charles Russell and tells many facts about his life. This kind of writing is called a biography. The word biography comes from two word parts—bio, meaning life, and graph, meaning writing, Biographies are found in your library in a separate section where the books are arranged alphabetically by the name of the person of which each book is written. Therefore, you would look on your library shelf for a biography on Clara Barton, not under the author's name, but in the B's under Barton. If you find an author you enjoy who writes biographies on many different people, such as Jean Fritz, you need to look up the author Fritz and then write down all the books you are interested in. Take your list to the shelves and look for each one under the name of the person written about.

Because *Cowboy Charlie* is not a long book there are many things about Charlie's life that the author did not include. Suggest to your student that someday he may read other books about Charles Marion Russell which have even more facts about his life and work.

Teacher's Note: There is another American artist who was born just a few years before Russell, named **Frederick Remington**. There are many interesting **parallels** between Russell's life and Remington's. It is amazing the wealth of information each of these men chronicled in their paintings and sculptures about a way of life of the Old West which was quickly disappearing. Depending on the age and interest of your student it may be too confusing at this point to try to introduce another artist. But, as the teacher, you may enjoy looking up Remington and learning a bit about his life and work for yourself.

Language Arts: Storytelling

Find Jeanette Winter's illustration of the men sitting around the campfire under the starlit night. Looking at the picture, remind your student that Cowboy

Charlie first learns about the Old West through stories his father reads and tells to him. Every new story makes Charlie want to see the West for himself! Later Charlie hears stories and tales from the cowhands around the campfire in Montana and he even tells some stories of his own.

Teacher's Note: There are various phrases to use that describe storytelling, such as spinning yarns, spinning tales, swapping stories, etc.

Discuss with your student the fact that storytelling is a wonderful craft or art form to attempt. Learning how to tell a good story has several facets. A good story always centers around a main incident.

To try a storytelling session with your student, have him begin with an incident that has made a real impression on him. Let him relate that incident to you verbally. (This could be something special that happened to your student or that he witnessed, or something that was scary like falling into a lake when he couldn't swim. It could be an incident from his own family history or something that he has seen.) If he would like you to do so, make an audio or video recording of his story.

After he is finished, relate some incident from *your* life that greatly impressed you. Then give him a list of storytelling points (see below) and see if he thinks your story has any area that could be improved according to these points, or embellished to make it a more interesting or exciting story. Remind him that critiquing someone else's work must be done respectfully, just as he would want his own work reviewed.

When the exercise is over, if he asks, let your student work on improving his own story. If he does not ask, tell him that you are so glad he thought of an incident and told his very own story. At another time, you might work with him on additional aspects of personal storytelling. Again, this is such a valuable craft to pursue both for the future storyteller and his listeners!

List of Storytelling Pointers:

• Remember a good story needs a beginning, middle and end. So, a story of falling into the lake might begin with the description of a beautiful day and all the wonderful plans that have been made then progress to the accident, and end with the resolution of the event.

• The storyteller should not try to memorize the story, but have the main points that he wants to cover in mind. These important points are divided into the beginning, middle and end.

• He should think of interesting descriptive words, and paint with his words a picture of the incident, the feelings, the smells, sounds, etc.

• He can use his voice to make the quiet parts of the story quiet and the exciting parts more lively. In other words, he can use a good expressive voice as well as facial expressions and hand gestures.

• The storyteller should keep some eye contact with his listeners. In Jeanette Winter's story, the cowboys knew that Charlie's eyes were twinkling because they could see them!

Family storytelling, as Charlie's father does when he tells his son stories of his great-uncle Bent, is a most precious memory-keeping device. Storytelling is an important tool to hold families together and keep them aware of their past and excited about their future. Encourage your student's family to work on incorporating family storytelling into their time together. Any family member can tell a story about another. An older sibling could tell the story of the first time the younger one walked, or smiled or fell off the bed. The children can tell stories about the parents or a visit by the grandparents. Parents and grandparents, as well as aunts and uncles can tell stories about the children. Yet it must be remembered that these stories should always be told with respect, and by treating the subject of the story *exactly* as the storyteller would wish to be treated if a story were told about *him*. Family storytelling can be a chronicling of events and history and fun but should never be a painful experience for the subject of the story!

If you have an aspiring artist in the family, he may wish to illustrate the stories told in the family circle, just as Charlie listened to the stories and drew his heroes, and painted the stories that he heard!

Language Arts: Creativity and Imagination

Teacher's Note: This lesson is just an enjoyable discussion that can take place anytime during the day.

When Charlie Russell is young, he pretends that he sees bears in the woods, and imagines he is roping cows. With your student, discuss the fact that Charlie's imaginings are full of excitement and color and will influence his art in the years to come. Does your student see that same kind of creativity and imagination in anyone around him—either adult or young, friend or relation? Does he, himself like to imagine? Do you? Share with each other the favorite things you've imagined and ways that your imagination has led to creativity.

To further your discussion, ask your student if he were walking through the woods, would he be more likely to imagine a scene from a jungle, the Old West, or a deserted island? If he were walking past a pond would he be more likely to imagine Captain Hook running from the crocodile, himself braving the ocean like Sir Francis Drake, or a happy fishing day with his dad? You can continue giving choices for imaginative play and discovering more about your student from his answers.

Language Arts: Describing the Jaunts of Imagination

Teacher's Note: This lesson is similar to the one above, but it is written rather than oral. You certainly can do both lessons, but perhaps not on the same day!

Discuss with your student the fact that when Charlie Russell was young, he had a desire to go west. He thought about it all the time. He imagined what it would be like to be there. He probably talked about it a great deal. His parents certainly were influenced by his strong desire and let him take such a trip with a family friend. Seeing the West for himself was all that Charlie had imagined and even more!

Is there a place that excites your student's interest? It could be somewhere in his own country or abroad. Have him write a short piece about his special place as he imagines how it would be to visit, just like Charlie imagined it would be to go west. Other topics for imaginings might be to think what it would have been like to go with Columbus on the New World voyages, to live during the time of legendary King Arthur, or in the reign of Queen Elizabeth. What would it have been like to be a pioneer in America? Has your student ever imagined being a part of the early explorations of Africa, or the Arctic? Would your student have enjoyed and dreamed of being in the airplane for the flight over the English Channel with Papa Bleriot (*The Glorious Flight*, FIAR Vol. 1) or on one of the space missions?

Language Arts: Poetry and Song

Below are a few suggestions for songs and poetry to go along with parts of *Cowboy Charlie*.

Sing the lyrics of "Home on the Range." Although they were written after the days of the Old West, they speak of many of the things that Charles Russell saw. Also, check a cowboy songbook for songs that were sung around campfires and songs that tell the stories of the West.

One excellent resource book is out of print, but you may be able to order it through your library. It is called *Songs of the Wild West*, with Commentary by Alan Axelrod and Arrangements by Dan Fox. This book was a publication of the Metropolitan Museum of Art, so that beyond the music, the book is filled with museum prints of famous western artists including Charles Marion Russell and Frederick Remington!

On the last page of *Cowboy Charlie* it says that the great herds of buffalo were gone. The poem "Buffalo Dusk" by Carl Sandburg, beautifully and poignantly describes this occurrence.

There are also famous "cowboy poets" you can search for online. (Be *sure* to preview these!)

Here is a poem written by a Paiute American Indian and translated by Mary Austin. It tells of the writer's desire, after a long winter, to see the summer months once again. The imagery of this poem is powerful.

The Grass On the Mountain

Oh, long long
The snow has possessed the mountains.
The deer have come down and the big-horn,
They have followed the Sun to the South
To feed on the mesquite pods and the bunch grass.
Loud are the thunder drums
In the tents of the mountains.
Oh long long
Have we eaten the chia seeds
And dried deer's flesh of the summer killing.
We are wearied of our huts
And the smoky smell of our garments.
We are sick with desire of the sun
And the grass on the mountains.

Art: Painting

Find a collection depicting Charles Marion Russell's paintings. There may be books of complete works at your library, or you can also find them online. With your student, marvel at the rich variety of expression and first-hand knowledge of his subjects evident in Russell's detailed works. If you can, visit a museum that has an original Russell painting. There is no substitute for standing in front of the real thing—a picture where the artist's *own hand* made the brush strokes certainly brings a sense of reality to these lessons. So, if it is in any way possible, see an original piece of Charlie's artwork!

Art: Panoramic Scenes

Based on the Greek words for "entire view," a panoramic scene is one that is wide and encompasses abundant scenery. In *Cowboy Charlie*, the fold-out scene of Charlie sitting on a horse overlooking the cattle crossing the river that stretches out over three book pages would be considered a panoramic view, Why does your student think that Jeanette Winter used this art form? (The broad vistas of the West could not be fully appreciated in short views, but filled the senses as far as the eye could see. Jeanette Winter used this type of painting to illustrate the grandeur of the wide-open plains and mountains!)

Cameras usually have a setting that allows for extremely wide panoramic shots as well as regular sized pictures. In the past, some extra-wide movie screens were built with a curve that caused the movie to seem as if it happening around the viewer. Movies made for this type of screen were sometimes called Pano-vision. Modern IMAX movies utilize some of these same techniques, as well.

Art: Painting and Color in Illustrations

Perhaps your student will remember Jeanette Winter's writings and art work in the *Five in a Row* Volume 2 lessons for *Follow the Drinking Gourd*. If you still have the book, look at the pictures along with those of *Cowboy Charlie*. You and your student will appreciate recognizing the same artistic style in both books.

Jeanette Winter painted the illustrations for *Cowboy Charlie* with acrylic paints. Remember, acrylic paints are much like oil paints but pictures painted with acrylics do not take as long to dry as oil paintings do, and the brushes can be cleaned with soap and water rather than turpentine.

Art: Sculpture - Modeling Figures

Cowboy Charlie modeled animals from leftover pieces of beeswax. Your student can try that if he has wax available. If there is interest and no beeswax, let him model figures the way Charles Russell did in the story using clay, Sculpey®, or Crayola's Model Magic®. He can experiment with modeling animals, houses, people etc. Perhaps you and your student could create a Wild West panorama complete with painted scenery (Jeanette Winter style) and figurines. Don't forget to model a few cacti!

Art: Researched Details in Illustration

If your student already knew the personalities of Davy Crockett, Daniel Boone and Kit Carson and had seen portraits of these men in the past, he would be able to distinguish which man is which in the illustration at the top of page two of *Cowboy Charlie*.

Jeanette Winter did not just paint some random figures dressed in buckskins for these figures, but she actually did research to bring the likeness of each man to her illustration.

Your student might find it interesting to look up each man online. Compare the portraits and then see if he can determine which figure is which. The man on the left is Davy Crockett, the one in the middle is Daniel Boone and the one on the horse is Kit Carson! Don't they bear a strong resemblance to their portraits?

Art: Drawing on Different Surfaces

Most of the drawing your student has done in his lifetime was probably on paper. Charlie Russell painted on anything he could find. Paper would have been quite scarce in the days of the West, so Charlie was creative. He painted on boxes, birch bark, the backs of envelopes and buckskin. It is entirely possible to find pieces of birch bark, or small pieces of buckskin for your student to try as a base for his drawing. What are other things around him that might be appropriate for use in drawing?

One thing is sure about Charlie—he drew. He drew all the time. He never stopped and though many times he probably was not satisfied with his work, he continued, always trying to capture the things he saw around him. The fact that he never stopped trying is one of the marks of a true artist.

Teacher's Note: The use of the back of the envelope is reminiscent of Abraham Lincoln who, it is said, penned the Gettysburg Address on the back of an envelope as he was traveling.

Art: Cooking and the Chuckwagon

In the life of the West, during roundup (or cattle drive) time there was at least one man designated to cook the food for the cowhands who were working hard all day long. This man was called the cook, or commonly Cookie. He had a wagon fitted neatly with food supplies and cooking utensils. This "chuckwagon" was a portable kitchen pulled by horses or mules, which could travel many miles from the home ranch and be right where the cowboys were actually working when mealtime came around. There are two pictures of a chuckwagon that Jeanette Winter has drawn. On the page where "Kid Russell" tells his stories in the starlight around the campfire, you can just see the corner of the chuckwagon. The next page has another view and you can tell how the back shelf drops down and is propped up by a single table leg. The cooking and washing up was done at the chuckwagon. Good cooks were highly sought after and chuckwagon cooks were paid more than the cowhands. The cowboys were respectful of the cook and even made sure they rode into meals from the downwind side so the food didn't get covered in the dust their horses kicked up!

Typical food from the chuckwagon included biscuits, meat (beef, deer or other fresh-killed meat), beans, coffee, pancakes (called flapjacks), etc. Flour or cornmeal was used for flapjacks and biscuits, and sometimes a sourdough starter was used as well.

Math: Figuring the Years in Between Events

There are many dates of events listed in the history lessons in this unit. Find some different combinations and have your upper elementary grade level student do the subtraction necessary to see how many years transpired between specific events.

Math: It's in the Presentation

Charlie has his mind so full of the West that he doesn't apply himself to his schoolwork. Show your student the page where Charlie is drawing on his math problems. Perhaps he needs some interesting illustrations for his math book, or some problems he feels are relevant, like figuring how many mules it would take to drive a team and how many pounds of food and water they would need for a month-long roundup.

Could your student, based on his knowledge of Charles Marion Russell (gleaned from this story) design a math curriculum that would excite Charlie's imagination and make him want to do his work? Let your student take a small segment of math work and try this idea. If your student were the teacher how would he try to present the material to Russell to attempt to capture his interest? How would he present the times tables or the subject of fractions? What kinds of word problems could your student write that would interest Charlie?

Science: Astronomy - Falling Stars

Talk with your student about the idea that as a boy, Charlie lay outside his home in St. Louis and looked up into the sky wondering what it would be like to see the stars in the west. Then he was able to watch the skies many times as he rode nighthawk (guarding the cowhands' horses at night) or was a night herder, singing lullabies to the cattle in the moonlight. Out in the western dark without any lights, and in higher altitudes (with its thin atmosphere) the stars appear more numerous and breathtakingly beautiful. Jeanette Winter paints beautiful night scenes and several times she depicts what we call a "falling star."

Show one of these illustrated scenes (including the picture on front cover) to your student and ask him if he knows what a falling star is. Technically, a falling star is a meteor shooting through the earth's atmosphere and is not a star at all! A meteor is a solid mass of material (from golf ball size to house size) which enters Earth's atmosphere. The friction of Earth's atmosphere causes the material of the meteor to heat up and glow. The meteor moves through the sky and sometimes burns up completely and sometimes, when not burning up completely, actually strikes the ground. People commonly call these meteors falling stars or shooting stars but they are meteors that look sort of like a star moving rapidly across the sky.

Maybe your student has seen a shooting star or maybe he would like to begin watching for one. During certain times of the year, meteor showers are more common and there is a greater chance of seeing shooting stars. You can determine when these peak viewing dates are by looking at nature calendars or by searching online for information on meteor showers and their dates.

Science: Animal Skeletons On the Prairies

During the time of the Old West, and still today in cattle country, one can find skeletons of cows that have died. These animals may have been taken by a predator, or been weakened by illness, but after their death the skeletons are left as a reminder of their hardships.

Ask your student if he knows how the skeletons become clean and white. The bones become cleaned of meat through the process of decay, which is sometimes helped along by scavengers. Meat (and plant life) **decays** through the action of bacteria, molds and yeasts that thrive under warm conditions and break down (or simplify) the chemical substances of dead animals (and plants). After the meat is decayed and/or scavenged from the bones, the bones become clean and white through the action of the wind, rain and searing sun.

Scavengers (you may have touched on this subject briefly in the lessons for *The Story of Ferdinand* featured in *Five in a Row* Volume 1) are animals who eat dead, putrefying meat (carcasses). While many animals will consume fresh kill, not every animal will eat meat that has been dead awhile and is already decaying. Therefore, since meat begins to decay quickly in the elements and heat, and since most animals won't eat such decaying food, scavengers are extremely useful in keeping the many carcasses of dead animals from remaining on the ground causing pollution.

Before naming some of the more common scavengers, guide your student's thoughts for a moment to observations he has made in the past. What kinds of animals will go through garbage cans for food? (dogs, raccoons, crows, gulls) What kinds of animals are seen near dumps and sewers? (rats, cockroaches, crows, vultures) If your student has noticed animals eating garbage and frequenting places of decay, these animals are probably the scavengers.

A few scavengers for the plains and mountain areas of the west include condors, vultures, seagulls, crows, opossums, coyotes, foxes, raccoons, bears and in higher elevations the wolverine. There are many more scavengers, including species of fish (such as catfish), etc.

Sharks, crabs and lobsters are just a few examples of marine scavengers. And don't forget the common rat and the magnificent cockroach. Both of these creatures are responsible for cleaning up much decaying animal and plant life. Many of the creatures that are the best scavengers are the ones most shunned by man. Partly because they like decaying carrion they are repulsive to some people, and even more because as these scavengers eat the decaying material, they are picking up dangerous bacteria which can often cause sickness to man. People try to keep their kitchens clean to discourage cockroaches and rodents and their accompanying germs from entering. Yet, out in the wild these creatures are invaluable in keeping the environment clean.

Science: Mountain Habitat

The Rocky Mountains have several different habitat areas, each with particular flora and fauna (plants and animals). These flora and fauna do overlap somewhat in each of the habitat areas, so the following information is general. In the foothills of the mountains there are shrubs and deciduous trees with deer, squirrels and many other species while down in the valleys live such animals as moose, beavers, coyotes, and muskrats.

As the elevation increases, pinion pines and junipers grow and there are deer, elk, bears, squirrels, etc., Higher up firs and pines grow in more abundance and this is the home of the bighorn sheep whose habitat extends above the timberline, as well.

Above the **timberline** there are no trees. The timberline is the designation above which trees do not grow due to higher altitude conditions, including cold temperatures, lack of moisture, and sometimes snow pack over many months, though not all year. Your student can see the timberline in pictures of the mountains, but it is so much more exciting when he catches the first glimpse of a real timberline for himself!

There are, on some mountains of high elevations, alpine areas where only a few types of plants and wildflowers grow. Finally, the peaks of some of the mountains have snow cover year round.

For a wonderful illustration of the mountain habitat, look at the picture Jeanette Winter paints—the one opposite Jake and Charlie in the cabin. There are beavers in the valley, trees on the slopes with bears and elk, and then in the higher elevations mountain sheep with far fewer trees and in the background above the timberline, no trees at all. Each creature that the author describes in her writing, she also paints and she adds a few that are not in the text for good measure. Look at other scenes and let your student have fun identifying the birds and animals.

Science: Rivers - The Mississippi and the Missouri Rivers

The Mississippi River handles the watershed from all the land east of the Rocky Mountains as well as a great deal of the land west of the Appalachians. The headwaters, or the source of the Mississippi River is in northern Minnesota and the mouth empties into the Gulf of Mexico at the New Orleans, Louisiana delta.

The Missouri River begins in southwestern Montana at a spot called Three Forks. And it actually flows all four map directions before emptying into the Mississippi River just north of St. Louis. Ask your student, as he is searching out this information on a map, if he can explain how a river could flow in these various directions? Let him consider this question for awhile. What is actually happening? Remember that water, pulled by **gravity**, flows downhill. The point at which the Missouri River is birthed up in the mountains of Montana is the highest point between the source of the Missouri River and its mouth (where the river empties into the Mississippi) just north of St. Louis. Therefore, the river flows northwest *downhill* then north-east *downhill*, then east *downhill*, then south *downhill*, east again *downhill* to the Mississippi! It might be interesting to find a raised-relief map of the United States, sold through some map stores, homeschool websites or at natural history museums to see how the river flows. If your student wishes, he could make a map with Play-Doh® or flour dough, to see how this actually works. With some help he could consult topographical maps which show the actual elevations and make a scale replica.

Science: Conservation - National Wildlife Refuge

In order to preserve natural areas of interest in the United States, National Wildlife Refuges as well as National Parks have been established. Your student may enjoy learning something of the history of these measures of conservation. A National Park or Wildlife Refuge is declared to be so by an act of Congress. In 1872 Yellowstone was declared the nation's first National Park! John

Muir, naturalist, was largely responsible for efforts to have Congress name Yosemite and Sequoia National Parks as well (1890). And President Theodore Roosevelt led various conservational efforts during his time in office.

Research online or with library books will help your student discover much about our National Parks and the many famous people who worked toward conserving America's areas of beauty and interest. Did your student know that in Montana there is a Charles M. Russell National Wildlife Refuge? Look for it on a detailed Montana map. Maybe you and your student could actually visit there someday!

Teacher's Notes

The *Five in a Row* lesson options for each unit in the manual are all you need to teach your child. The additional resource area provided below is simply a place to jot down relevant info you've found that you might want to reference.

COWBOY CHARLIE

Date:

Student:

Five in a Row Lesson Topics Chosen:

Social Studies:

Language Arts:

Art:

Math:

Science:

Relevant Library Resources: Books, DVDs, Audio Books

Websites or Video Links:

Related Field Trip Opportunities:

Favorite Quote or Memory During Study:

Name:

Date:

Science: **Rivers - Lengths**

The Missouri River and the Mississippi River are the first- and second-longest rivers in North America. Research and find the shortest river in North America to add to the rivers listed below. Also, if your student has rowed *Ping* from *Five in a Row* Volume 1 add the Yangtze River to the list. Using the length graph, chart the length of each river next to its name in a different color marker or colored pencil line. This will create a visual of the rivers' related lengths.

Missouri River ________

Mississippi River ________

____

____

____

____

____

____

____

____

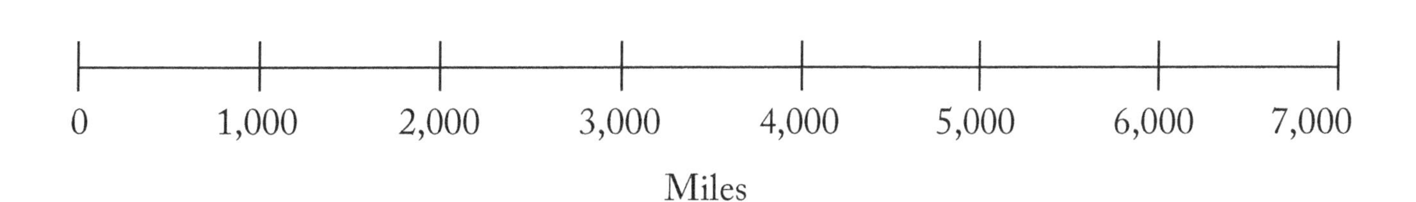

Name:

Date:

Geography: **Flags of Missouri and Montana**

The Missouri flag consists of three horizontal bands of red, white, and blue, with the arms of Missouri in the center. The red and white stripes represent valor and purity, while the blue represents three things: permanency, vigilance and justice.

The Montana flag consists of a blue field with the state seal in the center and the word "Montana" above it. Within the seal, a plow, shovel and pick rest in a field in front of the Great Falls of the Missouri River. The ribbon contains the state motto, Oro y plata, which is Spanish for "Gold and silver". *For more information, see Parts of a Flag on page 266.*

Color in the flags of Missouri and Montana below.

Name:

Date:

Social Studies: **History - Timeline of Charles Marion Russell's Life**

Using the timeline below, record important dates in Charlie's life. Research and find other important events and people that were influencing the world during the same time period. If your student researches other contemporaries of Russell they can plot their lives out along the same timeline. Add printed pictures if desired and use hash marks along the timeline to represent specific dates and mark accordingly.

1864 **1926**

Grass Sandals

Title: *Grass Sandals*
Author: Dawnine Spivak
Illustrator: Demi
Copyright: 1997
Summary: The true story of one of the most famous Japanese poets and his marvelous travels

Social Studies: Geography - Japan

Ask your student in what country the poet-traveler Basho lived. (Basho lived in Japan.) Does your student know where Japan is? Can she find it on a map? When she looks at Japan on a map, what can she tell about this country compared to other countries around it? (Japan is a relatively small country in area, and it is an island. Actually Japan is made up of many islands.)

Place the story disk on Japan; Spend time enjoying the map of things Basho sees on his travels, at the end of the book *Grass Sandals*.

Social Studies: East Meets West

The story *Grass Sandals* begins with a dedication in which the author's daughter says, "nothing happens in this book," to which the mother/author replies, "That is what Westerners say about Japanese writing." Through this story you may be able to very simply begin to show your student how Eastern and Western cultures have often differed in thought and philosophies.

The Far Eastern countries, which include Japan, have many aspects that are presented quite simply compared to the Western counterpart. The art, writing, preparation of foods, and clothes are often presented with graceful simplicity. That does not mean the writing, recipes, fashions, etc., are not complicated. Each one of them may take a great deal of time and effort to make or prepare, but the presentation is marked by simplicity. There is much discipline, control and calmness throughout Eastern traditions. Traditionally there has been no sense of "rush" in the cultures of Far Eastern countries. Many of these traditions are followed in the same way as they have been for centuries.

In contrast, the Western cultures tend to be active, fast paced, inquisitive, always willing to explore new methods, often adopting them in fashions, art, foods, etc. While Far Easterners have paid close attention to their past traditions, generation after generation, Westerners are more likely to shun their own past as old-fashioned. People of Western thinking are constantly looking for new (and to them better) ways of doing things and there is a recurring sense of rush to the pace of life. This explanation is quite simplistic but it is only the merest introduction to the ideas of differences in the two cultures.

How does Basho combine the two lines of thought into his own standard of living? He values simplicity in his possessions and his pace of life. He doesn't have too many possessions—at least he is able to leave his home to travel and he does not carry much with him. But, more like a Westerner, he does cover extensive areas of land, he is observant, inquisitive, creative and has many adventures.

Much of Eastern thought and expression has traditionally been subtle. A story, or art, or a play will unfold quietly and though many things are not said or shown; clues tell you what is happening. In contrast Western culture tends to be more graphic and less subtle.

Encourage your student by saying, "Let's see if we can read carefully enough to see all the wonderful events happening in this true story of Basho. If so we'll be reading more like an Easterner, and perhaps not in so much in a hurry like a Westerner!'"

Social Studies: Culture of Japan

Your student may have been introduced to the culture of Japan in the *Five in a Row* Volume 1 story selections *A Pair of Red Clogs* and *Grandfather's Journey*. If you studied these lessons, you will be ready to dig deeper into the present day Japanese life and culture.

Today Japan is a modern, bustling country with cities, offices, theaters, etc., much like the United States. One of the biggest differences between the U.S. and Japan is the smaller size of the country of Japan. Because Japan is not large geographically there is a greater concentration of people per square mile. In fact there are approximately 900 people per square mile, as opposed to United States approximately 93 people per square mile and Canada with about 8 people per square mile! (Remind your student that these figures are averages. There are densely populated cities in the U.S. but there are also miles and miles of unpopulated areas—farms, ranches, national forests, etc. The category was density per square mile—and that is found by dividing the total population of a country by the total area in square miles.)

In order to study modern clothing, homes, vehicles, etc., of Japan find some good simple books at your library, or look online. You will see that life in the cities of Japan has become just as fast paced as it is in American cities, and the differences in the cultures seem, on the surface at least, to be less than in the past.

Social Studies: Culture of Japan - Japanese Writing

Traditional Japanese writing, which your student can see on the back cover of *Grass Sandals*, is considered by many to be the most difficult writing system in the world. It is a combination of phonetic sounds and Chinese characters. The order of each stroke in the character is predetermined and has traditionally been taught without deviation. In other words, the children had to learn each brush stroke "in order" for each character in their language, with as many as thirty brush strokes per character.

Flashcards: Copy the back cover of *Grass Sandals* and cut out each Japanese character. Place one each on a file card and write the word it represents on the back. Have fun learning these Japanese words.

Matching Game: Another game you can play with these word characters is to make two photocopies. Cut the copies apart and glue each character onto an index card. You should now have nine pairs of cards—18 in all. Now place the cards (blank on the back) all face down and mix them up. Your student can play a matching game by looking at the differences in the marks of the figure. This would be an exercise in observation and memory!

Social Studies: Character Relationship - Friendship

Basho had friends and Basho made more friends. This traveling poet of Japan enjoyed people and he was willing to cultivate new friendships as well as maintain established ones. Ask your student if she thinks it is easy to make a friend? Discuss ways to meet people and how it is often through a common interest that friendships are begun. Talk about ways to maintain friendships. Discuss how to keep up with friends through visits, letters or phone calls, as well as helping when a friend is in need. Talk about the importance of making up after arguments, or clearing up misunderstandings, etc., and converse about what happens to a friendship if these breaches are ignored.

Language Arts: Biography

Grass Sandals is the story of a man who actually lived in Japan, who had adventures and who wrote poetry. Does your student remember the name for this kind of book (as opposed to a fiction work)? It is called a biography. The word biography comes from the Latin word for *life* (bio) and *writing* (graph). A biography is a book written about an actual person who is now living, or who has lived in the past. Biographies are wonderful books to read because through reading them you not only get to know a real person but you learn much about the places, events, people and times which surrounded him.

You can easily find a biography at your library. The Biography section is usually shelved alphabetically by the name of the *person they are about* rather than alphabetically by *author* as fiction books are.

Have fun with your student exploring the Biography section of your library and check out a few simple biographies to read together. (Three good authors to check in your library system are Robert Quackenbush, Jean Fritz and David Adler.)

Teacher's Note: You may want to ask your student if she has heard of an autobiography. How is it different from a biography? Auto means "self" or "same," so *autobiography* means a book written about oneself.

Language Arts: Details in Writing

Talk with your student about the fact that authors can make a reference to an idea early in a story and then complete that idea at a later time. On about the fifth page of *Grass Sandals*, Basho is painting on his hat. Does your student remember what Basho painted? Basho addresses his hat (like he would a person) and says that he will soon show it cherry blossoms. Three pages later the Japanese poet says that he has "kept his promise to his hat." This is not a critical point or lesson. It just demonstrates the well executed details in the writings of Dawnine Spivak. Your student can tell or write a story that has similar writing techniques included.

Did your student comment on the description Spivak makes as she compares Basho, walking along dressed in black robes, to a crow? Does she remember that this is a form of simile?

Language Arts: Poetry - Haiku

Haiku (HY koo) is a beautiful Japanese form of poetry that has a very specific form or pattern. Basho, in our story *Grass Sandals*, was a poet of Japan and he wrote many haikus. Let your student know that she, too can write a haiku like Basho did. All she needs to do is follow the pattern.

Teacher's Note: Before you try to explain how to write a haiku, make sure your student understands how words are divided into syllables and is able to sound them out. Let your student know that when she has mastered this information she can write a Japanese haiku for herself. For practice you can clap with your student—one clap for each syllable of a word. For older students, you may also use this as a Language Arts opportunity to explain how words are hyphenated at the syllable breaks. Explain that this information will help them in their writing when a word is too long for the end of a line—they will know how to properly divide the word and place part of it on the next line down.

A haiku is made up of seventeen syllables arranged specifically in three lines of verse. The pattern is 5,7, and 5 syllables. Each line has a specific number of syllables and somewhere in the words is generally hidden a clue about the season of the year. The word frog might mean summer while daffodils might mean spring, red-yellow leaves refer to fall, etc. The entire haiku is often about something very simple in nature or some event told simply with just a few words, but these few words paint a word picture that everyone can enjoy. Below is an example:

In the still evening	5 syllables
leaping out of a river—	7 syllables
splash five little fish	5 syllables

If your student enjoys departing from familiar form she may like the fact that the three lines often do not begin with capital letters and that she can use ellipsis (...) or a dash (—) at the end of the first or second line as a pause. Note the lack of typical punctuation such as commas and periods.

Enjoy experimenting with this wonderful poetry form and illustrate the finished results, if you wish, as Basho did.

Language Arts: Vocabulary

curve In a bending line (like fog curving over the hills).

satiny Smooth and shiny.

winding With many bends and curves, as in a river or path.

scribbled Wrote down quickly without regard for neatness.

restless A feeling of wanting to be up and moving rather than still.

Language Arts: Supplemental Books

The illustrator of *Grass Sandals*, Demi, wrote and illustrated a book called *The Empty Pot*. Although it takes place in China, not Japan, this is a thought-provoking and enjoyable book to read and would be a great go-along with *Grass Sandals* as well as giving you more chance to examine the illustrations of Demi.

Also, at this time, you might enjoy rereading *Grandfather's Journey* and *A Pair of Red Clogs* (FIAR Vol. 1) to pull together details from life of the past in Japan.

And, one last idea: A book called *Emily* by Michael Bedard, illustrated by Barbara Cooney. This is an interesting story of the reclusive American poet Emily

Dickinson. In the story *Grass Sandals*, Basho writes a poem and sends it back in a saddlebag to the farmer who let him borrow the horse. In *Emily*, Emily Dickinson gives a poem away as well. Let your student listen to or read this story and see if she observes the similar actions of these poets, even though one of them is very social and one of them is not.

Art: Action in Illustration

While the men in the trees sat still and went nowhere, Basho went many places and had many adventures. Look at the illustrations throughout the story and see how artist Demi has quietly and gently tucked a great deal of action into her illustrations. The end papers show Basho writing on a leaf. The title page shows the rush and flutter of many cranes ascending as Basho is again at work. On the page that describes a haiku (after the dedication page) notice the deer leaping, and Basho's feet in a happy walk. On almost every page there is water moving, or birds flying or animals running, fire blazing or wind blowing. Yet all of these illustrations still serve to highlight Basho's quiet personality with their calmness and beauty, even in action. (Maybe it is just Basho's quiet, delighted reaction to the movement around him that makes it feel like even the movement is calm.)

Art: Grass Paper and Calligraphy

The paper with fibers used in the background of the pages for *Grass Sandals* is grass paper. You can find grass paper in different colors and with different amounts of texture at art stores and possibly large hobby/art supply stores. Grass paper usually is not as absorbent as some other kinds of papers and is sometimes used for calligraphy.

Calligraphy is an art form that consists of beautifully rendered handwriting. The art form dates back to early Chinese times. Today there are many different styles of calligraphy (each having a different letter-form to its alphabet) and it is used to letter formal documents, greeting cards, posters and framed sayings and artwork. Calligraphy is accomplished with ink and a brush (as Basho uses) or pen. The ink will soak into paper that is absorbent, and fine, beautiful lines will not be possible. Therefore, calligraphy artists use grass paper and other non-absorbent papers for their work.

You can also take this opportunity to explore paper making. You can watch a video on how paper is made and then you may wish to try making some paper of your own. Handmade papers are beautiful and valued, as each handmade page is unique. There are paper making kits available at hobby and art stores.

Art: Painting a Hat

For a simple art project buy a few sheets of brightly colored poster board. Cut an 18"-24" diameter circle from the poster board. Now cut it from one outside edge to the centerpoint. Then twist (or wind) your circle into a cone hat. Either tape or staple the overlap to make the cone shape secure. Now attach shoestrings or twine on each side about halfway between the rim's edge and the cone's point to tie loosely under the chin.

Then with a brush (the type with a flexible, tear-drop shaped bristle cluster) and some black paint, let your student draw or write some figures on her hat.

Art: Illustrations - Colored Ink and Oriental Brushes

If you would like your student to experiment with ink and Oriental brushes, you can find these at an art supply store or sometimes at a large hobby store. Perhaps you may only wish to go to one of these stores and just show your student what the brushes look like. There is authentic Oriental ink available, but if you would prefer, you can inquire about inks that would work as well and still be washable. The handling of the brushes and ink might be an activity better suited for the older range of *Five in a Row* student.

Oriental brushes have long wooden handles, often made of bamboo, and bristles of different types of hair—wolf, rabbit, goat, etc. The tips of these brushes are not squared off but taper to form perfect points when the brushes are pulled from the ink. These brushes are held upright in the hand (at a 90° angle to the flat paper on a desk) when painting or writing. Look how Basho holds his brush in the picture on the end papers.

Experimenting with Oriental brushes is a great deal of fun. Find a book or video on Japanese painting techniques and let your student try some brush strokes and maybe even draw some bamboo! Plain white newsprint is the best practice paper for the ink. Cover the working place with plastic or an oilcloth and make sure a smock or old shirt covers the clothes! Teacher and student alike will have a great deal of fun trying out some new art techniques.

Art: Appreciating the Various Treatments of Water

Demi has used many different techniques in painting water for the story *Grass Sandals*. With your student look through the entire book, making note of rivers, ponds, streams, waterfalls, etc. Let your student try some of these techniques if she is interested.

Art: Sewing

Basho sews ties on his hat so it won't blow away. Take this opportunity to explain and demonstrate some simple sewing techniques. Find appropriate small projects suitable for your student's age and interests. A simple project might be binding a pair of moccasins (you can get kits at craft stores).

You may enjoy teaching a bit of history surrounding sewing, like how Native Americans used bone needles, or about seamstresses and tailors who hand sew and/or use sewing machines, or about the invention of the sewing machine. (The sewing machine was invented in 1790 but never patented or produced. In 1830 a Frenchman also invented a sewing machine. But it wasn't until 1851 that **Isaac Singer** patented and began producing the Singer sewing machine. Because of his patent and production, Isaac Singer's name is usually associated with the invention.)

Math: Century

With the background information that a century is a unit of measure, used for measuring years, and that a century consists of one hundred years, you can proceed to the lessons below.

The page after "What Basho Saw" at the end of the book *Grass Sandals* speaks of Basho living in the seventeenth century. The dates given for his life are 1644-1694. Ask your student to figure out how old Basho was when he died using subtraction. (Basho was fifty years old.) Now ask your student if she can determine why it says Basho lived in the seventeenth century while his life dates are in the 1600s. (Explain that the years one through one hundred after the birth of Christ are called the *first* century. The years A.D. 101-200 are called the *second* century, etc. Your student can see, for example, that the years of A.D. 106 and A.D. 149 were in the second century. In like manner the 1600s when Basho lived were in the seventeenth century!

How many centuries have there been from the seventeenth century to the present? Basho lived that many centuries (or groups of 100 years) ago. (Basho lived nearly four centuries ago.) The last information page says that there was another poet who lived a century after Basho. What century would he have lived in? (He would have lived in the eighteenth century or the 1700s.)

By knowing the date of the present year, can your student determine what century she is living in? (The twenty-first century.)

Science: Astronomy - The Milky Way

The Milky Way is actually a galaxy which includes multitudes of stars (our sun is one of them), as well as all the planets of our solar system. Though it is technically an entire galaxy, we also use the term Milky Way when speaking of the band of closely grouped stars which appear at night like a band crossing over the sky. In areas where there is little light pollution, these stars are so close together they look like a faint milky swath across the sky. If your student is interested, find a simple book on the Milky Way at your library or look at pictures online.

Science: Zoology - Frogs

If you have studied the FIAR Vol. 3 story selection *Andy and the Circus*, you may have already introduced the subject of amphibians and the life cycle of the frog. Ask your student if she remembers *Andy and the Circus*. Ask her what she can tell you about frogs and tadpoles.

Teacher's Note: Respect requires that this line of questioning not begin with, "You've studied this and you *should* remember—what *do* you remember?" but rather, "Wasn't that a great book—*Andy and the Circus*, and all the things Andy had to do before he could get to the big top? Do you remember that Andy had some tadpoles in a jar? Aren't frogs interesting? Do you have a favorite kind? What are some of the things you know about frogs?" This type of questioning is far more likely to produce a friendly response of any information that your child knows about the subject. Once you know how much your child already knows, you can proceed with new information.

If review is needed, give the introductory information over again. Frogs are considered **amphibians**. Amphibians are animals that are born in the water, breathe air through gills, go through life cycle changes and spend their adult lives mostly on land breathing air through their lungs. The general life cycle of a frog is egg, tadpole with no legs, tadpole with growing legs, and adult frog. A good simple book from your library or the information in Volume 3 of *Five in a Row* may be of help.

If review is quick or not necessary then you may deepen your study by discussing the **habitat** of frogs. Frogs live everywhere except Antarctica. Frogs usually prefer moist areas, but most frogs do not live in the water—they may jump in the water to get away from danger, but most frogs live on land. A frog has many **natural enemies** including snakes, hawks, and herons. A frog's **diet** usually consists of insects, worms, etc. There are many different **sounds** made by frogs which can be heard online. Or better yet, observe in person during the spring and summer months by ponds, streams, lakes, etc.

A frog both absorbs and loses water through its skin, especially its abdomen. Therefore, frogs need a moist environment and it may be that many kinds of frogs are active at night because the hot sun would cause them to become **dehydrated**. (Dehydrated is made up of the prefix de- meaning *remove* and the root word hydrate meaning *water* so that to **dehydrate** something is to remove the water or moisture from it.)

Try taking a field trip to a good pet store to see exotic varieties of frogs. You can also find books on frogs that continue beyond the "simple information" level with more detailed information if your student is interested.

In addition, your student may enjoy getting literature on amphibians from your state conservation department or nearby nature center. This type of literature will showcase the amphibians that are in *your* state—the frogs, toads and salamanders your student would be the most likely to see on a regular basis.

Remind your student that in the story *Grass Sandals*, the frogs about which Basho writes a haiku would be those frogs native to Japan. Some frogs that live in North America also live in Japan—the American bullfrog is one of them, though it would have a Japanese common name. But there are many others which you can learn about using a book or website that tells about frogs around the world.

It might delight your student to visit a pond in the summer and just walk around it near the edge. She may hear the frightened squeaking sound of a frog as it plops into the water ahead of your student's feet! It is sort of an "eek-plop" sound. If she stands quietly and searches, your student may be able to spot the frog in the water—eyes above the surface watching her. Does your student notice the frog's eyes? Can she understand through her observation how having the eyes at the top of the head helps the frog? With these eyes, a frog can see while most of its body is underwater, and it can see in almost any direction! Maybe your student could write a poem or haiku about her experiences observing nature, just like Basho did.

Science: Botany - Bananas

The famous Japanese poet was given a banana or basho tree. He planted it and watched it grow. It was so delightful to him that the author of *Grass Sandals* says he changed his name to Basho!

Technically or scientifically, the banana tree is not really a tree because it does not have a wood trunk or real boughs. Rather it is considered an extremely large plant! You and your student can easily see that this is true in the illustration of the banana plant next to Basho's house on the second page of the story. The illustration shows a plant with very large leaves. These leaves are not boughs but rather come up from the center of the plant. It is just the enormous size of the banana plant that causes some people to call it a tree. **Teacher's Note:** Your student can examine many plants, trees and shrubs and learn for herself which have woody trunks and boughs (or woody stems like some shrubs) and which have herbaceous or soft plant stems.

The banana plant produces the banana fruit which is considered to be one of the most popular fruits in the world, and ranks in the top five of the major food crops of the world. The banana plant needs a climate that is very warm and moist. Can your student determine, based on her knowledge of geography, where in the world might be a good place to grow bananas? (If a first thought is only a warm place, remember that it must be a moist climate as well!)

Does your student know about **tropical regions** and where these are located? Do the terms **Tropic of Cancer** and **Tropic of Capricorn** give her a clue? The tropics lie in a wide band around the world between these two parallels of latitude. On a map or globe have your student find these two parallels of latitude if she knows them. If not, show her where they are located and indicate the amount of land that lies between them. Let her examine what areas and countries are to be found in the tropics.

Maybe your student remembers studying *How to Make an Apple Pie and See the World.* In the lessons for that story in *Five in a Row*, Vol.1, your student learned that bananas grow in Jamaica. Can she find Jamaica on the map or globe? Is it within this band of lands between the Tropic of Cancer and the Tropic of Capricorn? Central and South America also grow bananas (Brazil is a large producer) as well as many other tropical areas around the world, including Hawaii, Florida, Mexico, etc.

Most of the bananas consumed in the United States are the yellow skinned fruit variety. There is also a darker, tough-skinned variety called a plantain that is starchy and used more like a vegetable, not as often in the United States, but more often in other parts of the world.

The banana plant produces one large bunch of bananas and then dies and is replaced by younger growing plants. Bananas are also picked green for a very important reason: If the plantation workers waited until the fruits were ripe the skins would begin to split and insects would eat the fruit before it could be harvested. The green bananas continue to ripen and tum yellow and become sweet *after* picking them at the green, unripe stage.

Science: Chemistry - Bananas and Oxidation

Your student may already know that when a peeled banana is exposed to the air it turns brown. If you don't think your student has already observed this phenomenon, cut up part of banana as if it were for a snack, put it aside where she can see it, and leave it on a plate while you talk about bananas. When the fruit has begun to turn brown, ask your student if she remembers how light and pale it was when first cut. Bananas have chemical substances in them which are protected by the skin, but when peeled and sliced and left in contact with air these substances actually go through a chemical reaction (oxidation) that turns the fruit brown. (This is also common reaction when potatoes and apples are sliced and exposed to the air.)

Citrus fruits have an acid in them that will slow down the enzymes which encourage the oxidation process. For that reason many cooks will add citrus fruit juice to a fruit salad that contains cut apples and bananas. The fruit will stay fresh looking for a bit longer until it is served.

Make a fruit salad (including apples and bananas) with your student. Add some fresh orange juice, lemon juice or pineapple juice and let her observe the results. Made an hour ahead of serving, and mixed well, the salad should still look fresh when it is eaten. You could also make a small batch of identical fruit salad without adding the juice and compare the two before serving.

Science: Botany - Bamboo

Bamboo is a plant that is a member of the grass family. Even though your student may have seen tall clumps of grasses, bamboo is a giant! It can grow over one hundred feet high! Used in hundreds of applications all over the world, bamboo can be eaten (cans of tender bamboo shoots can be found in the Asian section of your grocery store), as well as used to make homes, roofs, baskets, shoes, ornaments—the uses are endless.

Like bananas, bamboo grows well in tropical climates or in some warm temperate climates. If your student is fascinated by all the amazing uses for bamboo, she might enjoy a book from the library or doing research online for more detailed facts.

Science: Botany - Flowers

Basho was content to sit and drink tea "in the company of morning glories." Has your student ever seen the brilliant and soft blues of morning glories with the morning sun shining on them? Has she ever thought of a plant as "company?" Morning glories are indeed a beautiful sight worth savoring!

Morning glories are a flowering plant that is grown from seed. They form vines that cling to any support and climb more each day. The bright blue flowers open at dawn and close by afternoon. New flowers bloom the next day. Morning glories have provided cheerful displays of brilliant blue for countless generations of flower lovers. Try growing some morning glories with your student and enjoy them as Basho did! (Though these plants are grown from seed and you can find the seed packets easily at any big box store or gardening shop, you can also find starter plants at greenhouse garden centers. Take extra care in transplanting them!)

If you grow morning glories try this experiment. Have your student gently tie a string around the stem of the plant about six inches from the top point of the vine. Measure how far this is from the ground. As the plant grows upward, does your student think the string will stay in the same place or move higher? Wait a few days and observe. The string should be the same distance from the ground and the amount of vine above the string should be more than the original six inches. The vines grow by adding cells to the vine tip, not pushing up from ground level.

Later, when Basho gets new grass sandals from a friends, he writes a haiku about irises. Irises are usually bought as bulbs (the horticultural term is rhizome), which look something like a slightly flattened large cigar, and which run parallel to the ground (you may have to define parallel for your student) just under the soil's surface. These bulbs are planted in the garden in the fall or early spring for summer flowers. They can then stay in the ground year-round and will multiply so that in a few years there are more flowers than the first year. At this point the rhizomes themselves have multiplied. They are then dug up and divided so that the plants will stay healthy. If all the divided bulbs are replanted, with some space in between, there will be even more flowers for the next few years. Many of the old fashioned American varieties of iris have a lovely sweet bouquet or scent. (If you do not have a place to garden, you can sometimes find Japanese iris in florist shops or even grocery stores. Buy a few and enjoy them in a vase.) It is nice to think that whether you grow them or buy them you can usually find some Japanese iris (smaller in blossom than our common iris) to enjoy, just like Basho did!

The horse which Basho borrowed is seen eating hibiscus flowers. These are large blossoms (sometimes dinner plate sized) which can be grown in some areas of the United States as well as in Japan. Check your gardening stores and ask if they have hibiscus plants and what type of growing conditions and care they need.

Teacher's Note: If you are able to view or grow morning glories, irises, and hibiscus flowers, review the simple parts of a flower and compare the two types of flower by color, number of petals, number and look of stamens, differences in look of pistil, and other defining characteristics.

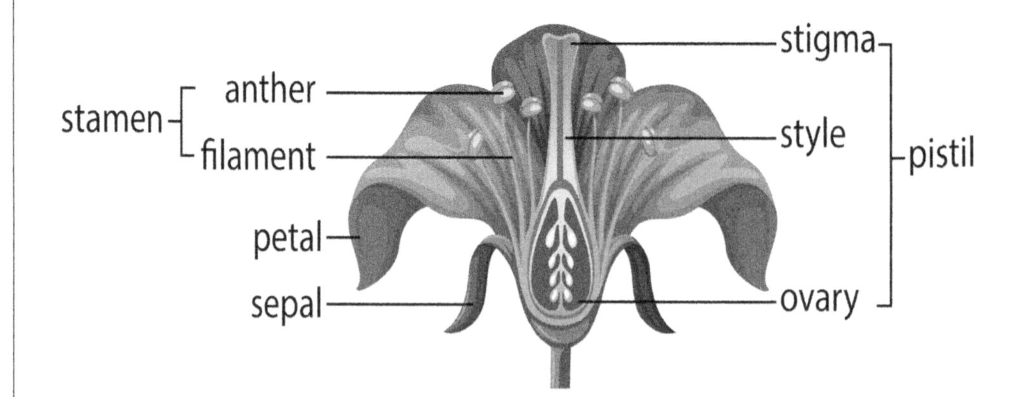

Science: Zoology - Cranes and Crickets

In the illustrations for *Grass Sandals* you can point out the cranes to your student. (You can find them on the title page, dedication page as well as the last page of the story.) These are the Tancho (also called red-crowned or Japanese) cranes. These beautiful, graceful birds have the sharply contrasting white with black edged feathers, and red "cap." The cranes have long legs and necks. Can your student think how these features might help the birds in their habitat? (The long legs are necessary for wading in the water to find food, and the long necks to stretch down and feed on snails, frogs, etc.

Ask your student if these birds remind her of any that she sees on occasion? Depending on where she lives, she might have seen a sandhill crane—which are the most abundant cranes on earth, or the great blue heron, or great snowy egret. Tell her that cranes are easy to distinguish from herons by looking at their necks in flight. A heron's neck is doubled up in an "S" curve while the cranes stretch their necks out straight as they fly.

Cranes, of different varieties, are prevalent in much of Japanese art and decorating. Once your student has become aware of them she will notice cranes in Chinese restaurants, at museums, or as garden decorations, whereever decorative Japanese art is featured.

On the last page of the story, we are told that Basho notices a cricket. Perhaps he heard the cricket or perhaps he only saw it among the grasses. Basho was what some people call "in tune with nature" which means he was always noticing the birds, plants, animals and insects that lived around him. As soon as he noticed he would stop and watch (observe) for a while and he learned from everything he saw! He enjoyed being outside and enjoyed experiencing the wildlife around him.

Does your student remember how to tell a male cricket (the ones that sing) from a female cricket?

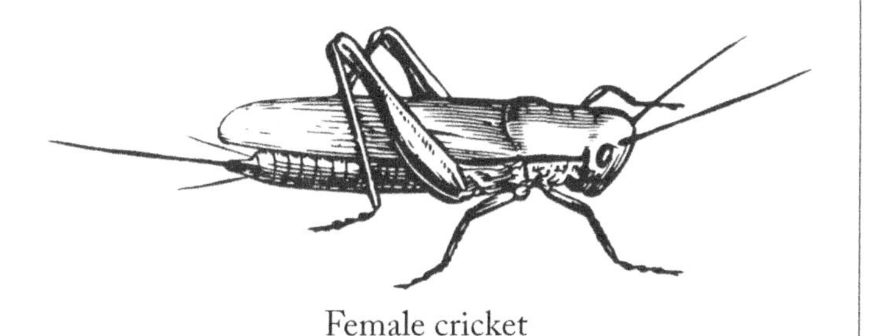

Female cricket

Crickets were covered in *Five in a Row* Volume 3 during the study of *The Salamander Room*. In a later volume of *Five in a Row*, you will have the chance to study crickets in detail during the book selection *A Cricket in Times Square*. For now, you might add the information that crickets generally hide during the daylight and come out at dusk to feed during the night. Crickets eat insects, bits of grains, etc. There is also the wonderful sound that a cricket makes by rubbing the bases of its wings together. But, did your student know that if she quietly waits outside after dark and listens carefully, she will be able to hear the crickets chirp *within* an entire orchestra of other night singing insects? How many different sounds can she hear? Does each insect stop and start again, or do they keep up a constant trill? Are there any frog choruses tucked into the night's performance?

A wonderful book on this subject is *Discover Nature at Sundown* by Elizabeth P. Lawlor. This is a treasure of a book for those truly interested in the animal behavior of the night. There is a bit of evolutionary material included so use it for your own teaching research and present what you desire to your students. Read this book and you will have many fascinating pieces of information which will astound your students.

Science: Geology - Hot Springs, Cold Streams and the Sea

Did your student notice that on his travels Basho bathes in hot springs, splashes in streams that are cold and swims in the sea?

Can your student tell you how hot springs become hot? Hot springs occur when underground water is heated by areas of hot rock or lava deep in the ground. This may be an opportunity to quickly cover the four divisions of the earth's make up and core. The earth is covered in a thin layer called the *crust*, below that the *mantle*, then the *outer core* and deepest inside is the *inner core*. A simple book or diagram online will have more information on this topic and colored illustrations which can be copied by hand or printed and placed in a notebook.

Where does your student think the cold streams come from? If she cannot tell you, find a picture of a mountain with snow at the top (there is one on the blue iris page). During the seasons when the snow melts, streams are created which flow downhill, icy cold! Can your student tell you a main difference between the springs and streams, and the waters of the sea? (The hot springs and cold streams are considered fresh bodies of water, while the sea contains salt water.)

Science: Astronomy - Moon

Basho was content to live alone and travel alone, but he also enjoyed meeting new people and seeing old friends. In *Grass Sandals* Basho meets some friends and they enjoy watching the full moon, drinking tea and writing poems about the beautiful sights they see. Remind your student of this story tie-in as you begin your lesson on the moon.

In *Five in a Row* Vol. 2 you may have studied the phases of the moon during the story lessons for *Owl Moon*. If you need to, review this information briefly. (The moon's phases are: waxing crescent, first quarter, waxing gibbous, full moon, waning gibbous, last quarter and waning crescent. You can find a picture of these phases online. Some new information: new moon rises at sunrise, first quarter at noon, full moon at sunset, and last quarter at midnight.

Add some information about the topography of the moon. When a person looks at a full moon she sees some areas of light and some areas of grays. With a telescope one can begin to see that the gray areas are vast plains and that there are many craters on the surface of the moon. Most of the numerous craters were formed as meteors moved through the moon's thin atmosphere and crashed into its surface. (The earth's atmosphere keeps most meteors from ever reaching the ground. The friction caused as a meteor moves through Earth's more protective atmosphere burns most of the objects up before they crash into its surface.)

The plains areas of the moon's surface were mistakenly called "seas" by early astronomers who thought they looked like bodies of water. Thus a topographical map of the moon would list some of the main plains areas of the moon as Sea of Tranquility, Sea of Rains, Sea of Serenity, etc. With a map of the moon's surface, can your student figure out which plains areas make up the "facial features" which have traditionally been called The Man in the Moon?

You might also want to discuss briefly the lunar landing which took place by U.S. Apollo 11 Astronauts on July 20, 1969. A simple library book on this fantastic accomplishment might be extremely interesting to your student.

Science: Astronomy - Moons on Other Planets

Remind your student that when Basho and his friends drink their tea by the light of the moon, each friend saw a tiny moon reflected in his tea. Since Basho lived in Japan, on the planet Earth, the moon that all the friends see is Earth's moon.

But did your student know that there are other planets in our solar system? Some of these planets have many moons! With today's advances in astronomy, other planets' moons are being discovered often. Of course, they don't all look like our moon and wouldn't all be visible in a teacup if you were having tea on that planet!

Mercury 0
Venus 0
Earth 1
Mars 2
Jupiter 79
Saturn 82
Uranus 27
Neptune 14
Pluto (dwarf planet) 5

Science: Weather - Rain and the Sense of Smell

Basho says he can smell the rain. Has your student ever noticed the smell of rain drifting in on the wind before a storm actually arrives? Or the fresh damp smell after a rain? The next time there is a storm on the way, remind your student to be using all of her senses to experience the storm!

Science: Earth Science - Mountains

Remind your student that Basho travels over much of his country. He sees beautiful mountains and writes about them and paints them. Look with your student at all the paintings of mountains that the illustrator Demi has done for this story. You can also look in library books or online for pictures of actual mountains in Japan. Can you find the Japanese Alps? There are many other chains of mountains covering the islands that make up Japan.

Does your student know the names of the mountain ranges in her own country? Cover these if necessary and then do a quick study on the names of the main mountain ranges of the world. This exercise is not for memorization but for the introduction to the sounds of the names, and information about various countries or continents. Show your student the difference between an entire mountain range and a famous peak. For instance, she may hear someone speak of the Himalayas and not know that Mt. Everest is the famous peak that draws so many to climbing adventures there. Or she may think that Mt. Everest is the range when it is only a single peak! Let her know that the abbreviation "Mt." when it precedes the name usually designates a single mountain.

If your student is interested, find the *Rand McNally Picture Atlas of the World*. In it you will find a wonderful graphic of many famous mountain peaks of the world lined up so that you can see which is the tallest, the smallest, etc. From this graphic you will be able to match famous peaks with their mountain ranges. The picture also shows how each famous peak has its own "face" or profile (familiar side). That is, some may be easily recognizable in pictures just because of the way the peak is formed. The Matterhorn, Mt. Kilimanjaro, Mt. Cook and Mt. Fuji (in Japan!) are rather distinctive in their shape.

Mountains also present a chance to study volcanoes. This may or may not be the time you would like to present this information, but it is mentioned for your consideration. A volcanic eruption can change the face or profile of a famous mountain, as it did in 1980 for Mount St. Helens in the state of Washington.

Teacher's Notes

The *Five in a Row* lesson options for each unit in the manual are all you need to teach your child. The additional resource area provided below is simply a place to jot down relevant info you've found that you might want to reference.

GRASS SANDALS

Date:

Student:

Five in a Row Lesson Topics Chosen:

Social Studies:

Language Arts:

Art:

Math:

Science:

Relevant Library Resources: Books, DVDs, Audio Books

Websites or Video Links:

Related Field Trip Opportunities:

Favorite Quote or Memory During Study:

Name:

Date:

Language Arts: **Biography - Research**

Choose a person living, or who lived in the past, to use for this biography research activity sheet (someone of current or historical significance is a good choice). Before you can write a biography you must research your subject (person) to learn details of their life that you would include in your story. Fill in the blanks below to gain a bigger picture about your subject and the things that shaped their life. Older students may want to use their research information to write a short story or paragraph about the person they chose to study.

Name:

____

Picture/Portrait

Date and Place of Birth:

____

Events during childhood (illness, family, opportunities, etc.):

____

Events during adulthood (marriage, children, jobs, opportunities or losses, etc.):

____

Contributions to Society (scientific discoveries, inventions, ministries, notable actions, etc.):

____

Date of Death, Cause of Death:

____

Name:

Date:

Art: **Calligraphy**

If your student has interest in learning a simple calligraphy-type alphabet, here is one to try. The lines show exactly how high each letter should be. Your student can use a chisel point magic marker or for even more fun and control, try using a broad tipped cartridge ink pen made especially for calligraphy and available at an art store or hobby store in the art department.

a b c d e f g h i j k l m n o p q r s t u v w x y z

A B C D E F G H I J K L M N O P Q R S T U V W X Y Z

0 1 2 3 4 5 6 7 8 9

Name:
Date:
Language Arts: **Is It a Haiku?**

After completing the Language Arts: Poetry - Haiku lesson you may choose to have your student complete the following activity. A haiku is made up of seventeen syllables arranged specifically in three lines of verse; the syllables per line pattern is 5, 7, and 5.

Have your student clap, or raise their fingers to indicate the syllables for each line of the haikus below and decide if they do or do not follow the 5, 7, 5 pattern. Have your student mark the box next to haiku, fewer syllables (not a haiku), or more syllables (not a haiku) for each haiku below.

1. the black bee stings me—
it doesn't hurt too badly
I don't like it though

☐ haiku ☐ more syllables ☐ fewer syllables

2. butterflies are colorful
and flit all over
high above the clouds

☐ haiku ☐ more syllables ☐ fewer syllables

3. brown rabbit waits for
the cabbages to grow round
so he can eat them

☐ haiku ☐ more syllables ☐ fewer syllables

4. red maple leaf falls
slowly down from up above—
a damp chill is in the air

☐ haiku ☐ more syllables ☐ fewer syllables

5. the inchworm
moves up and down
scrunching as he goes

☐ haiku ☐ more syllables ☐ fewer syllables

Answers: 1. haiku 2. more syllables 3.haiku 4. more syllables 5. fewer syllables

Name:
Date:
Art: **Brushes and Ink - Kanji**

Kanji is one of three Japanese writing systems, along with hiragana and katakana, that include symbols representing words or ideas having different meanings and sometimes different pronounciations.

Below is sampling of several common kanji symbols. On a separate sheet of paper help your student copy the symbols using brushes and ink.

The following Bonus Unit Studies utilize books that are currently out of print. See "Finding the Books" at the end of this manual for more information on locating and using these and other excellent but harder-to-find titles.

The Hickory Chair

Title: *The Hickory Chair*
Author: Lisa Rowe Fraustino
Illustrator: Benny Andrews
Copyright: 2001
Summary: As a boy, Louis has a special relationship. The events of that relationship involve a mystery which is finally revealed when he is an old man.

Social Studies: Family Relationships

In the story *The Hickory Chair*, we see a large family. Louis' family was made up of Gran as the oldest, her three children Candy May, Lofton and Louis Senior, and their spouses and children, Louis being the youngest grandchild. This family spent time together—at least we know they were together on Sundays. The children played together and we know the adults had a close relationship based on their reactions to Gran's death and how they worked together to take care of her estate.

Talk about your student's family. How do they spend time together? What are their traditions? Let your student write a piece for his notebook about a special family gathering he remembers. Remind him to try to recall all the sights, sounds, colors, tastes, aromas, feelings, personalities and events that he can think of.

Social Studies: Family Relationships - Grieving Together

Has your student's family ever gone through a deep sadness as Louis' family did when Gran died? How did they react? In this story they all cried together, apparently for a length of time. Finally, the story says, "when every eye was cried out" they commenced to read her will. It is important that the family allowed everyone time to grieve. Then Gran's playful heart, coming up with the idea of hiding notes, gave everyone a sense of adventure even in the sadness and they continued to be bathed in wonderful memories of her.

Social Studies: Family Fun - Games

Begin by reminding your student that Louis has a very special time playing hide and seek with his cousins and his grandmother. Hide and Seek is a game which has been played for generations and one that needs no game board or pieces, just a few places to hide. Played with two or more, one is chosen to be the seeker. He covers his eyes and counts to the agreed upon number. While the designated seeker is counting, the others run to a hiding place where they think they will not be found. At the end of the count, the seeker begins to hunt for those in hiding. In some games the rules are that the players hiding can wait until they think they can make it back to the starting base without being caught, and they try to get there before the seeker can tag them. In this case the first one found or tagged, will be the seeker of the next game. In other games, the last one found is declared the winner and the first found is the new seeker. This game can be played inside with hiding places such as under the bed or in a closet, or it can be played outside where there is a great variety of places to hide. **Teacher's Note:** As a safety precaution, warn children about hiding in places that may prove dangerous.

The title of this story *The Hickory Chair* is reminiscent of another game that children sometimes play called Musical Chairs. In this game there are chairs set up side by side in a line but with each chair alternating facing frontward or backward. There are enough chairs for the number of children playing—minus one! The game begins as music starts and the children march in a circle around the line of chairs. All of a sudden the music stops, everyone grabs a chair and the one left without a chair is out. (As children go out they can join with the person in charge of starting and stopping the music.) One chair is removed and the game continues until there is only one chair left, the music stops and one of the two people left gets the last chair and becomes the winner. Even though this is a game usually played with younger children, an entire family could have fun playing together as well!

Social Studies: Architecture -Attics and Wardrobes

Remind your student how Louis and Gran spent time sitting on Gramps' trunk in the attic and listening to the wind singing on the roof.

Does your student know what an attic is? So many recently-built homes have not been designed with attics, that many children don't even know what an attic is! Homes used to be built with an area above the top floor of living space. This attic area was usually unfinished with the exception of possibly electric wiring for a light, and stairs to reach it. Occupants of the homes used the space to store trunks, furniture, and other items not in use at the moment. In an attic one might find some old clothes, souvenirs of past vacations, the old baby crib and stroller and old toys all saved from the children of the past for the grandchildren to come.

Often attics had steep sloping roofs because they were created in the space above the rooms of the house where the roof beams joined. In climates where the summers were warm, the attic was the hottest place in the house, due to the fact that warm air rises!

Many stories have exciting adventures that began when children find some wonderful thing stowed away in the attic. Again in *The Hickory Chair* Louis and Gran sit in the attic, and talk and shed a few tears, play games and listen to the wind in the roof.

Also, in the picture opposite the first page of text in *The Hickory Chair*, Benny Andrews, the illustrator, has drawn a wardrobe. A wardrobe is a large piece of furniture that functions as a closet and makes room for both hanging clothes and folded clothes. Wardrobes were common in most houses before built-in closets became the fashion. Yes, it is true, for many years from the beginning of our country until well after the Civil War, many houses (especially rural) did not have built-in closets and clothes either hung on pegs, or in wardrobes!

Language Arts: Supplemental Book

Miss Hickory is the tale of a doll, left behind by her owner, who must "make it on her own." This story by Carolyn Sherwin Bailey was the 1947 Newbery Award Winner and has been a childhood favorite for generations. As a tie in to this week's story lessons, *Miss Hickory*, the little apple twig doll with a hickory nut for a head, might be fun for children to read after enjoying *The Hickory Chair*.

Language Arts: The Adventure of Making Lists

The story of *The Hickory Chair* inspires making lists! Remember the note Louis thinks is his? What is it really? (a grocery list) Try making a list of the clues in the story that tell of Gran and another list of those that tell you about Gramps. (Gran's list might contain some of these: she is a good hider, is cheerfully visited by her family on Sundays, smells of lilacs and a whiff of bleach, has a warm face, owns a tattered Bible, etc. Gramp's list could have: carved a bed for his son, carved the hickory chair from their own tree, went to a workplace, was in the army, etc.) If you are enjoying list making, try making a list of all the "favorite people:" favorite youngest grandchild, Louis; favorite grandson born on Tuesday, Cousin Bill-Bob; favorite tallest son, Louis, Sr.; favorite eldest grandson whose father snored here, Louis' brother; favorite middlest grandchild, Cousin Lucille. List Gran's three children: Candy May, Lofton, and Louis Sr. And last of all make a list of all the places that the grandchildren found notes: mirror, trunk, bed, Bible, hickory chair. That Gran sure *was* a good hider!

Language Arts: Descriptive Prose

Lisa Fraustino writes with a prose style that is often like poetry. When she describes the great hickory tree from which Gran's favorite chair was carved, she writes Gran's reminisces, "I ... see that old hickory tickling the belly of the sun." In this line the author uses personification for both the hickory—that *it* did the tickling, and of the sun—that it had a belly and could be tickled.

Fraustino also uses imagery when she describes Gran's voice as a molasses voice. Pair this discussion with the science lesson on molasses below. When your student sees how thick and rich and slow pouring molasses is they will better understand the description of Gran's sweet, smooth, rich, slow voice.

In addition, the author of *The Hickory Chair* writes about Gran's salty kisses, when she and Louis are in the attic. Ask your student why he thinks her kisses are salty. If he doesn't know wait and don't tell him right away. Perhaps after a day or two of rereading the book your student will suddenly realize that it might have been because Gran was sitting on her husband's trunk and missing him! The salty kisses came from her tears. It is exciting for a student to make these kinds of observations on his own, if possible.

Language Arts: Vocabulary

molasses (also see Science: Sugar Cane and Molasses) A dark, sugary syrup obtained as a result of sugar refining.

connive To cooperate secretly, to conspire together.

commence Begin (as in commencement).

to no avail A saying which means something was not accomplished.

curdled To coagulate (changing into a thick mass), or become curd.

collage Method of creating a work of art with combinations of paint, fabric, string, paper scraps, etc.

Language Arts: Reading and Speaking Practice

For fun, both you and your student try reading and then just speaking with your best "molasses" voice. Can you attain that rich, smooth drawl as you read the story or just talk together? As a point of observation, listen together for people speaking with various accents and voice rhythms. You might notice someone speaking at a grocery store or on a bus, or on the radio. As Fraustino describes Gran's voice as molasses, encourage your student to think about how he would describe the different voices, accents and patterns of speech that he hears. Have him use descriptive words and keep a list if this seems like fun. Also, your student can pretend to be a radio or television announcer or advertiser and act out a scene (which you've written) with a molasses voice!

Art: Learning About Museums

Looking at the information on the dust jacket, your student will discover that the illustrator of *The Hickory Chair* has his works in the permanent collections of many different museums. Museums listed on the dust jacket include: The Museum of Modern Art, The Metropolitan Museum of Art , and the Brooklyn Museum, all in New York, and the High Museum in Atlanta, Georgia along with the Ohara Museum in Kurashika, Japan.

(You may want to include for older children the names of other famous museums such as the Chicago Art Institute, the Guggenheim Museum, and the Louvre in Paris, as well as any famous museums which may be located near you or in a city you have visited.)

What is a museum? A museum is a place where collections of paintings, sculpture and artifacts are displayed. There are different kinds of museums where instead of paintings you may see other displays, such as natural history museums where you can see live and preserved animals on display as well as rocks, shells, etc. There are also topical museums that concentrate on trains or planes or the circus, etc.

In this discussion now, however, we are talking about art museums or galleries. In this type of museum you will find paintings, drawings, sculpture and sometimes artifacts. Museums of this sort often own a number of paintings, etc. Sometimes they own so many that they cannot display them all at once. The museum curators will display some and then change their displays, rotating their permanent collections. A permanent collection (such as the collection which houses Benny Andrews' artwork) means that it is owned by the museum and you can expect to see the work there on a regular basis.

Once in a while such a museum will host exhibits that have been traveling throughout the country and are just at the museum for a short time—usually from one to several months.

Find a museum (even a small gallery will do) and take your student to see the work of various artists. If you begin such trips at an early age you will find that on subsequent trips your student will develop personal favorites which he will enjoy seeing each time you go!

Art: Medium

The copyright page of our story tells us that Benny Andrews, the illustrator, used oils and fabric collage for the pictures of this book. These illustrations, then, would be considered **mixed media** works of art.

Look at the dedication page. Can you see the brush strokes in the light colored oil paint above the woman on the bench? Now look at the page where Gran and Louis are in the attic sitting on Gramps' old trunk.

Under the rafters it looks as if the artist used linen or cloth of some kind and painted over it. Look for other examples of brush strokes in oil, and of fabric in his illustrations. If there is interest, let your student try some paint and fabric collage art. Using either watercolor or acrylic paint (much like oil except it dries faster) and a pile of scrap fabric (you can buy scrap fabric at the big box stores, if you don't have any) let your student experiment with this media! If you don't have stretched canvas to work with try a heavy piece of cardboard as the surface for the picture. Your student can draw his picture right on the cardboard and then paint and apply fabric right over the drawing.

Art: Color

Talk about the colors Mr. Andrews used in his illustrations for *The Hickory Chair*. Beautiful greens, pinks, blues and yellows are seen throughout the illustrations of the story and tie the story together simply through the theme of color. Look with your student at the last picture of the text. Have him notice the pink color in Louis' coat. Can your student see how this color is also on the top of the chair cushion and in the granddaughter's dress and again on the rug? In how many places is the yellow used in this picture? And blue? Try this exercise with any of the pictures in the book and your student will realize that with the thousands of colors available to an artist to use, a good artist will limit his palette. He will use just a few colors (light and dark values of the same color) over and over in his painting to keep the work from being too busy and distracting.

Art: Details and Observations from Illustrations

Look with your student at the title page. Ask your student what he sees in the picture. (He may say that he sees Louis looking out the window.) Perhaps he wonders why Louis would be at a window if he is blind. Maybe he can think of some reasons why this might be so. (The sun is warm and Louis would be able to feel that. There is a bird on the windowsill reminding the reader that there would be all sorts of noises coming from the outside that might interest Louis as well.)

Then look at the picture on the back cover of the book. This picture is the heart of the story, what the author wants us to remember—that Louis had a special relationship with his Gran and that they loved each other. The way their bodies are leaning toward each other with Gran gazing down at Louis, gives us insight to the loving depth of that relationship.

Art: Sayings in Art Form

Notice the first illustration of the story where Gran hides Louis in the bed that Gramps had carved long ago. Above the bed is a wall hanging with the saying, "Home Sweet Home." Perhaps your student would like to create a wall hanging with this or a similar saying on it to place somewhere in his own home.

Just for fun, brainstorm other sayings with the word "home" in it: home for the holidays, no place like home, my old Kentucky home, home run, home base, home is where the heart is, etc.

Math: Learning About and Making A Graph

Discuss with your student the concept of making a graph. Why does he think we use this type of communication? A graph is a *visual* representation of gathered or complied information. A graph can quickly show in visual form a great deal of numerical information. There are several different types of graphs including a bar graph, a pie or (circle) graph, and a line graph.

Have your student take the lists he made in the Language Arts lesson on List Making, and make a graph to chart the number of items in each group. This would be a graph showing how many items were on each type of his lists. Grocery list—three items; number of places where Gran's notes were hidden—five; the children's names—five; the number of hiding places, etc. When your student is finished with his graph, which of the lists was the longest? Which one was the shortest? He would know the same information by reading the results of each list, but with a graph he can see it instantly! Ask your student if he thinks his information would fit better into a bar graph, a pie graph, or some other type of graph? He might want to make one of each and see which he thinks is the eastiest-to-understand visual representation of his facts.

Math: Understanding Generations

The story of *The Hickory Chair* begins when Louis is a young boy and his Gran is still alive. Louis' family then, would consist of three generations: grandparents, children and grandchildren. There is, on average, approximately twenty to twenty-five years between each generation in a family.

Louis grew up and is shown at the end of the story with a granddaughter of his own. That would mean that Louis had been a father to at least one child of his own. So, there would be the addition of two more generations in Louis' family. From the beginning of the story to the end there were five generations represented from Louis' family.

Remember that Gran was no longer alive when Louis' child(ren) and grandchild were born. How many generations are currently represented in your student's family?

Science: Bleach and Lilacs

Teacher's Note: This lesson is for your older student. Chlorine bleach is poisonous in quantity and can do damage to fabrics, rugs, etc. Please keep bleach out of reach of children.

Lisa Fraustino writes that Louis described Gran as smelling "like lilacs, with a whiff of bleach." Does your student know what bleach is and what it is commonly used for? Why might Gran always smell a bit like bleach? (Gran was used to using this household product for laundry days.) Put a drop of bleach on a cotton ball or paper napkin and let your student smell what bleach is like—don't put it too close!

Chlorine bleach and oxygen bleaches are used for whitening and brightening colors in the laundry. Chlorine bleach can take the color completely out of colored fabrics and so it is used sparingly on these darker clothes, or the less harmful oxygen bleach is used instead. Chlorine bleach is used on whites to take out stains and brighten garments. Look through the illustrations of *The Hickory Chair* with your student and notice in how many pictures Gran has a white collar and sometimes cuffs. If these were removable garment pieces (which is likely), she might have bleached them to keep them bright white. Even though the collar and cuffs could have been well rinsed, there would still be a faint whiff of bleach discernable to Louis.

Small amounts of chlorine bleach are used to purify drinking water and chlorine bleach is also used as a disinfectant. So, Gran might have used bleach in her cleaning water. If she cleaned some every day, she might have smelled a bit like bleach from that activity.

A lilac is a shrub with pinnacles of small purple flowers that bloom in the spring and it has a lovely fragrance! Louis' Gran may have had lilacs growing in her yard, but the fact that she *always* smelled like this flower was probably due to using a cologne or bubble bath, powder, etc., that had the lilac fragrance.

Science: Chemistry - Testing for Acids and Bases

This lesson is an introduction to acidic liquids, which are a key element in the next lesson on curdling.

Litmus is a substance that scientists use to test the acidic or basic quality of a solution, in other words to find whether it is an **acid** or a **base**.

Litmus paper is composed of strips of paper with the litmus substance on so that it can be dipped in a solution for testing. The strips are either red strips or blue strips. Red litmus paper will turn blue in the presence of an acid but not change in the presence of a base or neutral solution, while blue litmus paper will turn red in the presence of a base and not change if the solution tested is an acid or neutral.

Have your student use red litmus paper strips to test small amounts of orange juice, lemon juice and vinegar in small separate bowls. (Remind your student that all **citrus juices** are acidic, such as lime, grapefruit, etc.)

Science: Chemistry - Chemical Reaction: Curdling

Put 1/4 cup milk in three separate glass dishes. (Glass is suggested so that you can see the process, but any type container can be used.) Add one tablespoon of lemon juice, to the first dish, then a tablespoon of orange juice to the second dish and one tablespoon of vinegar to the third dish. Leave for 5 minutes and then examine. What happened? (The milk will curdle, or begin to separate into curds or lumps.) This is the same chemical reaction that is used to turn fresh milk into buttermilk and cheese.

Remember from previous FIAR story lessons that a **chemical reaction** is one in which two or more substances react together to form a new compound. If your student stirs some sugar into a glass of water, he will have two substances mixed together—a **mixture**, yet both substances remain the same and can be separated from one another (by physical means like evaporation). In a chemical reaction, such as stirring a citrus juice into milk, the two compounds react together and change into another compound, as sour milk, something like buttermilk. It is not possible to return the substances to their original forms—they have made a new substance. Curdling then, is a chemical reaction that produces a new substance.

Now that you have done this experiment, why does your student think the author of *The Hickory Chair* described Lewis' reaction in this way, " ... and the air curdled in my throat." Just before in the story when Lewis thought he found his own note, he said the air tasted sweet—now he says it "curdled." Discuss this with your student and see if he has any ideas. Talk about the fact that when we are terribly disappointed, we sometimes have an acidic taste in our mouth. Just like our feelings the very saliva in our mouths becomes a little thicker and sort of sour tasting!

Science: The Human Body - The Eye

Teacher's Note: As you read through this lesson, note that in a later volume of *Five in a Row* one of the biographies studied is about Helen Keller. During this study the human eye and other related topics will be presented in a manner appropriate for older students. Therefore, you may decide how you wish to cover the following lessons—perhaps in just an introductory way.

The story of *The Hickory Chair* brings up the subject of human sight as well as blindness. First, if you have not covered the eye in past lessons on the human body, then take the time to give a simple explanation of the eye and how it works before tackling the subject of blindness.

Ask you student if he knows that the human eye is an incredible optical device that is something like a camera. There is even a part of the eye we call the lens! (It's always good to find out, through interesting leading questions, what your student already knows about a subject and then add on from there. For instance maybe your young student knows that bright light hurts his eyes and makes him want to shut them. Or he might say that he knows that you have to be careful with your eyes because when they are poked they hurt! Your student will let you know what he knows and that can lead into lessons and avoid needless repetition. This method also gives your student confidence in his gathered knowledge, and an encouraging beginning to his lesson—he already knows something about your topic! He will then continue to take in the new information with even greater enthusiasm.)

The eyeball is really a sack filled with liquid. This jelly-type liquid is called vitreous humor. There are also parts on the front of the eyeball which allow light to come through. The **pupil**, which is the actual opening, the **iris** which is the part that gives each eye its color, blue, brown, gray, etc., and which contracts and expands to allow more or less light to enter the eye through the pupil according to the need of the moment.

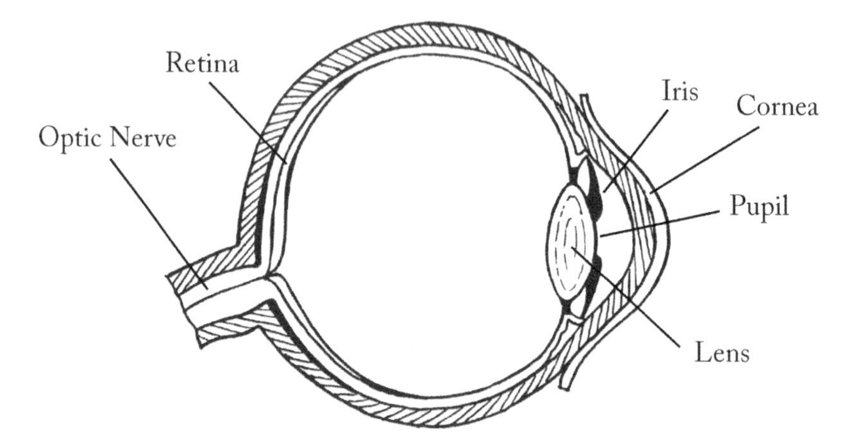

After describing the pupil and the iris and pointing to the illustration, ask your student if he has noticed when a light is turned on at night it seems too bright and makes him want to close his eyes? Sometimes the sunlight itself is too bright.* There are times when there is too much light and the iris of the eye contracts to close down around the pupil and only let a small amount of light in. In the same way, at night we need to have all the light available to see objects in the darkness. (In pure darkness we could not see.) However, the kind of darkness in a bedroom at night or outside at night still has enough light to let us see objects. At these times the pupil of the eye will look much larger because the iris has expanded to let all the light that is available in through the pupil. Your student can see the difference in the pupil size if you go into a moderately dark room. Wait a few moments. Then let him look at your eyes and have him pay attention to the pupil size. Then while he is keeping his eyes on yours, turn on a light and have him notice what happens. The pupil size will become much smaller.

Covering the pupil (again, the hole through which light enters the eyeball) is a very clear **lens** and over that a protective clear **cornea**. Both the lens and the cornea help focus the light rays into the eyeball and toward a specific point at the back of the eyeball called the **retina**.

Often the **optic nerve** is also pointed out to students at this time as an introduction to the concept that the images seen through the eye are coded and transferred by the optic nerve to the brain for processing.

You may want to find a simple book at your library to go over these ideas and allow your student to make some notes and illustrations for his science notebook. ***Safety:** Make sure that your child knows it is truly dangerous to stare directly at the sun. Talk about wearing sunglasses (he still cannot stare directly at the sun even with sunglasses) and about how he can take good care of his eyes.

Just for fun, notice how at dusk, just before dark, it seems as if the colors have gone away? Everything—the trees, birds, house—looks more like a black and white picture than the glorious color picture seen in the daylight. This is because it takes light to allow us to register colors. This is a lesson in light, but the brief preview of such understanding through observation can begin now as we talk about the human eye. Later when you come to a lesson on light and color it will be more familiar to your student.

Science: The Human Eye and Tears

When Gran and Lewis sat on the truck in the attic, Gran had tears in her eyes. How did Lewis know this? (Lewis said she had salty kisses.) Eyes do so many things. They let us see in the daytime and help us see even when it is darker. Our eyes open and shut protectively and they tear up both for protection and during times of great emotion.

First, the tears of protection are what happens when an eyelash or bit of dirt get in your eye. The eye tears up to wash away the intruding matter. When the eye is poked or hurt it also tears to wash away harmful bacteria. Another critical feature of tears is that they lubricate the eyeball and keep it from drying out which would be very dangerous.

But why are tears salty? The fluid that makes up our tears has in it substances that help fight infection. Salt is a part of that solution. (Has anyone ever suggested to your student that he gargle with salt water for a sore throat or soak an injury in Epsom salts? Salt is used to help disinfect and provide an environment that is not healthy for dangerous bacteria.) Salt is part of a regimen that helps fight infection.

Science: The Human Eye and Blindness

A few sentences into the story of *The Hickory Chair* we find out that Louis is blind. Louis himself states that he was born blind. Sometimes children's eyes do not develop properly and they are born blind. More frequently, blindness is a result of an illness, disease or an accident. With your student, talk about the differences in being born blind and losing sight later in life. What would be unique about each situation?

Ask your student if he knows the wonderful advance that was made into the lives of the blind by a man named Louis Braille. Briefly describe how this man invented an entire new language of writing (a system of raised dots) which allows the blind to read. A blind person who has been taught to read by this method can read anything that has been translated into Braille. They can also write in the Braille language as well.

If possible show your student the Braille words on elevators and other public places.

Teacher's Note: You don't have to go into great detail with this lesson. In a later *Five in a Row* volume there will be a unit on Helen Keller with detailed information on the human eye, and Louis Braille, appropriate for older students.

Science: Botany - Hickory Tree

Remind your student that Louis and Gran discussed the hickory tree that "tickled the belly of the sun." How many different trees does your student think he can recognize? Maybe he would like to start a nature journal with drawings and facts about the different trees that he sees around him. We recognize and identify trees by their shape (of trunk and branches), their bark, the arrangement and shape of their leaves, and their fruit or nuts. We can also pay attention to their typical size, whether or not they produce good shade, whether they are colorful in the fall, their longevity, etc.

Point out to your student that the leaves of a hickory tree are not single leaves on a petiole as on a maple tree or an elm tree, but a collection of five leaflets together on a single petiole. This is called a simple compound leaf. The hickory tree has compound leaves. If you can, go on a walk in an area with diverse trees and see if your student can identify trees with simple leaves as well as trees with compound leaves. For this exercise, he may need to examine the petiole. Provide him with a simple tree identification book or print out a few diagrams of different types of leaf arrangements. Let him draw these for his notebook or nature journal.

The hardness of the wood (density) is another variable in different types of trees. Has your student ever handled a piece of balsa wood, the almost feather-light pale wood? A similar-sized piece of hickory would feel much heavier, and while you could push a nail into balsa with your fingers it would take a hammer to put a nail into a piece of hickory. A hickory tree has strong, hard wood used often to make handles for tools such as rakes, shovels, axes, etc. From this information, does your student think that a rocking chair made from a hickory tree would be strong and last a long time? Remembering the illustrations on the last page of the story your student will know that the rocking chair lasted through Louis' lifetime and will probably last through the life of his grandchild! Many pieces of furniture that have been made from various hardwoods have survived generation after generation for hundreds of years. Perhaps your student could visit a museum and see pieces of furniture that were hand carved back in colonial times, and other pieces that were manufactured long, long ago.

Besides the valuable product of hardwood, a hickory tree has edible nuts. Pecan trees are related to the hickory and pecans are an extremely popular food nut.

Science: Sugar Cane and Molasses

Does your student know what molasses is or where it comes from? Has he ever thought about where sugar comes from? How many things are all around us that we so take for granted that we never even wonder what they are or how we obtain them? Have your student pause for a moment and be filled with wonder that there are so many interesting things to learn about!

Molasses is a by-product that comes from the process of converting sugar cane into sugar. It is a thick, sweetish brown liquid. Some children may not find molasses as tasty as honey but you can make a good table molasses by mixing two-thirds golden molasses with one-third corn syrup. The subsequent taste is not quite as strong as straight molasses and it is a real treat on fresh buttered cornbread. Try some while you're reading *The Hickory Chair* and think about how rich and smooth and velvety Gran's voice was!

For further research check online or in a library book to find out how molasses and sugar are made and which countries grow sugar cane. Where else can we get sugar? (Sugar is also refined from sugar beets.)

Teacher's Notes

The *Five in a Row* lesson options for each unit in the manual are all you need to teach your child. The additional resource area provided below is simply a place to jot down relevant info you've found that you might want to reference.

THE HICKORY CHAIR

Date:

Student:

Five in a Row Lesson Topics Chosen:

Social Studies:

Language Arts:

Art:

Math:

Science:

Relevant Library Resources: Books, DVDs, Audio Books

Websites or Video Links:

Related Field Trip Opportunities:

Favorite Quote or Memory During Study:

Name:

Date:

Language Arts: **List Making**

Use this activity sheet to list the clues in the story of Gran and Gramps.

Gran	Gramps
____________________	____________________
____________________	____________________
____________________	____________________
____________________	____________________
____________________	____________________
____________________	____________________
____________________	____________________
____________________	____________________
____________________	____________________
____________________	____________________
____________________	____________________

Name:

Date:

FIELD TRIP

Art Museum

Using the list of art museums from the Art: Learning About Museums lesson, help your student search online to find a virtual tour of one of the museums listed in that lesson.

Print out pictures from the museum that your student chooses for their virtual field trip. Let them paste the images into the space provided below and fill in some information they may learn during their virtual field trip.

Museum name and location: ____

Date it was founded: _______________

Most famous piece of artwork on display: ___________________________________
(if this is not discovered on the virtual tour, search "most famous piece of art displayed at [museum name]")

Personal favorite piece of art you saw on this field trip: ___________________________

Current exhibit (name/date): ____

Name:
Date:
Math: **Family Tree of 4 Generations**

Fill in the ovals with names from your student up through four generations of family members. Also write their ages on the lines below their names. Then calculate the years between each generation by subtracting the average ages of each generation from the preceding generation's age. Write the answers in the spaces at the bottom.

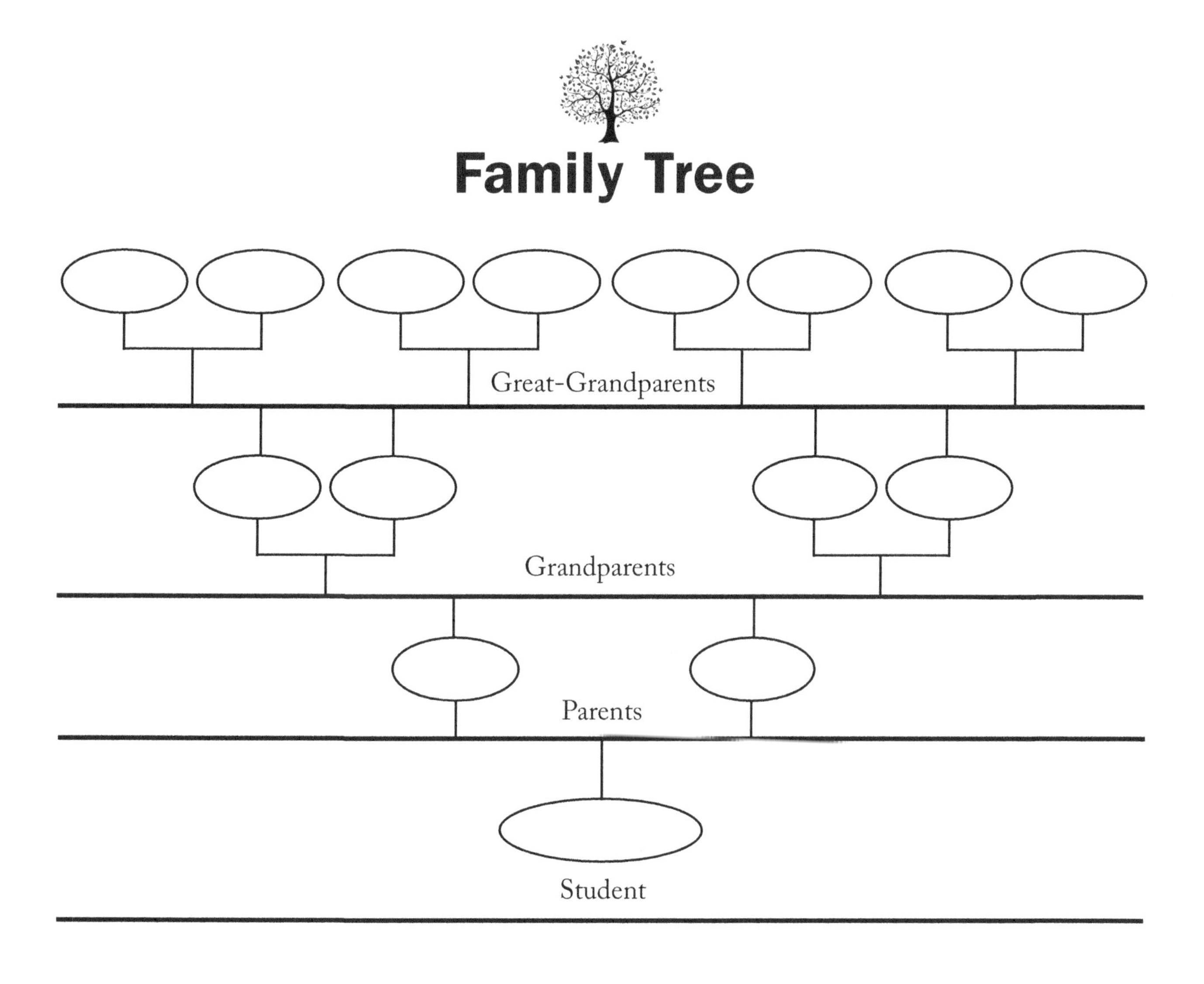

Years between first and second generations: ________________

Years between second and third generations: ________________

Years between third and fourth generations: ________________

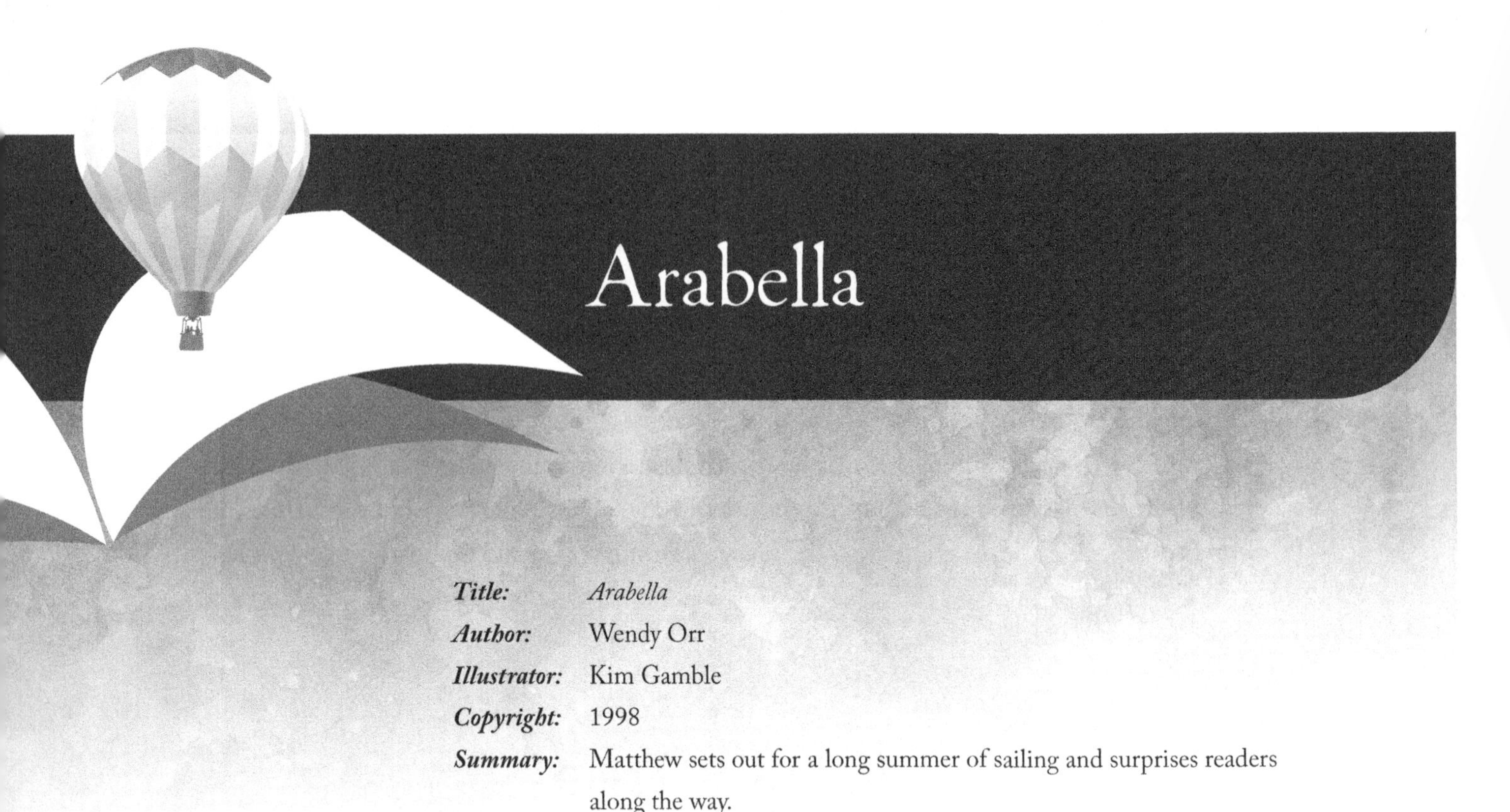

Title: *Arabella*
Author: Wendy Orr
Illustrator: Kim Gamble
Copyright: 1998
Summary: Matthew sets out for a long summer of sailing and surprises readers along the way.

Teacher's Note: In preparing to present this story, you may want to find some pretty shells, a model sailboat, a lighthouse or any other nautical theme items that you have. You could set them out all at once as a "teaser" for the next story or you could bring them out a few at a time as you progress through your week.

Social Studies: Geography - Islands Around the World

Grandpa lives on an island. Yet, the story never tells exactly where this island might be. Try looking for clues with your student. There are large deciduous trees in the illustrations but there are also palm trees. So if the island is off the east coast of the North America it probably would be in the southern part. Depending on the age of your student you can talk about all the areas that could provide the setting of our story: Hawaii, Florida, the Caribbean, etc. In fact, there are islands around every part of all the continents and some islands are out in the oceans away from land. Still, there may be a further clue besides the illustrations. On the copyright page it says that the book was originally printed in Australia. Maybe the island is off the coast of Australia. The dust jacket doesn't provide specific information about the island location, but it says the author had learned to sail when she was young and now her children sail in a different ocean. The exact setting of this story remains a mystery but you can have fun learning about the different places where it might have been set. You could use this story as an opportunity to study a location that is new to your student! Place your story disk wherever you decide the story could have taken place.

Social Studies: Relationships and Learning

In the book *Arabella*, Grandpa and Matthew have a close relationship. Grandpa loves sailing and introduces Matthew to it hoping that he will learn to love sailing too. Spend some time thinking about the way that Grandpa accomplishes his goal with respect, gentleness and patience.

On the left-hand page illustration with the pink sunset and the "round white moon" it says, "Every day Matthew learned a little more about Grandpa's boat." Talk with your student about learning something new. Most people can't learn everything about a new venture at once. Generally the best way to teach or learn is a little bit at a time. If your student is already reading, talk about how that process came about. First she learned letters, then sounds, syllables, words, sentences and finally paragraphs and stories. (For younger students pick any progressive activity and use that as an example.)

It was wise of Grandpa not to try to teach Matthew too much too soon. The boy might have burned out. Have a discussion about what the common phrase "burned out" means. This will help her understand these words and concepts when she hears them in conversation.

When Matthew asks, "How do you steer?" Grandpa quickly gives him an answer without making Matthew feel silly for asking and without Grandpa acting in a superior way. Later, Grandpa lets Matthew bring the boat to the wharf all by himself. Grandpa's words are so encouraging: "Couldn't have done better myself!" Talk about how important encouragement is when you are trying something new. Amazingly, one word of harsh or teasing criticism can wipe away many words of praise. A good teacher is careful and wise in her choice of words!

The above discussions and lessons are designed to help your student process information about teaching methods. She can think about these topics as they relate to her and the things she tries to learn. But also, she can begin to practice good leadership-teaching skills herself. Whether she is helping a younger sibling learn something new (like tying shoelaces) or dealing with an employee when your student is grown, the material in these lessons provides a foundation for important life skills.

Social Studies: Relationships and Loss

Sooner or later everyone experiences loss. Sometimes it is the loss of an object that is cherished like Grandpa's *Arabella*. Sometimes it's a beloved pet or acquaintance or relative. Take some time to discuss the process of grief: Often when we lose someone or something important to us there is an initial denial or refusal to believe it has actually happened. Then with the realization of the reality of the situation (perhaps days later) there is sometimes a deep period of depression or profound sadness—a deep sense of loss which may linger for a time. In most cases this period resolves into a feeling of acceptance and an emerging desire to get on with the tasks of life. In cases where people find it difficult to progress to the next step in the grief process in a reasonable length of time, counseling may help.

Talk with your student about a time when you lost

something important to you and some of the steps of grieving which you went through.

If you studied *The Rag Coat* in *Five in a Row* Volume 1, you might remind your student of Minna and the way she worked through her grief.

Social Studies: Relationships - Being Away From Home

In *Arabella* Matthew leaves home for a long summer. Does your student think it would be fun to visit grandparents or cousins, or go to camp for the entire summer? Why or why not? What kinds of things would be fun? What would be difficult in being away from home for so long? (Answers will vary because every child is wonderfully different!) Ask your student if there is an age where she thinks this kind of summer away from home would be fun? Our story does not say exactly how old Matthew is. Have your student guess how old she thinks Matthew is and why.

There are many reasons why people, at times, have to be separated. Sometimes fathers or mothers have to travel. Sometimes parents, grandparents or siblings are hospitalized. Talk with your student about coping during times of separation.

Tell her about times when you have been separated from family or friends, how you felt and what you did to cope.

During a long period of separation, a mother once told her son, "Whenever you look up and see the moon shining, know that I am looking at the same moon, too." These kinds of thoughts along with good memories help keep people close even during times they have to be apart.

Social Studies: Sea Lore

If you choose to introduce this topic you will want to begin by saying that you're going to talk about sea lore. Does your student have any idea what that is? The word *lore* means traditions, ideas, stories, songs, superstitions, etc.—in other words, folk knowledge and customs gained through experience. If you were studying mountain men there would be stories, traditions, etc., about them. However, in this case you say, "But we are studying things related to the sea—boats and sailing, nautical terms (terms having to do with the sea), customs, etc."

For instance, Grandpa makes several comments in the story about the *Arabella* bringing him luck. In many books you will read about happenings at sea and you will recognize sailors talking about what brings them luck. It is a part of seafarer's lore. Interestingly, the name of Grandpa's model boat is the *Arabella* which means "prayerful." So, perhaps it was just out of sailor's habit that he talked about luck.

Another tradition of the sea is that many boats are named for women. Did your student notice that the *Arabella* and Grandpa's red boat with the white sail are both referred to as "she"? If your student is a reader, let her find the places in the story this is so. Have her look for the pronouns "she" and "her" when one of these boats is mentioned. There are at least twelve references. Let your student point out a few. (**Teacher's Note:** You can talk briefly with your older student about pronouns being one of eight parts of speech at this time if you desire.)

In addition, when a boat's name is used it is usually preceded by the article "the" which is not in italics. We speak of Grandpa's beloved model ship as the *Arabella*. Your student will find countless references to this convention whenever she reads about boats and boating. Mentioning it to your older student now, and letting her see the words in the story will also help her learn to write theses kinds of descriptions correctly.

You may also want to mention the traditional aspect of sea lore where sailors tend to personify boats, the wind, the sea, etc. Personification is giving human traits or personality to non-human things. (Remember *Five in a Row* Volume 1, in *Mike Mulligan and His Steam Shovel* how Mary Anne, the steam shovel, had lots of personality?) The phrase "what the wind and sea take they don't give back," sounds like the wind and the sea have human motives. "She's gone," referring to the boat is another example. Traditional sea lore has many references to boats, the sea and the wind having a human personality. Your older student may enjoy watching for such references when reading tales of the sea.

Social Studies: Living on an Island

Would your student enjoy living on an island? What are the advantages and disadvantages? Did you notice what Grandpa carries into his house at the beginning of the story? (He carries in a box of groceries.) Some islands do not have stores and other conveniences. If you live on an island you may have to get in your boat and go to a larger island or the mainland to get groceries, see a movie or get a haircut. You may also need a boat to get to transportation on the mainland, to go to hospitals, schools, etc.

Grandpa and Matthew's breakfast on the wharf looks like fun. Is there a place where you could go to eat breakfast or lunch beside some type of water? Perhaps you might be near a river, lake, pond or ocean and a breakfast out would be memorable! Yes, life on an island could be interesting.

Social Studies: Through the Generations

Grandpa said *his* grandpa carved the *Arabella*, which means the *Arabella* could have been fifty or sixty years old! Does your student know of any items in her family that have been handed down from generation to generation? Are these items particularly valued by her family?

Grandpa also handed down stories to Matthew, and a love of sailing. He says to Matthew: "You're a sailor now. Just like me, and my grandpa before." Do you have similar experiences from your grandparents to share with your student? Do you know anyone who has followed in her grandparents footsteps, in profession, trade or hobby?

Social Studies: Relationships - Inferred Information

Ask your student how she knows Matthew cares deeply for his grandfather. Answers might include that Matthew is respectful and enjoys time spent with his grandpa. But the one great way Matthew shows his deep love and concern is when he decides to rescue the *Arabella*. Matthew knows the boat can't be replaced and that it is his Grandpa's most treasured possession. Matthew risks hardship and danger to bring the *Arabella* back. Action like this shows deep feelings and care.

How does your student know Grandpa loves sailing? He never says exactly, "I love sailing!" Look for examples in the text and pictures that help you know how much Grandpa delights in sailing.

Language Arts: The Art of Storytelling

Grandpa tells Matthew stories of the sea. Some of these stories were probably of events Grandpa had himself experienced. Many may have been traditional (older) tales of the sea.

Telling stories is a wonderful art to perfect. Encourage your student to begin to try storytelling. Often young children whose vocabularies are much greater than their abilities to write, will perfect their storytelling skills before ever putting pen to paper. When they eventually catch up, they will know the elements of stories and have wonderful tales to write.

Historic events lend themselves to storytelling and can truly make the subject come alive. Learning about family events and being able to recount these stories in an entertaining and interesting way encourages close family ties. As a teacher, try sketching out some family stories of your own and present these to your student. By doing this, you demonstrate that *you* value storytelling.

Have your student make sure her story has a beginning, a middle and an end, just like a written story. Like written stories, a told tale is more interesting if there is a conflict of some variety, action and a climax. Another facet of stories told orally is repetition. Every story doesn't use this device but often having a familiar refrain in a tale helps keep continuity and interest. A told tale should not be memorized verbatim. Rather the storyteller should have in mind an outline of the story and fill in the necessary information with lots of descriptive sentences, especially ones that help the listener see, hear, taste, and touch the incidents of the story. For instance, when telling of a trip to Grandma's your student might say, "and when Sarah skipped into the kitchen she could smell the rich aroma of apple pie baking in the shiny white oven. 'Ohhh!' Sarah exclaimed, 'I'm glad I came to Grandma's.'" (The sentence, "I'm glad I came to Grandma's," could be the refrain of the story.) Stories for young children may be kept short and whoever tells the story (teacher or student) needs to think about whether or not the subject matter will be captivating for their audience.

Unlike written stories, there are different skills for storytelling that need to be addressed. A good storyteller uses suspense, good good eye contact, dramatic gestures, voice control (dynamics, both soft and loud), pacing, and she is always careful to use extremely clear speech.

Try telling a story to your student. Let her work on a story to tell you. There are many benefits to learning the art of storytelling!

Teacher' Note: A wonderful beginning to the art of storytelling for a young child is the wordless book. There are many great wordless books whose illustrations give a structure for a story and then the student can fill in a myriad of details as she follows the pictures. Two good wordless books are *Follow Me* by Nancy Tafuri and *Tuesday* by David Wiesner. Mercer Mayer and Marianna Mayer produced the extremely popular *A Boy, A Dog and A Frog* wordless series. Wordless books are only a *preliminary* step to storytelling because the dynamics of eye contact and gestures, etc., are not present, but it is a good way for a young child to have a beginning framework for oral interpretation.

Language Arts: Review for Italicizing Names of Ships

If you have used many *Five in a Row* lessons, your student has had many opportunities to notice that the names of ships are printed in storybooks in *italics*. Review this lesson with your student and remind her that if she is writing a story by hand, a ship's name is underlined. This underlining in handwritten work is comparable to italics in a printed book.

You may want to take this opportunity to explore and list other categories that are italicized in print (or underlined in handwritten work) including titles of books, full-length plays, motion pictures or musical compositions, names of magazines and newspapers, and personalized names of aircraft and trains as well as ships.

Language Arts: Joy of Words - Alliteration, Simile and Repetition

Teacher's Note: One of the most pleasing aspects of FIAR teaching is that the lessons have so much opportunity for review. As the teacher, you present a topic then let your student ponder it and try it a little. You don't have to drill and drill an idea because it comes around again in another lesson. Soon your student recognizes a concept and will begin to notice examples in her own reading. She will begin to enjoy the lesson concepts and someday even use them in her own writing. Voilà! True learning! So, present the information like a spoonful of sugar, in little amounts. You will find these concepts being reviewed many times.

Author Wendy Orr has carefully chosen her words for this story. Look over the pages of *Arabella* with your student for literary devices like simile and the use of alliteration. (**Simile** is the comparison of two unlike things using the connecting words *like* or *as*.) Examples from the story: (speaking of the boat that shot past) "*like* an arrow from a bow." Another example would be "sails lifting *like* a seagull's wings."

Alliteration is the succession of similar *sounds* (not necessarily the same letters). Examples from the story: spray splashed; wild white sail; brown bobbing; flew faster; wharf and windows.

Where in the story do you hear **repetition**? Have your student listen for it. Repetition can be of words, phrases, sentences or ideas. Several times Orr writes of a "small red boat with wild white sails." This refrain of repeated words is as subtle and gentle as a lapping wave. It ties the story together and when you encounter the phrase you sense a comfortable, familiar feeling. In fact, the way the author uses repetition in this story actually creates a rhythm. Wendy Orr's story has a definite rhythm of rolling waves so appropriate for a story of the sea! (To enrich this lesson locate John Masefield's poem "Sea Fever" and read it to your student. It can be found online and in the excellent poetry anthology *Favorite Poems Old and New*, edited by Helen Ferris. Can your student hear the beautiful cadence of the rhythm of the sea? Compare this to Orr's writing. In addition, search for music that has rhythms of the sea, for example, John Denver's "Calypso." Sea shanties such as "Shenandoah" and "Michael Row the Boat Ashore" might be fun here.)

Language Arts: Reading Comprehension - Inferred Information

Teacher's Note: This might be a good lesson to do near the end of the week after several readings.

Ask your student why she thinks Matthew (early in the story) is so taken with flying. "I wish I could fly," he says. Can your student think of a possible reason? Could the reason that Matthew is so enamored with flying be because he can't walk or run? Maybe his desire to fly follows his desire to be able to move about at will. Does your student have any physical disabilities? Does she know someone who does? If your student can walk and run, how would she imagine life with a wheelchair would be? Through this story we find that if Matthew is any example, even with a disability, life can be full and exciting!

Now, discuss Grandpa's cheerful answer to Matthew's wish to fly: "Sailing's the next best thing." Grandpa sees sailing as a way for Matthew to become adept at a skill and have a way to go wherever he wants. "The wind filled the sails and the boat flew wherever Matthew steered her." Grandpa doesn't think anything needs to hold Matthew back. In fact Matthew seems to live a wonderfully full life, even to a heroic rescue of the *Arabella* at sea!

(An excellent read-aloud story for your older students to go along with this theme is *The Door in the Wall* by Marguerite de Angeli.)

Language Arts: Writing a Good Story - The Use of Suspense and Climax

Teacher's Note: If you have rowed *Lentil* in FIAR Vol. 1, now would be a good time to review the elements of a story as discussed in that unit.

Author Wendy Orr writes a good story by setting the stage and then coming up with a conflict. The loss of the *Arabella* creates a problem to be solved—a conflict to be resolved. As Matthew decides what to do about the missing boat, and then ventures out into the storm we see the rising action becoming more suspenseful. For page after page we see Matthew struggle with his boat. Have your student try to find words of suspense. Some might be: "waves crashed over the deck" or "wind became a roar"; "waves turned to mountains"; "his boat wouldn't stop"; "tossed on the waves and slid down their valleys"; "a wild crazy dance on the crest of the waves"; "yanked the rope"; "the wind snatched it from his hands"; "fight the tug of war"; and more! These are words of danger and suspense and they make an exciting story.

Finally, abandoning hope of saving the *Arabella*, Matthew struggles just to stay alive. Where is the climax of the story? The scene where Matthew says, "I'll never get home!" and strains to turn the boat around, seems to be the height of action. Will he ever see home again?

Then we begin to sense a falling action, the waves and wind begin to quiet and the shore comes into sight. As he scoops up the Arabella the conflict is also solved. Have your student try writing a story that has a conflict or problem and also an element of danger or suspense. Remind her that she can choose words to heighten the feeling of suspense, just like Wendy Orr does in *Arabella*.

Language Arts: Descriptive Sentences

The author of *Arabella* has written some refreshingly descriptive sentences. In the story, find the passage "... towards the dot of Grandpa's island." Then "the dot grew into a wharf and a man with waving arms." This description is so familiar to anyone who has ever been out on the water. At first you just see a speck of land and then familiar objects appear and finally you can discern people!

Also, the description of Grandpa's house on the fourth page is marvelous. The words are full of smells (the salty ocean air) and sound (the whisper of the woods) and on the next page the poignancy of an elderly man's most treasured possessions. Together with your student, try crafting a sentence describing something on each side and then tell what is in between, just like the description of Grandpa's house. For example: The kitchen counter was a merry mess with half empty spice bottles on one side, dirty measuring cups on the other, and a glorious unbaked banana cake perched precariously in the middle! Another simple example could be the description of a hot dog inside the bun and condiments on each side. Try to include descriptive words of sight, sound, smell or touch.

Wendy Orr also uses **parallel construction** in her descriptive writing. Look at the page where Matthew is lying on his belly in the red boat during the storm. The second sentence on that page reads, "His arms ached, his hands hurt and his fingers bled ...". These descriptive phrases are parallel "arms-ached, hands-hurt, fingers-bled." Each phrase has a subject-verb similarity called parallel construction. The next page has a sentence that says, "Matthew's arms were so tired they wanted to sleep. His eyes were so sad they wanted to cry." Again we see parallel construction; this time the first sentence is constructed exactly like the second sentence. Print out the two sentences on a piece of paper, one above the other. Now draw a line from the words in the first sentence that match the words in the second sentence. For instance, draw a line from Matthew's to His. Then draw a line from arms to eyes, from were to were, from tired to sad, etc. Talk about the fact that the words themselves may be different (if they weren't it would be repetition!) but each part of speech in one sentence corresponds exactly to the word below it in the second sentence. This type of literary construction establishes a cadence (a rhythm of sounds or inflection) to the story as well as providing interest. Have your student try to develop some paired sentences and/or phrases that have a parallel construction. Example: The cat moved so quickly it was nearly invisible. The dog moved so slowly it seemed to be sitting still.

Remind your student that she is practicing a new way to add interest to her writing, just like the author of *Arabella*!

Language Arts: Lists

Find the list on page five of *Arabella* where Grandpa is bringing in the groceries. Many times writers use lists as a technique of description. For a younger student just explain that a good author sometimes uses an interesting list in her writing and read the list in this story. Think up a several topics and let your student dictate to you things that could be put on a list of that topic. Also, if there is interest let your student make up a short story making use of a list somewhere in it.

Language Arts: Complete Sentences

Your older reading student may have recognized that *Arabella's* author, Wendy Orr, doesn't always use sentences that have both subject and verbs. In other words, she doesn't always use complete sentences. This book is an excellent one to use as a grammar review. Can your student find the sentence that is not a complete sentence? (This type of sentence is called a sentence fragment.) The page where Grandpa's possessions are described begins, "Ships in glass bottles ..." and continues with a list of possessions but no verb for the list. It never says Grandpa's treasures *consisted* of ships in glass bottles, etc., which would have used the verb *consisted*.

Now discuss with your student the concept of writer's (or poetic) license. Sometimes, for specific reasons, writers decide to suspend regular grammar rules and write phrases that are not complete sentences. We call this writer's license. In *Arabella* Orr used license partly to establish the rhythm of her story, making her writing a kind of poetic prose. It isn't poetry but it pushes the traditional conventions to establish a poetic quality. A good writer knows exactly when she is breaking the rules of grammar and has a good reason. With a good writer, using a phrase for a sentence is not just a mistake!

Language Arts: Vocabulary

Teacher's Note: The following words are defined in nautical terms. There may be other uses of these words not defined here. Your older students may also enjoy finding other definitions of these words, i.e., different uses for the word board, hoist, tiller, deck, wheel, drift, etc.

board To get on a boat or ship. "Please board the *Stanley* at 6:00 P.M."

hoist To haul or raise up. In this story, hoist means pulling to raise the sails.

wharf A dock or platform built out into the water at which boats may tie up (dock) or unload cargo or passengers.

tiller A board or handle near the stern (back) of a boat used to move the rudder.

rudder A control surface in the water under a boat used for steering or turning the boat.

mast A pole set upright (perpendicular to the deck) on a boat to which sails and rigging are attached. A boat may have more than one mast.

sails Cloth attached to the rigging to catch the wind and propel the vessel through the water.

deck The part of a boat sailors walk on, like the floor of the boat.

wheel The large spoke circle the captain turns to steer the boat. The wheel is connected to the rudder.

drift To be carried along by the water currents and wind.

figurehead A carved statue or bust placed on the bow of the ship for decorative purposes.

yachts Boats used for pleasure or in racing. They can be powered by sail (wind) or engine or both.

jumble Thrown together without much order (not a nautical term).

whitecap The white tips of the waves when the wind has stirred them up.

Art: Medium

Australian artist Kim Gamble used watercolors to capture the feel and flow of the water's waves. Notice with your student the edges of each picture and the beautiful colors, especially on the cover picture. The blue of the sky contrasts sharply with the white clouds and moves into purples at the horizon and into deep blue-greens for the water. The brown wood window frames the outdoor scene at the same time making a shelf for shells, bottles, feathers and the *Arabella* herself!

Notice the blue glass bottle on the windowsill. Does your student realize that Gamble has painted this object so well that it appears as if you can see through the bottle to the water beyond?

Throughout the story there is action and suspense in the artist's paintings and then, Kim Gamble ties it all up neatly with his oval picture on the outside back cover!

Art: Model Ship Building

In the story *Arabella* there are two different kinds of model ships. One is a ship in a bottle. It is sitting on the table in front of Matthew as Grandpa is bringing in the groceries. The other is the model of the *Arabella* herself, which sits on Grandpa's windowsill.

Has your student ever seen a ship in a bottle? You may be able to find a shop where she can view such a wonder, or at least look at a few pictures online. Building a ship in a bottle takes much time and patience—and a very old trick. Does your student know how a ship is built in a bottle? (The ship isn't actually *built* in the bottle, but rather built and then carefully inserted *into the bottle*. A thread remains outside the bottle attached to the hinged masts which are then pulled to an upright position!) The dust jacket says that Wendy Orr's grandfather sailed a ship with tall masts and that he built ships in bottles! Authors who write about "what they know" often include personal bits of information in their stories.

The model ship that sat on the windowsill was built from wood, had cloth for sails and pieces of cord for rigging.

People build models of many things (cars, planes, homes, buildings, tractors, etc.). Through modeling projects people learn a great deal about their specific field of interest. Model-building is also a great vehicle for learning patience, developing eye-hand coordination and for learning to finish what we begin. If your older student would like, she can search for books on boats which show the specific parts and make her own model of a ship. She could make a model of clay, or wood. For this model small masts could be fashioned of sticks or toothpicks with string glued on for the rigging. A project such as this one can be as simple or difficult as your student wishes. Depending on the age and interest of your student, model and hobby stores carry many different model boat kits at various levels of difficulty. You may wish to work on a model boat project together. Or, if a relative is interested in creating a gift for your student, let the model maker know it would be greatly appreciated. Have fun learning through modeling!

Art: Observing the Details

Two items you would often find in a nautical setting include binoculars and barometers. Binoculars (or telescopes) are often used for looking out over the water. In this story however, only binoculars are found in the picture. They are hanging on the wall at Grandpa's house. Also, Grandpa's house has a barometer (on the bookcase). If you have access to a barometer let your student examine it and see how it differs from a wall thermometer. (See the Science lesson for explanation of how a barometer works and its basic use.)

Art: Subtle Use of Detail

Discussion: Was your student surprised after reading *Arabella* to find out that Matthew uses a wheelchair? By now you have probably gone back through the illustrations and noted that the wheelchair was in almost every illustration all along! Only in a few pictures is it absent. The illustrator, Kim Gamble, made a choice to be subtle (not show everything) with the information that Matthew needs the wheelchair. Instead he hid most of the chair from sight in many of the illustrations. There is no mention of the wheelchair in the text by the author, and for the most part, the illustrator also chooses to keep this information a secret until the end of the story. Does your student think this is a wise choice? Why? It does seem that by partially hiding the picture information about Matthew, it gives the ending of the story a deeper emotional punch. All of a sudden the reader realizes what a truly great effort it took for Matthew to rescue the boat!

If this type of artistic subtlety intrigues your student, she could write a story with an element of surprise. Then she could illustrate her story, perhaps hiding some of the clues in the pictures or withholding a surprise till the end. This is a more difficult exercise and you might consider working on it together.

Art: Drawing a Boat

If you have a student interested in drawing, have him try to draw a simple rowboat. *The Drawing Textbook* by Bruce McIntyre has simple instructions for drawing a rowboat. (*Draw Squad* by Mark Kistler is another excellent drawing resource. You'll also find an activity sheet on drawing a sailboat at the end of this unit.) As your student's interest increases, you can probably find wonderful, helpful books on drawing more intricate boats available at your library.

Art: Dots, Lines and Curves

The story text reads, "... the dot of Grandpa's island," and "the curve of the beach ..." Take this opportunity to explore two-dimensional drawing components. What can you make with dots (or points), lines and curves? Use pen and ink, or felt tip markers to make some designs. They can be free form or symmetrical designs, in monochrome (one color) or multicolor. When your student is finished, mount the best one on some black poster board and hang it up where she can see it.

Dots, lines and curves can also be used to draw pictures of real objects. Now perhaps your student would like to try drawing houses, toys, animals, etc. When she is finished help her notice where dots, lines and curves have been used.

Art: Inferred Information Through Illustrations

After a reading of the story, turn to the page where Grandpa is carrying in the groceries. Why didn't Matthew help with that chore? He seems the kind of boy who would gladly help anytime he was needed. Perhaps Matthew's disability prevented him from helping carry the groceries. Look at the expression on Grandpa's face. He seems happy to be taking care of that task himself. Never in the text or pictures does Grandpa seem to overreact to Matthew or coddle him, but rather treats him with respect and dignity. The reader can tell this by the way Grandpa encourages Matthew and teaches him to sail. Again Matthew's disability is never mentioned but rather conversations with Grandpa provide a helpful sense of, "You can do this!"

Math: Quarters, Halves and Wholes

In the story, Wendy Orr writes of a round white moon. We call this a full moon. As the moon waxes (appears to grow larger) and wanes (appears to grow smaller) we also talk about a quarter moon. Spend some time presenting or reviewing concepts of whole, half, quarter, etc. You can talk about the moon, musical notes, time on a clock (quarter hour, half past) or talk about money (quarters, half dollars), etc. If this is new information use blocks or measuring cups to demonstrate "parts to make a whole."

Math: Seasons- Parts to a Whole

At the beginning of the story, Matthew is leaving home to spend a "long" summer with his Grandpa. The use of the word *long* here probably means the entire summer. Talk about how the months are generally divided into seasons and how many months are in each category. For instance, in the Northern Hemisphere the summer months are considered to be June, July and August. With four seasons having three months each (use blocks to group for young student and let them count) that makes twelve months for the whole year. How many months are there in half a year? What would be the three months of the other three seasons—fall, winter and spring?

Science: Human Body - Blood Cells

Find the place in the story where Matthew attempts to rescue the *Arabella* and the text says that his arms ached, his hands were hurt and his fingers were bleeding. What does your student know about the subject of human blood cells?

Does she know that in her own blood there are red "donut shaped" cells which carry life-giving oxygen to all her cells, and also removing carbon dioxide from her body? These red cells have no "hole" like a donut, but instead have a depression, Does she know there are also white cells which help fight infections, and platelets which help in clotting? Does she know a fluid called plasma surrounds the red and white cells as well as the platelets? Thus the plasma, red cells, white cells and platelets together make up human blood.

Has your student heard of the medical term used when a person, in extreme need of blood (due to injury or disease), is given blood donated by someone else? (transfusion)

Fortunately, Matthew isn't seriously injured so he doesn't need a transfusion. Perhaps if his fingers were badly cut, when he arrived back at Grandpa's he might have cleaned his hands, put on some anti-bacterial ointment (to help fight infection) and possibly a few bandages to keep out the dirt.

There is no end to the wonders of this subject—the blood and the intricate ways that it moves through veins, arteries and capillaries and all the work that it does for the human body.

Science: Health - Physical Activity

Look through the story and see how many pictures of ropes your student can find. The ropes are used for rigging and mooring. Also, during Matthew's rescue of the *Arabella*, the story says that Matthew has to slide along the deck until he catches the rope and fights a tug of war with the wind. Has your student ever played the game tug of war with a rope? Use this opportunity to find a long rope, gather some willing participants and play a game of tug of war. Don't forget to make a center line mark. When one team pulls the other over this mark the pulling team wins. Sometimes a game can go on for quite a while before this goal is accomplished. Take care to monitor the game and stop it if someone is caught in the rope or being hurt. This game is a great way to get exercise while remembering Matthew and his fight with the wind!

Science: Sun and Moon

"One night [Grandpa and Matthew] sailed till the sun sank red and the stars came out, and by the round white moon they sailed her home." Grandpa and Matthew enjoyed the lights in the heavens. Often sailors use the sun, moon and stars to navigate—to know where they are and to quickly pinpoint direction. Today it is becoming more common to use GPS or *global positioning satellite* that takes its triangulated readings off of several satellites and quickly gives the sailor his exact location.

The sun and moon are fascinating to study. Wherever your student is in her knowledge of these heavenly bodies take her a step or two further. Find simple books at the library and explore the wonders we see almost every day. Have her draw pictures of the parts of the sun and the moon, adding facts about sunspots and moon craters to her previous knowledge.

Science: Reefs

In our story we learn that Matthew steered around rocky reefs. Reefs can be areas of rock, sand or coral which are just beneath the water. Sailors must make sure that they know the charts for the waters they are sailing. The charts tell them exactly where hidden sandbars, rocks and coral reefs are located. Lighthouses are often located near reefs to show the sailors dangerous areas where they cannot come too close.

Coral reefs are magnificent areas to scuba dive or snorkle. They have lovely formations and they provide habitat for enormous numbers of fish and other creatures of exquisite beauty and interest. Coral is formed by small animals (polyps) that live in colonies with many others of their kind. When the animals die they leave behind connected limestone skeletal remains. The result is what we know as coral reefs—large areas of limestone formations under the water. Watch a video of a coral reef with your student. Enjoy the beautiful fish and other colorful components of a coral reef. Also look for a simple book for more understanding, if your student expresses interest.

Teacher's Note: You may also include this lesson when you study the Great Barrier Reef of Australia from the book, *The Pumpkin Runner*, also in this volume.

Science: Weather Forecasting, the Barometer, Clouds and Signs

Grandpa didn't think of going out in a storm (he went back to bed) and Matthew wasn't planning on going out on the water either, but he saw the *Arabella* and wanted to save her. A good sailor knows the weather signs, reads a barometer and doesn't go sailing or boating in potentially stormy weather.

How does someone learn about the weather? Weather forecasting has different indicators. One good forecasting tool is the air pressure or pressure of the atmosphere. A **barometer** helps to predict the weather by measuring the air pressure. During times of approaching storms a barometer will show falling **air pressure** levels. As the barometer reading begins to fall, people who use the waterways will take notice and watch for other signs of approaching storms. **Teacher's Note:** Barometers record air, or atmospheric, pressure. Atmospheric pressure is also called **barometric pressure** because it is recorded by barometers! In most weather-related science activity or experiment books from your library there are directions for homemade barometers.

Another facet of weather prediction is learning to recognize the clouds in the sky—which clouds mean fair weather and which mean stormy weather on the way. There are even particular cloud formations that indicate severe weather. Find a simple book on clouds or check online and begin to learn cloud formations.

There are many additional signs that indicate approaching bad weather. Often you can smell rain coming when it is still a long way off. Sailors have long used signs such as rings around the moon, red skies in the morning, and smoke curling low and staying low to predict approaching bad weather. Even odd signs such as crickets calls seeming sharper, hills seeming closer, and damp walls or stinking ditches, all can portend wet weather ahead. It is fun and important to become familiar with the signs of nature as well as the technologies of our time in order to know the coming weather. Again, wisdom can make the difference between life and death. A good sailor *does* wait out a storm before setting out!

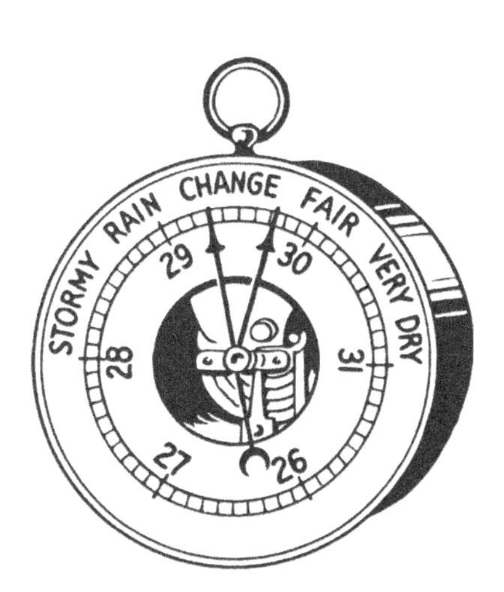

Another way to know what weather is expected is consulting your local media forecasts. The Coast Guard also produces a continuous weather broadcast that sailers would find helpful.

If you have an older student interested in learning more about forecasting, Eric Sloane's *Weather Book* is full of interesting facts and drawings. Eric Sloane has several other weather-related books, as well, with beautiful drawings and useful information. (**Teacher's Note:** Also, the *spelling* of the word forecasting can be taught to your older student by reminding her that sailors need to know the weather ***before*** they set sail. This may help her remember to include the "e" in the word **fore**casting!)

Science: Rope and Knots

Matthew had to learn about ropes and rigging as he learned to sail the "small red boat with the wild white sail." Rope is traditionally made by twisting together thinner cords to form a thick, strong length of cord. It can be made from cotton, hemp, nylon, etc. Sailors always check their ropes for signs of wear. It is no good to tie up a boat, even using the best knot, if the rope is frayed and breaks. The boat could be lost!

Also, learning which knots, hitches and bends to use and when to use them is essential for a good sailor.

Even if the rope is fresh and strong, a wrong twist at the pier and the boat floats away! This can happen because as the waves bounce the boat, much stress is put on the mooring rope and a loose rope unties easily. So, the correct knot makes all the difference. Besides, it is fun to learn to tie many different kinds of knots. Each one has its own uses. Matthew spent hours learning to tie knots well. Besides looking online, many different books will have instructions on knot-tying, including a Boy or Girl Scout manual, camping book, or book exclusively on knots from the library. Most books on sailing, etc., have chapters on learning to tie knots, also. Get some rope at a hardware or big box store. Or for even more fun if you have a marine store nearby, go there for the rope. It might cost a bit more but that is made up for in the "museum"-like fun of seeing all the boating equipment. (If you do go to such a store, look for a barometer and point it out! How many other pieces of nautical equipment can you find?)

Teacher's Note: If you introduce the subject of knots and how to tie them during this story, your student will return with pleasure and a sense of familiarity to this subject as she studies the lessons in *Hitty, Her First Hundred Years*, a book selection in a later FIAR volume.

Science: Common Animals of the Sea

Common animals of the sea can cover the spectrum of the animal kingdom. If you have an older student you may want to see how many familiar examples you can find of ocean life that fit into all the classes of vertebrates and invertebrates. An online search or a simple book on animal classification will help you place animals like jellyfish, starfish, crabs, and sponges, as well as dolphins, whales, swordfish, sharks, gulls, etc., in their proper classes.

For your younger student, introduce her to whales and dolphins (mammals), just like Matthew saw as he sailed with Grandpa. Talk about gulls (birds), fish, and shelled creatures (crustaceans). Again, wherever your student is in her understanding of marine life, introduce her to something new! Much of this new information you student can draw and write about, adding pages to her science notebook, or nature journal, if she is keeping one.

Sea animals make and live in the beautiful shells we sometimes find on a beach. On the cover of the book there are some shells. Can your student find a simple book on shells and identify them? (On the cover of our story there is a nautilus, a cowry and possibly a limpet.) What is your student's favorite shell?

Again, encourage your student to learn a little more about shells than she has known before. Have your student add facts and illustrations to her science notebook, even drawing or sketching some of these beautiful shells and learning a few facts about the animals that live in them.

Science: Tides

Tides are not specifically mentioned in this story, but anyone living near the sea experiences the phenomena of the tides. The *tides* are the daily rise and fall of the waters in our oceans and seas. They are caused by the pull on the earth from the moon's gravity. There are two high tides and two low tide periods every twenty-four hours. In the illustration on the second page where the story describes Grandpa's house you can see the water and some sand showing by the wall. It could be that the water is receding in a low tide in this picture. Low tide is an interesting time on a beach. Often you can find shells, sea animals (especially in tide pools—depressions in the sand), seaweed, driftwood, etc., that have been left on the beach by the receding tide.

To show your student how tides work, get a large flat-bottomed bowl. Put an inch of small gravel on the bottom of the bowl. Pour in two inches of water and cover the bowl tightly with a clear food wrap. Now show how the tide goes out by tipping the bowl gently and leaving wet rocks behind on one side. Now carefully let the water come back. Explain that this happens rather slowly on a beach. Still, some tourists can be trapped in areas like caves and on peninsulas because they are not mindful of the incoming tide! Learning about tides makes a good science lesson but it makes a good survival and life skills lesson, as well!

Science: Waves on Large Bodies of Water

Matthew had to battle the waves of the storm and then saw them quiet as the wind died down. Waves are swells or moving ridges across any type of natural water expanse. These waves are caused by wind. Depending on how strong the wind is, how much water space the wind crosses over and how long the wind blows determines the height of the waves. Waves have a high point called a peak, a low point called the trough,* and are measured by their height from **trough** to **peak** and their length from peak to peak. Wave action moves in a constant up, over and roll under, movement. Find a simple book at the library or look online for illustrations of the fascinating wave cross sections and **wave action**.

*As Matthew struggles in the storm the text says his boat was tossed on the waves and "slid down their valleys." Valleys are the same as troughs—the lowest part as the wave falls.

Science: Sailing

The science of sailing includes topics such as wind and weather, sailing skills, water safety and much more. If your student is passionate about this subject, you may want to find a good simple book at your library to answer some of her questions. Sailing may look easy, but there is a great deal more to the science of sailing than one might think!

Sailing involves several principles of physics such as **aerodynamics** and the use of **simple machines**. Aerodynamically the sail is shaped to not only have the wind push against it but also to create a lift, like the shape of a bird's wing or an airplane wing.

The side of the sail away from the wind is curved like the top of a bird's wing. As the air rushes past it, a lift is created on the convex side of the sail which happens at the same time as the wind is filling and pushing the sail from the concave side—a lift and push to propel the boat ahead. Isn't it interesting that the author Wendy Orr knows from her own experiences in sailing about this phenomenon? She writes on the second page of the story about the "sails lifting like a seagull's wings," and later "the wind filled the sails and the boat flew over the water."

There are so many terms and interesting facts regarding sailors and sailing that your student will notice in songs, movies, and books (some of which are listed below). Sailing is indeed the stuff from which adventure is made. Enjoy finding out more about this interesting subject and dreaming of adventures on the seas.

If your student has enjoyed studying the book *Arabella*, here are some other stories she might love as well:

Island Boy by Barbara Cooney

One Morning in Maine by Robert McCloskey

And for older students listening in, or for family read aloud:

Swallows and Amazons by Arthur Ransome

We Didn't Mean to Go to Sea by Arthur Ransome

The Swiss Family Robinson by Johann Wyss

Treasure Island by Robert Louis Stevenson

Teacher's Notes

The *Five in a Row* lesson options for each unit in the manual are all you need to teach your child. The additional resource area provided below is simply a place to jot down relevant info you've found that you might want to reference.

ARABELLA

Date:

Student:

***Five in a Row* Lesson Topics Chosen:**

Social Studies:

Language Arts:

Art:

Math:

Science:

Relevant Library Resources: Books, DVDs, Audio Books

Websites or Video Links:

Related Field Trip Opportunities:

Favorite Quote or Memory During Study:

Name:

Date:

Science: **Weather Forecasting, the Barometer, Clouds and Signs**

Have your student chart weather information for one day, or make copies for multiple days. If you don't have an outdoor thermometer or barometer at home you can help them find the information for your local area on a weather app or website.

Weather for (Date): __________

High Temperature ____________

Low Temperature ____________

Barometric Pressure ____________

Steady ☐ Rising ☐ Falling ☐

— 100
— 80
— 60
— 40
— 20
— 0
— -20

°F

Current Temperature

☐ Sunny

☐ Partly Cloudy

☐ Cloudy

☐ Rainy

☐ Snowy

☐ Foggy

☐ Windy (direction and speed) ____________

☐ Hazy

Notes:

____

____

____

____

____

____

____

____

____

____

Name:
Date:
Art: **How to Draw a Sailboat**

Follow the steps below to learn how to draw a sailboat. Remember to draw lightly with your pencil as you go so you can erase lines as needed.

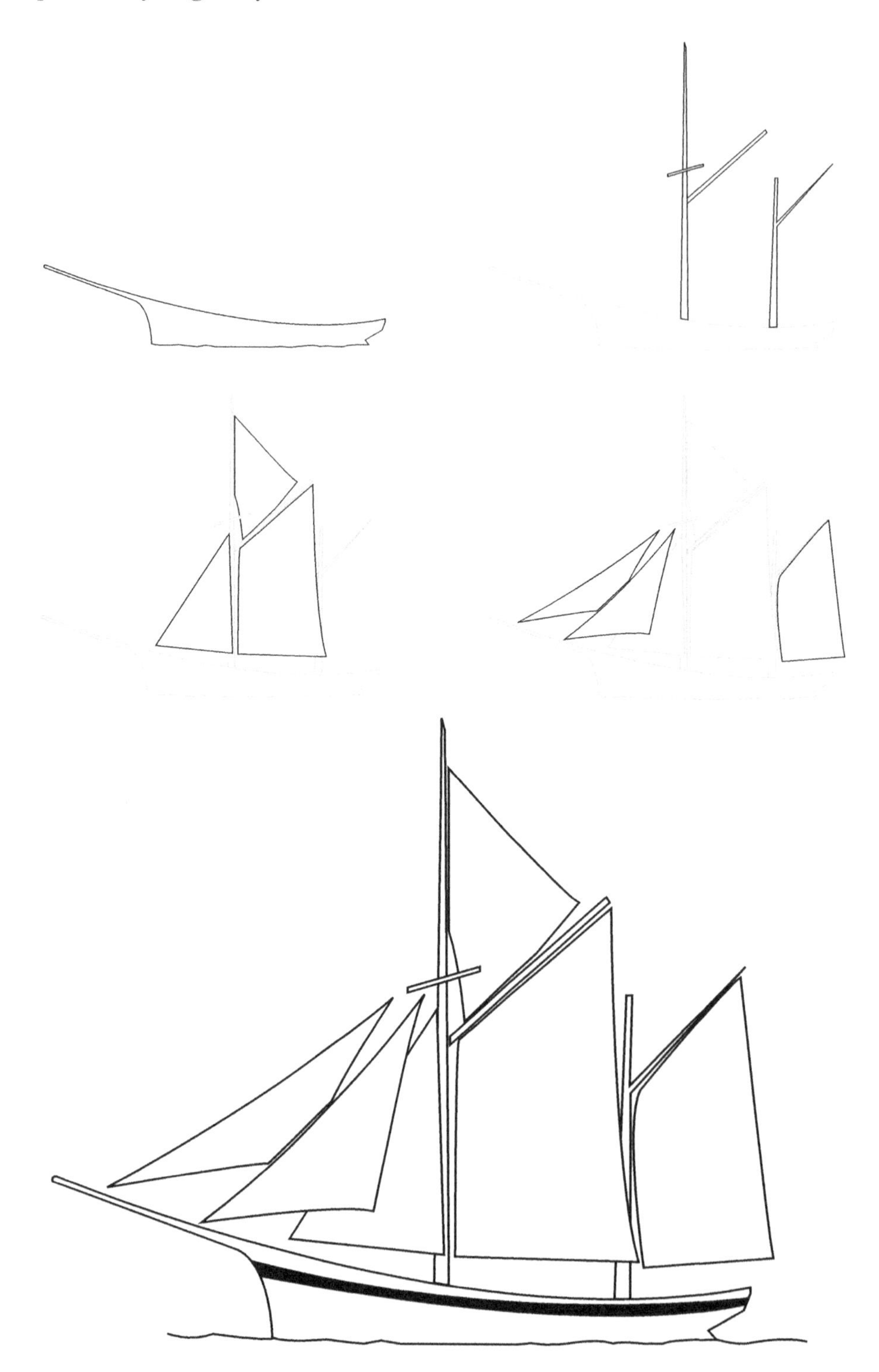

Name:
Date:
Social Studies: **Geography - Islands Around the World**

Have your student pick an island to research via a virtual field trip. Fill in the blanks below with information they discover in their search.

Virtual FIELD TRIP

Name and Location: ______________________________

Local Foods: ______________________________

____

Flora and Fauna: ______________________________

____

Weather/Temperature: ______________________________

Print and glue in pictures of the island.

Higgins Bend Song and Dance

Title: *Higgins Bend Song and Dance*
Author: Jacqueline B. Martin
Illustrator: Brad Sneed
Copyright: 1997
Summary: This is a fish story—the *whopper* kind!

Social Studies: Geological Term - Bend or Meander

The title *Higgins Bend Song and Dance* has a word in it you could discuss with your student. What is meant by the word *bend*? Your student probably knows what a bend (or a curve) in the road is like, but what is the bend in this story? In *Higgins Bend* it is a bend in a river! If your student has ever flown over rivers in an airplane he knows that most rivers are twisting and winding and have many curves in their paths. If your student has not seen rivers from the air, try finding a high bluff or building where a river's course can be viewed (hopefully a river with at least one bend that can be seen). You can also simply look at a map to see the many bends in a river's path or look at aerial views online.

Why do rivers have bends in them? How do they get that way? Most of the time a bend in a river's course is due to the force of the water against the bank that wears away the sediment, creating a scooped-out area or bend. The water hitting the bank is pushed back toward the other bank and creates a bend on the other side. As the force of the water continues to hit the curves it makes them even larger. This is a very simple explanation, but it explains why a river has bends in it and how rivers, over time, move in their course.

A more technical **geological term** for bend is "**meander**." You could discuss this term with your older student at the end of this lesson, tying it in with the idea of bends or curves in the river banks. This discussion might lead to other ways we use the word meander—for instance, to wander off of, or away from, a path, etc.

Social Studies: Character Relationships - Rejecting Community

Jacqueline Martin creates a complex character in Simon Henry. We know that he does not like to join in with others to sing or dance or hear stories, but we don't really know why. Potato Kelly says "too much work and tight boots have pinched her friend inside and out." But as with all people there is probably more to his story than that—perhaps some hurt, we just don't know. Simon Henry is what people call a loner and according to the story, " ... all business—fish business." All he did was work and fish and that made him really happy. Look at the illustration opposite the first page of the story. Does your student think that Simon Henry looks happy? He even has a butterfly on his hat but does he notice or care? The story says he never laughs and he doesn't even smile one day out of seven!

Discuss with your student the life of a loner. Yes, it is true that without a lot of others around you can pick exactly what *you* want to do when *you* want to do it. No one will be telling you what to do. But what is the result of such isolated living? Was Simon Henry helping others? Was he allowing others to help him or even to have fun with him? Does it look like Simon Henry has made a good choice by rejecting all the community functions and relationships?

Continue talking with your student about the concept of desiring to live life with others—in a family, with friends, in a marriage. Living with others around isn't always easy. You do have to share, and compromise now and then, doing things that other people want to do. Also, people don't always treat one another with consideration. Sometimes they tease or say or do something hurtful. However, in the long run, having people around you to share stories, hard times, and triumphs is essential to human nature.

Remember *The Rag Coat* by Lauren Mills in FIAR Vol. 1? Minna, the main character in the story, comes to believe for herself an important truth that was taught to her by her father: "People need people."

Perhaps Potato Kelly's loving, patiently offered friendship has something to do with it, and maybe a traumatic encounter with a fish—but Simon Henry does change. Follow his expressions from the dust jacket cover through the story until he tangles with Oscar and watch the change. This is a good example of how the illustrator is faithful to the author's story and you get a good look at the new Simon Henry—a man who is now willing to be with people.

Social Studies: Running a Business

Potato Kelly had a business. It was a bait shop and restaurant. It was also a meeting place—a place where people congregated and swapped stories and became friends.

Simon Henry had a business too. It was the business of fishing!

If you have previously studied *Night of the Moonjellies* in *Five in a Row* Volume 1, you could continue talking about the topic of family businesses and comparing Potato Kelly's Bait and Chowder shop to

Mar-Gra's. Discuss similarities and differences. (The setting for one restaurant is the ocean while the other is a river bend. In *The Night of the Moonjellies* the restaurant is just for food, where Potato Kelly's is a store of fishing supplies and bait as well as a place to get something to eat. The food itself is different. Families patronize both places. We see lots of help in one restaurant while it looks as if Potato Kelly runs her place alone. From the pictures and text we can't really tell. Mar-Gra's restaurant is an open-air food stand with tables outside while Potato Kelly's has an inside building with some outside dining, etc.)

What skills would be helpful in running a successful business? (Keeping an inventory system, having a servant's heart and good relational people skills, finding out what people like and need, and keeping a clean and neat store would all be helpful. In addition a food service store would have to be very careful about germs, etc.)

Another fantastic book about small business to read at this time is *Once Upon a Company* by Wendy Anderson Halperin. This is a true story of a family of children who develop their own company, learning along the way all about how a company works and grows. The money made by these children goes into their college fund. A truly remarkable book that is currently out of print but available used.

Language Arts: Tall Tales

See the Language Arts lesson on tall tales in *The Pumpkin Runner* unit earlier in this volume for introductory information on this type of exaggerated story. There is also mention of tall tales in the *Albert* unit.

After thinking about ways that *Higgins Bend Song and Dance* has elements of a tall tale, your student might want to create a tall tale of his own. You can brainstorm together with your student or have him try by himself, if he'd rather. He could make a tall tale about how something was created, or like *Higgins Bend Song and Dance,* about a particular incident blown out of proportion. A tall tale could be about himself, a member of his own family, a pet, or just about anything else he can think of! Your student might think about making it into a book with illustrations. Enjoy this opportunity for letting the imagination run wild!

Language Arts: Supplemental Story with a Similar Theme

Joan Blos writes a wise and witty story of a man who doesn't seem to fit into his neighborhood. The book *Old Henry* has an interesting similar theme with a surprise ending.

Art: Medium and Style

Brad Sneed illustrates *Higgins Bend Song and Dance* with beautiful **watercolor** illustrations of the river, its residents (like Oscar) and the people who live along its banks. Spend a few moments with your student looking at the illustration on the title page. Can your student see the fisherman? Let him examine the way the trees and leaves are painted, and the reflections of the trees in the water. Then gaze at the broad expanse of river to the bottom of the page. This picture is a preview of a "watery" story to come! Now, look at the last picture with the soft, brown dirt bank and its reflection in the water and the river as it flows around the bend. Have your student point out other illustrations in this story that are his favorites.

You and your student may recognize Brad Sneed's unusual, exaggerated artistic style from *The Pumpkin Runner* earlier in this volume. In that book, as in *Higgins Bend Song and Dance*, the characters are elongated in a sort of caricature (exaggerated figures) effect. Look up some paintings done by the Missouri artist Thomas Hart Benton. You and your student will be able to see similarities in these two artists' painting styles.

Art: A Cross Section Image and an Underwater View

For those of you who have the dust jacket on your book, look at the front picture. Have your student study the picture for a few minutes and then ask him to tell you about it. The unusual thing about this picture is that you can see the fish and the bobber and the fisherman's legs as if you had sliced down through the water! There are not any other pictures exactly like this one anywhere else in the story. This type of illustration is called a cross section. In many applications, from art to architecture to science (the "cross section" of a leaf slide for instance). Cross section images are often used in books that explain how things are built and how they work. Stephen Biesty has several books that have cutaway or cross section views of castles, ships, etc.

There is another unusual view painted by Brad Sneed, and that is the view from below Oscar as he is looking up at Simon Henry's raft. Now *there* is a picture! If this was the only scene your student could look at as he listened to the story, who does he think would win this fishing contest—the fish or the fisherman? Why? (No particular correct answer here, but your student might say the fish because the fish certainly *looks* bigger than the fisherman!)

Maybe your student would enjoy planning and executing a drawing or painting of something in cross section or something from another unusual view point.

Art: Potato Stamping

Potato Kelly was Simon Henry's friend and she was famous for all sorts of wonderful chowders and dishes which she made from potatoes. In honor of Potato Kelly and her friendly, cheerful disposition, show your student how to make carved potato stamps. You might even try one with a fish, one with waves, one with a boat, etc.

Make designs on the cut halves of potatoes. Remember carving is cutting away all that *isn't* the boat or fish, etc. To make a stamp just cut down about a quarter inch, so the figure which remains is raised enough to make a good stamp.

Using fabric paint for cloth, or tempera or dark watercolor paints for paper, make stamped designs. You can decorate the edges of the paper and use them for centerpieces, wrapping paper or stationery. Fabric rectangles can also be hemmed for placemats to be stamped, or t-shirts can be decorated with potato stamp designs.

Math: Store-Keeping Skills

Potato Kelly runs a store. She has a cash register. If you haven't already covered this topic, teach about money denominations or making change. For older students, discuss figuring discounts or the amount to add for tax or a tip. You might want to discuss how to set up a simple inventory system for a small store and how today, many stores manage this facet of business through computerized systems.

Math: Rivers and Their Water

It might be fun for your student to learn how much water weighs. A cubic foot (remember that cubic measurements are measurements of **volume**) of water weighs approximately 60 pounds. That means that if you had a box measuring **one cubic foot** and filled it with **water**, that volume of water would weigh a little over 60 pounds (**62.4 lbs.**) Water is heavy! Your student will know that if he has had to carry buckets of water to a garden, pool or fountain.

Each river has its own length, width, and depth. All of these can be measured. Your student can look up the measurements of famous rivers' lengths and compare them. What river is the longest in the world? (While the Nile River in Egypt is the *longest* river in the world, the second longest river, the Amazon, empties an impressive 4.2 million cubic feet of water into the ocean every second, much more than the Nile! Did your student remember that the Yangtze River is the third longest river in the world?) Your student may like to make a chart of rivers of the United States or rivers of the world showing their statistics. He may already have information that he used for the River Lengths activity sheet for *Cowboy Charlie*.

How many feet deep is a river? Some are very shallow, just a few feet deep, while the Congo River, for example, is so deep that it's difficult to even measure it! In the days of the steamboat, rivers were measured or "sounded" by dropping a line or rope into the water and measuring the depth. A famous American author named Samuel Clemens used the pseudonym (pen name) Mark Twain for his writings. The term **mark twain** was a measurement desired by riverboat captains to *safely* navigate the rivers. If the person measuring the depth called out "mark twain," it meant that the riverboat was in 2 fathoms (a nautical unit of measurement; each fathom equals 6 feet) of water. Twelve feet was the least amount of depth at which a riverboat could safely pass without running aground. A riverboat captain needed to know his river, the bends, the sandbars, and the depths at various places along the way.

Science: Astronomy - Morning Star

When Potato Kelley and Simon Henry set off on the raft under the morning star, little did they know Oscar would pull them all the way down to Higgins Bend!

Has your student ever noticed a very bright looking object in the sky near the horizon just before sunrise or just at after sunset? There's a good chance he has seen the planet Venus. The term *morning star* usually refers to this planet (seen early morning) which is the brightest celestial object in the sky after the sun and moon. (Some other planets can also be seen in a similar fashion at certain times of the year, but are not nearly as bright and noticeable as the planet Venus.) Venus is blanketed by thick clouds that reflect sunlight, making it extremely bright in the night sky. Venus was viewed for thousands of years before there was a telescope to help its viewers understand that it is a planet and not a star. Thus generally Venus is still known as the "morning star" even though it is not a star at all. It's amazing that your student can see this same "morning star" for himself.

Science: Physics - Rafts and Buoyancy

A raft can be made of boards, logs, pieces of Styrofoam, rubber, or of materials which are air-filled. When a raft is placed in a river or pond, tbe weight or density of the water holds it up and allows it to float as long as the raft has less total density than the water in which it is floating. Your student will have an opportunity in a later FIAR volume to make a small raft of his own in an art lesson for *The Raft*. For now, enjoy learning about different types of rafts and what they can be made of.

(**Teacher's Note:** Did your student notice the bobber on the front cover of the dust jacket of *Higgins Bend*? It is floating. Another example of buoyancy! Once your student understands a concept he may see many examples of it around him.)

The scientist Archimedes is considered the person responsible for defining the principles of buoyancy. Your student might enjoy learning more about this ancient Greek mathematician online or with simple library books.

A raft features prominently in the books *Tom Sawyer* and *Huckleberry Finn*, by Mark Twain. If you enjoy Twain's writings, you might want to find abridged or illustrated copies and read just the raft portions, or finish it if your student loves the story, as a read aloud.

Science: Fish and Fishing

Let's learn about the fish's place in the animal kingdom (review the kingdoms when you teach a new one or keep a running chart and keep adding to it). For a teacher who is able to keep charts, simply adding information to an existing chart is such a practical way to review past lessons with your student. It just takes a moment to review previously learned facts before you add new information to the existing chart.

Did you know that catfish are named because they have what appear to be two to four pairs of whiskers—reminiscent of cats! These whiskers are, in fact, actually called barbels, or feelers. Catfish come in many sizes ranging from a few inches to over ten feet and are found all over the world in both salt and fresh water. The kind of catfish that Simon Henry wanted to capture was probably a channel cat. These catfish live in the rivers of North America. There are also catfish that live in lakes and ponds. Record catfish of 120-130 pounds have been caught in the United States.

Many people consider catfish to be so delicious that catfish farms are operated in several states. These "farms" raise fish specifically for human food consumption. The farm-raised fish are popular for being sweeter and less fishy tasting than the river cats.

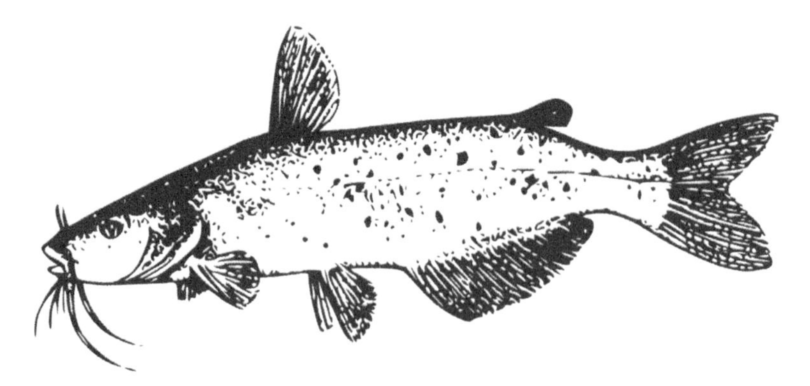

Higgins Bend Song and Dance offers a chance to have a discussion about fishing. If there is an avid fisherman in the family, or in the neighborhood, this would be a great opportunity to have him share this subject that he (or she) knows and loves, with your student.

Some topics to choose for discussion could be: types of fishing poles and rods, types of reels, and different kinds of bait, as Simon Henry found out! Baits can be live (such as minnows, worms, etc.), and there are also artificial baits and lures of many descriptions. Just for fun, visit a bait and tackle shop or the fishing department of a big box store and examine the myriad of bait and lures used for fishing.

Discussion topics for this subject might also include different species of fish in your area, and how to fish a stream, river, pond, etc. If you are not expert in this sport find information at your local conservation department. At your conservation department you will probably be able to collect pamphlets about fishing. These pamphlets include information on fishing regulations, and the types of fish in your area—where to find them (in ponds, rivers or lakes, and whether they live in shallow, medium or deep areas) as well as what is currently used in each case for bait.

Science: Biology - Flies, Butterflies and Worms

Simon Henry is all fishing business and as you and your student look at the picture opposite the first page of text, you can see Simon's bait bag hanging at his waist. There are some flies buzzing around it and some worms peeking out, as well as butterflies on Simon Henry's hat. (And yes, there is a dragonfly on the river plants below.)

Both the butterfly and the common house fly have **jointed legs** so they are both members of the **phylum Arthropoda**, and they both are of the **class Insecta** because they have **three body parts, antenna, and six legs**, even though the fly will be in a different order (Diptera) than the butterfly (Lepidoptera).

Your student may enjoy beginning a simple insect collection with some of the common insects, labeling them with their classification names and defining characteristics. It is critical, no matter what type of display case you use for an insect collection to put in a moth ball or two or a piece of insect pest strip to prevent weevils from destroying the collection. These preventatives will have to be replaced periodically, every eight months or so. Because both moth balls and pest strips are poisonous, care must be taken when using them and with where the collection is stored—not in small children's reach.

Common Orders of the Class Insecta

Lepidoptera
(scale wings)
butterflies
skippers
moths

Homoptera
(same wings)
cicadas

Diptera
(two wings)
house flies
mosquitoes

Hemiptera
(half wings)
bugs, i.e., cinch

Hymenoptera
(membrane wings)
ants
bees
wasps

Onodata
(toothed)
dragonflies

Coleoptera
(sheath wings)
beetles

Orthoptera
(straight wings)
crickets
grasshoppers

These are just a few of the common orders of the Insecta class. (There are 26 orders altogether.) This lesson is for those who are *interested* in learning about and categorizing insects. Your student may not yet be ready to find the enjoyment in such a project. If not, it is fine to wait till upper grades to do this sort of exercise. However, if *you* are interested, you can make up a sectioned box of specimens and label them for your classroom use. Whenever you find a new insect, like a silverfish, for example, add for it a new section: the **order Thysanura**. Yell out loud and strong that you "Found a new one!" and your student will at least be amused if not intrigued by your interest. Your collection will grow and review will be fun. Being able to see insects at close range, examining the legs, eyes, wings, etc., is an important part of learning about nature.

The worms that Simon uses for bait are probably night crawlers, also called an earthworm. (A few other types of worms are used for bait, but the earthworm is certainly the most common.) An earthworm is in the phylum Annelida.

(**Teacher's Note:** The following guided questions are to help your student learn how the classification system works and how he, himself can tell which creatures fit into which categories, by observing and thinking through a creature's defining characteristics.)

Phylum: Annelida - Segmented Worms

Does a worm have three segmented body sections, head, thorax and abdomen *and* have six legs? (No) Then it is *not* in the class Insecta. Does an earthworm have segmented legs? (No) Then it could *not* be classified in the phylum Arthropoda. Your student may say, "It's not an insect—it's not even an arthropod! What is it then?"

Your student will need to look for a new category in which to fit the earthworm. You can lead him to the discovery of the large phylum **Annelida** (uh NEL ih duh) or segmented worms! There are four groups of worms but the one group of segmented worms is more than enough information for now.

The common earthworm, Lumbricus terrestris, is a scavenger, feeding on decaying plant material. Encourage your student to find some great fun facts about this creature, including that it has five pairs of hearts, and no lungs or gills! Simon Henry sure had interesting things in his bait bag!

Teacher's Note: A reminder to you to help your student: Grubs and caterpillars are not worms, but rather the larval or juvenile stages of certain insects such as beetles or butterflies, etc. Later in life, the former grubs or caterpillars do not resemble a worm, but rather creatures with the characteristics of true insects: legs, wings, etc.

Science: River Life

Flora: Rushes are grass-like plants that grow in damp areas. Yet, not every grass-like plant that grows in damp areas is a member of the family of rushes! Let your student ponder that idea for a moment. (Learning to differentiate one species from another in the world of nature is important. Each time your student carefully observes something in nature, he will continue to learn more about it and see how it fits into its very own proper niche in the plant or animal kingdom.)

Watery areas have many different kinds of plants, grasses, cattails and other weedy growth. If you have a pond, river or lake area nearby, you might enjoy exploring and seeing how many different kinds of plants you can find near the water, or at the water's edge. Do wear proper clothing and boots for your explorations, especially if there are snakes in your vicinity. Let your child explore, discover, draw and write about what he sees. He can add this work to his science notebook or to his nature journal if he is keeping one.

Fauna: Red-winged blackbirds, herons, loons, otters, peepers (frogs), dragonflies, worms, and bees are a few of the fauna listed or illustrated in *Higgins Bend Song and Dance*. Of this list, how many has your student actually seen himself? Where did he see them? Using illustrated field guides, try to find examples of these birds, animals and insects and learn some new facts about them. Have your student record these facts in his science notebook. For students who enjoy drawing, they may wish to make up a composite picture of many of these river plants and animals that might have been seen from Higgins Bend in the river!

Common Orders of the Insecta Phylum

Lepidoptera	Diptera	Hymenoptera
Coleoptera	Homoptera	Hemiptera
Onodata	Orthopera	

Common Orders of the Insecta Phylum

____________	____________	____________
____________	____________	____________
____________	____________	____________
____________	____________	____________

Teacher's Notes

The *Five in a Row* lesson options for each unit in the manual are all you need to teach your child. The additional resource area provided below is simply a place to jot down relevant info you've found that you might want to reference.

HIGGINS BEND SONG AND DANCE

Date:

Student:

***Five in a Row* Lesson Topics Chosen:**

Social Studies:

Language Arts:

Art:

Math:

Science:

Relevant Library Resources: Books, DVDs, Audio Books

Websites or Video Links:

Related Field Trip Opportunities:

Favorite Quote or Memory During Study:

Name:
Date:
Art: **Social Studies - Running a Business**

After discussing the skills needed to run a food service store/business, use the spaces provided below to take inventory of (and record) some of the most-used items in your own refrigerator or pantry.

After several days or before grocery shopping occurs, take inventory again and note anything that needs to be restocked or purchased again.

Inventory Count Record

Date: ____________ Taken by: ____________________

Item	Quantity	Location	Buy
milk	<1 gal.	fridge	✓

Name:

Date:

Art: **Math - Rivers and Their Water**

Every river has its own length, width, and depth. All of these can be measured. Help your student look up the measurements of famous rivers' lengths and compare them using the space provided below.

River Name and Location	Length	Width	Depth

Name:
Date:
Art: **Language Arts - Create a Tall Tale**

Using the questions below, begin the brainstorming process of writing a tall tale. Afterwords, using the answers to the questions, write or dictate a tall tale of your own on a separate sheet of paper.

Who is the main character?

What makes them larger than life?

What is the conflict in the story?

What interesting details will you include?

How will the details be exagerated beyond belief?

What is the resolution?

Five in a Row Volume Four Story Disks

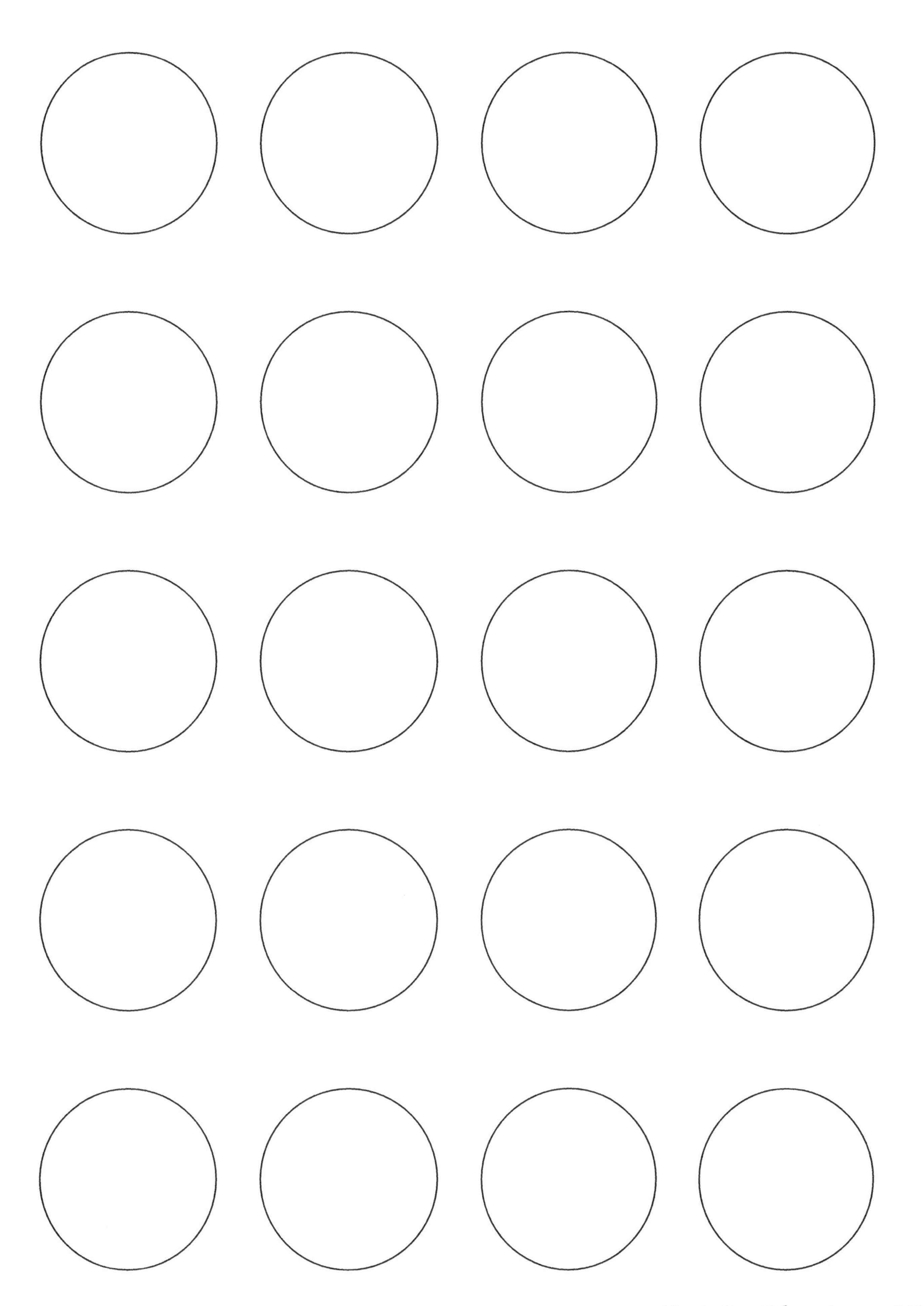

Sample **Lesson Planning Sheet: Week 1**

Sample Lesson Planning Sheets: *The Pumpkin Runner* has 34 suggested lessons in the lesson portion of this manual. The sample planning sheets below and on the following pages show ideas that *could* be chosen for a two-week study. You are free to choose *any* of the 34 lesson ideas and keep track of your choices by noting them on the reproducible, blank Lesson Planning Sheets (following pages). For more ideas on making the best use of your *Five in a Row* curriculum, be sure to read the *How to Use Five in a Row* section beginning on p. 10, and especially *What's Different About Volume 4?* on p. 21.

Week 1	Monday	Tuesday
	Social Studies	**Social Studies**
Title: *The Pumpkin Runner* **Author:** Marsha Diane Arnold **Illustrator:** Brad Sneed	Find Australia on map, place story disk Color flag, identify states and territories Discuss continents: Australia is the only country that is a continent Explain Hemispheres: Cut apples as example of hemisphere	Disagreeable people/characters in book -Cheating -Bragging How to react? Recall previous FIAR titles Share a personal story and ask for one Motivation for racing

Wednesday	Thursday	Friday
Language Arts	**Language Arts**	**Art**
New vocab: annual anticipation attire bearings lanky spectators Common sayings/meanings: shoo-in looking down his nose	Tall Tales and Fables, explain both Davy Crockett and "The Tortoise and the Hare" Using true incidents to create a good story Cliff Young (activity sheet)	Variety: Daylight and dark illustrations Viewpoint: Looking from Yellow Dog's eye level Elements of perspective: Ways to create depth in pictures

Sample **Lesson Planning Sheet: Week 2**

Week 2	Monday	Tuesday
	Math	**Math**
Title: *The Pumpkin Runner*	Metric system: Millimeters, meters, and kilometers	Division Use 8 runners to divide money
		(Prepare money beforehand/ activity sheet)
Author: Marsha Diane Arnold	Convert kilometers to miles	
	Unit measure of land acre 10,000 acres	Then do the problem on paper
Illustrator: Brad Sneed	Catching the clues for figures: How old is Joshua?	

Wednesday	Thursday	Friday
Science	**Science**	**Science**
Flora and fauna of Australia: Go through story for examples Use activity sheet	Physics: Hot air balloons (look online, too) Buoyancy Hot air: Molecules spread, forcing air out of balloon	(Buy pumpkins and get rock/ pumice ahead!) Botany - Pumpkins: Classification of plants, Cucurbitaceae Cucurbita Physics: Buoyancy and density Pumpkins in water, float? Rock and pumice in water, float?

Lesson Planning Sheet: Week 1

Week 1	Monday	Tuesday
Title: **Author:** **Illustrator:**		

Wednesday	Thursday	Friday

Lesson Planning Sheet: Week 2

Week 2	Monday	Tuesday
Title: **Author:** **Illustrator:**		

Wednesday	Thursday	Friday

Literary Glossary

Literary Devices

Alliteration
A succession of similar *sounds* (not letters) that occur at the beginning of a group of successive words. "The *d*og *d*ug a *d*eep *d*itch."

Foreshadowing
A literary device that suggests what is to come later in a work by giving hints and clues.

Hyperbole
An overstatement or exaggeration: "*I've told you a thousand times!*"

Irony
An event or outcome which is opposite what would naturally be expected: "*It was an irony of fate that the girl arrived just as her date left.*"

Italics
Letters slanted to the right, used for emphasis or to identify book titles, ship names, etc.: "The *Queen Mary* can sail so *fast* compared to ships long ago!"

Mood
The feelings a work of literature brings to the reader: sad, foreboding, buoyant, etc., derived from the particular descriptive words chosen by the writer.

Onomatopoeia
Representing a thing or action by a word that imitates the sound associated with it: *zoom, ping, ding-dong, buzz.*

Personification
Giving a thing, animal or abstract truth human characteristics: "*The moon smiled down on me.*"

Repetition
The repeating of certain words, phrases or ideas throughout a story or poem: "And I will take you home with me; yes, I will take you home with me."

Rhyme
In lines of poetry, where the ending *sounds* (not necessarily the letters) are the same: "Don't blame *me* / go and *see*..."

Simile
The comparison of two dissimilar objects, using the word *like* or *as*. "*When the lights went out, he was as brave as a lion.*"

Symbolism
Writing that suggests more than the literal meaning. "*The innocent girl wore a white dress.*" (White being a symbol of purity.)

Elements of a Story

Characters
A person, animal or thing (wind, for example) that inhabits a story.

Point of view
Who narrates (tells) the story:

First person: using I, me, etc.

Third person: using he, she, they, etc.

The point of view is usually the same throughout a short story, but you may find some stories where it changes. Ask, "who is telling this story?" Is the story told from only one character's viewpoint? (first person), or from the wider view of a narrator? (third person)?

Mood
The feelings a story stirs in the reader: calm, happy, sad, fearful, etc. The mood of a story can change; for example, from an ominous beginning to a happy ending. Sometimes there is a pervasive mood throughout a story such as wistfulness, etc.

Plot
The action or story line, which includes:

Conflict - the main problem of the story
Rising Action - events that create rising interest
Climax - the high point of action or tension
Denouement - the resolution or final outcome

Theme
The general idea or insight revealed in the story. The *heart and soul* of the story.

Setting
Where does the story take place: geography, town, a room, etc.? The time frame for the story: an hour, a day, a certain year or period of years, a season, etc.

Style
Someone once said, "Style is the *clothes* the words wear." In other words, how they are dressed—what *fashion* of words and sentence structure a writer uses to *outfit* his story. Many famous writers have distinctive styles. You can often tell by reading only a few paragraphs who wrote a passage. You might say, "Oh, that story sounds like it was written by ...."

Dictionary of Art Terms

Principles of Design

A picture usually follows certain basic *principles* of design including:

Center of Interest: the point emphasized in the picture. It should be differentiated by:

- Being larger or smaller than the other things in the picture.
- Being around or near the center of the picture but not usually in the exact middle.
- Being a different color, like a slightly darker red apple amid other apples, for instance.
- Being a different shape, like a boat with the sail up on a lake full of boats with their sails down.

Unity: Any element of design which holds components of a picture together and guides your eye around the picture: line, color, etc.

Rhythm: Repetition of an element in a picture: the line, color, shape, etc.

Balance: How the elements of a picture are constructed by use of symmetry or asymmetry.

Elements of Design

The *elements* of design are the tools an artist uses to follow the *principles* of design, which include:

Line: The path traced by a moving point. Lines can be straight, curved, zig-zag (as in lightning), broken - - - -, dots ...., or wavy.

Shape: The outward contour or outline; form; figure.

Space: *Positive space:* The house and the tree (the objects drawn or painted) are positive space.

Negative Space: The space *around* the objects drawn. All the space in this picture that isn't tree or house. An artist makes choices in the amount of positive and negative space in a picture to make a pleasing work. Look at lots of examples of pictures and find positive and negative space and notice how much of each the artist uses.

Texture: Artistically representing an object's surface and how it would *feel* (bumpy, smooth, etc.). Surface texture is unrelated to color, shape, etc.

Color: There are many components which make up the element of color including:

Color Hue: The name of the color: red, blue, etc.

Shade of Color: Black added to a particular color hue produces a *shade*.

Tint of Color: White added to a particular color hue produces a *tint*.

Tone of Color: Gray (black and white together) added to a particular color hue produces a *tone*.

Primary Colors: Red, yellow, blue. These colors cannot be obtained from mix. All other colors are produced by mixing these three *primary colors*.

Secondary Colors: Orange (made by mixing red and yellow), green (made by mixing yellow and blue) and violet (made by mixing blue and red).

Tertiary Colors: Made by mixing a secondary and a primary color. Yellow orange, red orange, yellow green, blue green, red violet and blue violet are made by mixing the colors that the names suggest. (Brown, *not* considered a tertiary color), can be made by mixing orange with a little blue and in other ways.)

Complementary Colors: Sometimes called opposites because of their place on the color wheel. In other words, on a color wheel, the opposite color from red is green. Green and red are complementary colors. As red is added in small amounts to green and visa versa, the effect is a graying or neutralizing of the original color.

Warm Colors: Colors that give a feeling of warmth, including yellows, oranges and reds. These colors are chosen by the artist when she wants to show the warmth of the sun, a light, a fire, etc. and when she desires to show symbolically the warmth of a scene, such as a homey scene. (This is an *enormous* subject with many subtleties, but this is a simple, working definition for young students.)

Warm Palette: Limiting colors used for a picture to the warm color hues (listed above), without using cool colors.

Cool Colors: Colors that give a feeling of coolness, including blues, greens and purples. (Again, this is a *simple* definition for primary students.)

Cool Palette: Limiting the colors used for a picture to only the cool colors (listed above) without using warmer colors.

Full Palette: Using both warm and cool colors in the same picture.

Perspective: Principles of Drawing for Depth

Size: Drawing some objects larger than others will make them appear closer to the viewer.

Foreshortening: A method of shortening the lines of *any* object, distorting the image to give the impression of depth. Let's look at circles and squares as examples.

Foreshortened Circles

Forsehortened Squares

Overlapping: Drawing objects behind and partly obscured by the front objects in order to make the front objects appear closer.

Placement: Making objects seem closer by drawing them closer to the bottom of the picture than the other components of the composition.

Surface Lines: Lines used on objects to give a 3-dimensional look, like the "wrapping around" of short lines to make a pencil seem round.

Intensity: Creating depth by drawing or painting close objects with more color and detail than objects that are in the background. The background objects are drawn with less detail and often have *grayed color*, made by adding to the color used on the main objects mixed with a little of their complement (opposite on the color wheel). This *grayed color* is used to paint objects in the background.

Shadows: Shadows give depth to a drawing and are often used to cause the subject to stand out more clearly. Shadows cause the object to *come forward* in the drawing or painting, and also indicate the direction of the picture's light source.

With shadows, it is important to remember the light source in your drawing and keep it consistent by having the shadows all flowing in from the same direction. The shadows will be on the *opposite* side of the light source.

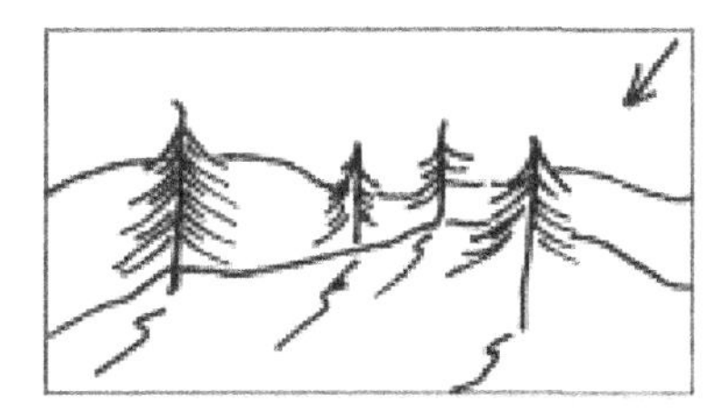

Shading: Helps make things appear rounded or three-dimensional by the use of shadows.

Additonal Terms

Medium: The type of art material you use to create a picture. For drawing, you might choose: pencil, pen and ink, charcoal, chalk or oil pastel, crayon, colored pencils or markers. For painting, choices include: oil paints, watercolors, acrylic (a water-based pigment that works like oil but dries more quickly), tempera (pigment is mixed with egg or other substances instead of oil), gouache (*opaque* watercolors made by mixing pigments with water and gum) or finger paint (probably a type of tempera). We might say, "This artist chose oil paints as *her medium*."

Viewpoint: The point from which an artist views her subject. In some drawings and paintings, we find ourselves looking down on the subject as if we were perched in a tree (called a bird's eye view). In other pictures we might feel as if we were seeing everything from the viewpoint of sitting or lying on the ground, looking up.

Finding the Books

Much has changed in the library system, due to internet access, since *Five in a Row* was first published. The books for the Bonus Unit Studies in this volume are currently out of print, and your local library branch may not own all the titles that are in print. However, it is easier than ever to search your library's online catalogue and request/hold titles. Even Interlibrary Loan (ILL) is something you can search from your home computer, through your library's website.

Not all library systems are exactly alike, but most online searches work in a similar way. You will sign in to your library system online with your library card number. Your personal account will show books you've requested or placed on hold and books you've checked out. Some systems even have virtual bookshelves where you can place titles for the future or that you've completed. If your online library system has this, it would be convenient to place the FIAR titles on your "future shelf" so that you can quickly go there to request a title or two for your upcoming studies.

When searching your library system's catalogue or the ILL catalogue, here are a few tips. Sometimes a book title won't be found when you search for it. Before giving up or moving on to ILL, try searching the author's name instead. Many times a book can be found listed with all of the author's other books even if it isn't found through a title search. This is true of the ILL catalogue system as well.

Placing several titles on hold every week or two will bring a consistent flow of books cycling in and will allow you to choose which one to use next. By requesting titles online you save yourself the time and effort of searching for books in person. The librarians will locate the book, shelved or misshelved. They will flag the computer to automatically hold the title for you when another library patron returns the book. The ILL requests will automatically happen through the libraries' computer systems. The requested book will be placed on hold for you and shipped to your requested library to be picked up next time you stop by. All of this will save you valuable time and energy!

As your local library collects your requested titles, they will notify you to let you know another book or two is being held for you. What could be easier?

If your library does not carry a *Five in a Row* title, or any book, that you wish they had on their shelves, it's a good idea to request it. The reason for this is that a library will sometimes eventually purchase a book if it's requested often enough. So if the library comes up empty-handed on a particular title, keep requesting it every few weeks. Encourage your friends to request it too! You'd be surprised how many wonderful books end up in the system that way. (Your library may have a quick and easy way to do this: check their website to see if they have an option for "Make a purchase request.")

A personal anecdote: A dear friend who began reviewing *Five in a Row* many years ago obtained *Who Owns the Sun?* via ILL. When she returned it, she suggested the librarian consider purchasing a copy for the local library. The busy librarian brushed her aside saying, "I'm sorry, but we've already spent our budget for this year; it's out of the question." Our friend simply opened the book and began reading it aloud to the librarian right at the check-out desk! Before she was halfway through, the librarian was wiping away tears as she listened to the poignant story, and by the time our friend finished reading, the librarian grabbed the book from her saying, "I'm going to take $15 from our office supply budget and order this book immediately!"

Sadly, many of the most wonderful books being written today, as well as marvelous classics like *The Story About Ping,* are being supplanted on limited library shelf space by books of far less merit. The library system is designed to respond to patron usage and requests. They buy and maintain what the most people are reading. One of our more subtle opportunities is to bless our communities with wholesome, solid books by requesting them, sharing them with local librarians, or even donating a copy of a special title from time to time. Our libraries are what we make of them!

One final note on the titles used in *Five in a Row.* We know that some of the books are difficult to locate or currently out of print for those who wish to purchase them. While we struggled with this issue, in the end, we concluded that we wanted to offer the very best of the more than 5,000 children's books we've explored and examined. In the first four volumes of FIAR, we've supplied dozens of complete unit study lesson plans—more than enough for three or more years of schooling.

For those who are willing to leave no stone unturned in their search for every FIAR title, we're sure you'll be blessed and rewarded for your trouble. Some of the more difficult titles to find are some of the richest! And, since publication of the first edition of *Five in a Row,* many previously out-of-print titles have come back into print, most notably from our friends at Purple House Press. So keep on the lookout for hard-to-find titles by trading with friends, having relatives check their libraries, requesting again and again locally, exploring used bookstores and thrift stores, etc. Many parents find that they enjoy the excitement of the search!

In the final analysis, we've tried to give you the very "best of the best" from the more than 5,000 children's books Jane has explored in the hopes that each one will be a present joy and a lifetime friend for both you and your children. God bless you and your children as you set out on the wonderful adventure of learning with *Five in a Row.*

Parts of a Flag

Throughout the *Five in a Row* stories, your student will learn about many countries and their flags. This page will help your child learn the parts of a flag.

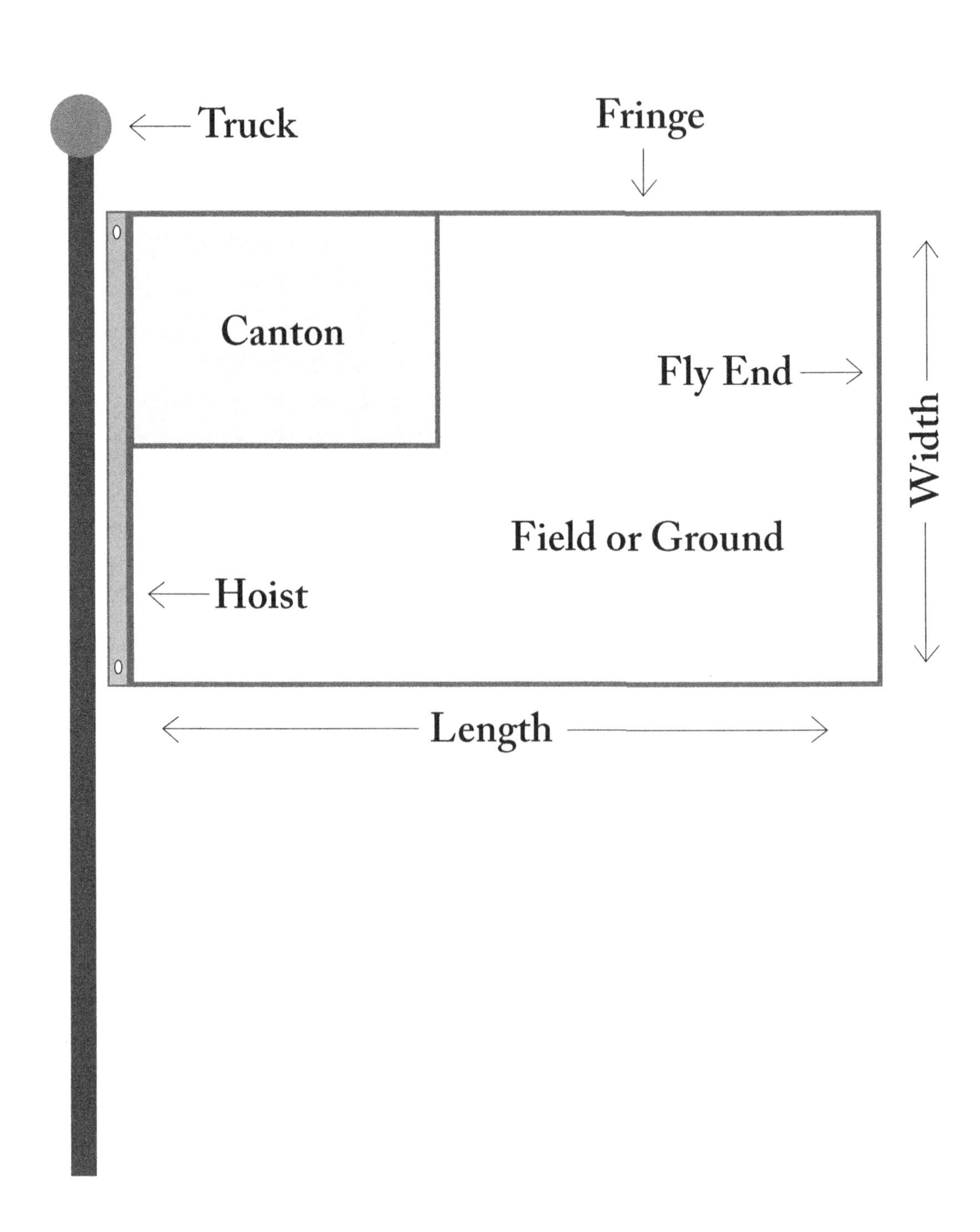

Index

Social Studies

Language Arts

Art

Music

Math

Science

Botany

Physics

Animals, Birds and Insects

Supplemental Book List

Blood and Guts: A Working Guide to Your Own Insides by Linda Allison (*The Pumpkin Runner*)
Boy, a Dog and a Frog, A by Mercer Mayer (*Arabella*)
Cactus Desert: One Small Square by Donald Silver (*The Tree Lady*)
Cloudy With a Chance of Meatballs by Judi Barrett (*Albert*)
Discover Nature at Sundown by Elizabeth P. Lawlor (*Grass Sandals*)
Draw Squad by Mark Kistler (*Arabella*)
Drawing Textbook, The by Bruce McIntyre (*Arabella*)
Emily by Michael Bedard (*Grass Sandals*)
Empty Pot, The by Demi (*Grass Sandals*)
Eric Sloane's Weather Book by Eric Sloane (*Arabella*)
Favorite Poems Old and New by Helen Ferris (*Mailing May, Arabella*)
Follow Me by Nancy Tafuri (*Arabella*)
Gardener's Alphabet, A by Mary Azarian (*The Tree Lady*)
Grandpa Green by Lane Smith (*The Tree Lady*)
Human Body for Every Kid, The by Janice VanCleave (*The Pumpkin Runner*)
Island Boy by Barbara Cooney (*Arabella*)
Miss Hickory by Carolyn Sherwin Bailey (*The Hickory Chair*)
My Great Aunt Arizona by Gloria Houston (*Roxaboxen*)
Old Henry by Joan Blos (*Higgins Bend*)
Once Upon a Company by Wendy Anderson Halperin (*Higgins Bend*)
One Morning in Maine by Robert McCloskey (*Arabella*)
Rand McNally Picture Atlas of the World (*Grass Sandals*)
Songs of the Wild West by Alan Axelrod and Dan Fox (*Cowboy Charlie*)
Start Exploring Gray's Anatomy by Freddy Stark, Ph.D. (*The Pumpkin Runner*)
Swallows and Amazons by Arthur Ransome (*Arabella*)
Swiss Family Robinson, The by Johann Wyss (*Arabella*)
Tom Sawyer (also *Huckleberry Finn*) by Mark Twain (*Cowboy Charlie, Higgins Bend*)
"Tortoise and the Hare, The" traditional fable (*The Pumpkin Runner*)
Treasure Island by Robert Louis Stevenson (*Arabella*)
Tuesday by David Wiesner (*Arabella*)
We Didn't Mean to Go to Sea by Arthur Ransome (*Arabella*)

Inspired learning through great books.

Five in a Row is a complete,* well-rounded, literature-based curriculum that takes your child from pre-K through middle school.

Current print products available from *Five in a Row* approved retailers:

For ages 2-4:
Before Five in a Row, Second Edition – Available from fiveinarow.com and Amazon.com

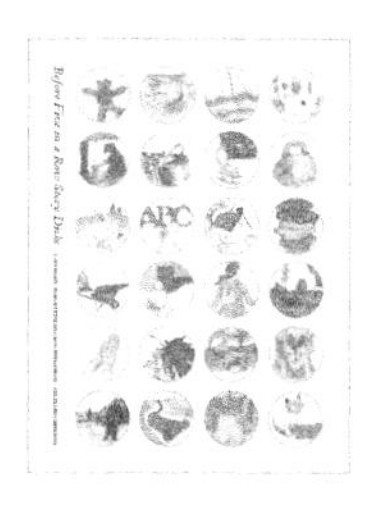

Before Five in a Row Story Disks (full-color, laminated) – Available from fiveinarow.com

Before Five in a Row Storybook Map (full-color, laminated) – Available from fiveinarow.com

For ages 3-5:
More Before Five in a Row – Available from fiveinarow.com and Amazon.com

More Before Five in a Row Story Disks (full-color, laminated) – Available from fiveinarow.com

More Before Five in a Row Storybook Map (full-color, laminated) – Available from fiveinarow.com

For ages 5-9:
Five in a Row Volume 1, Second Edition – Available from fiveinarow.com and Amazon.com

Five in a Row Volume 1 Story Disks (full-color, laminated) – Available from fiveinarow.com

For ages 5-9:
Five in a Row Volume 2, Second Edition – Available from fiveinarow.com and Amazon.com

Five in a Row Volume 2 Story Disks (full-color, laminated) – Available from fiveinarow.com

For ages 5-9:
Five in a Row Volume 3, Second Edition – Available from fiveinarow.com and Amazon.com

Five in a Row Volume 3 Story Disks (full-color, laminated) – Available from fiveinarow.com

For ages 9-10:
Five in a Row Volume 4, Second Edition – Available from fiveinarow.com and Amazon.com

Five in a Row Volume 4 Story Disks (full-color, laminated) – Available from fiveinarow.com

Five in a Row Starter Kit: Vols. 1, 2, 3 (First Editions) plus
Five in a Row Bible Supplement

Five in a Row **Supplements:**
Five in a Row Story Disks (full-color, laminated)
Five in a Row Bible Supplement (for Vols. 1, 2, 3)
Beyond Five in a Row Bible Supplement (for Vols. 1, 2, 3)
Five in a Row Cookbook (for Vols. 1, 2, 3 of both *FIAR* and *Beyond FIAR*)

For ages 8-12:
Beyond Five in a Row: Volume 1

Beyond Five in a Row: Volume 2

Beyond Five in a Row: Volume 3

For ages 12 and up:
Above & Beyond Five in a Row

Rainbowresource.com currently offers most *Five in a Row* print products as well as Literature Packages that go along with each of the *Five in a Row* and *Beyond Five in a Row* volumes.

Digital resources available from fiveinarow.com

Visit www.fiveinarow.com for additional digital resources and more information on the products above.

FIAR Notebook Builder
More than 120 pages of notebooking templates for all ages, appropriate for any topic or unit of study.

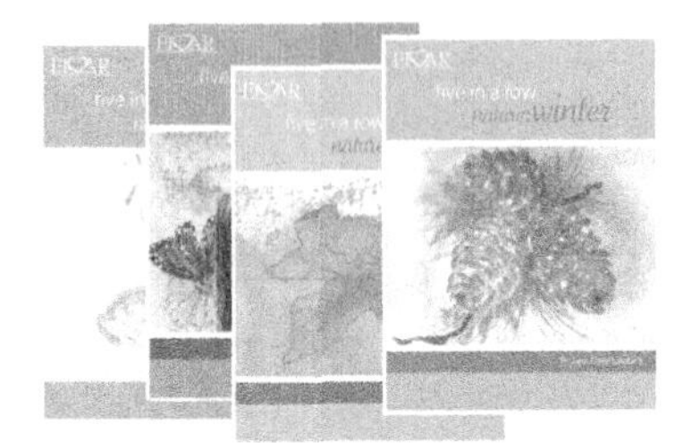

FIAR Nature Studies (Spring, Summer, Fall, Winter)
The *FIAR Nature Study* encourages your entire family to enjoy and explore the outdoors in all four seasons; it is a topic close to Jane's heart. Resources are provided to ensure that you can be a nature mentor to your child! It is a true unit study approach to nature studies; suggestions introduce you and your child to poetry, music, and art that tie in to the season.

FIAR Holiday: Through the Seasons
A treasury of traditions, ideas, and more for making your own special holiday memories.

Homeschool Encouragement Messages (Audio Files)
Inspiring messages from Steve on often-requested topics: Where Do I Begin, I Can't Teach All the Grades at Once, Making Your Children into World Changers, On Becoming Great Teachers, and High School and Beyond.

More digital products available at fiveinarow.com

You'll find other digital products at www.fiveinarow.com, as well, including a *FIAR Planner* and bonus units for Volume 4, as well as other *FIAR* products in digital format: *Above & Beyond FIAR*, the *FIAR Cookbook* and *Holiday* volumes, individual *FIAR Volume 4* units, and *Fold & Learns* for select *FIAR* and *Beyond FIAR* units.

You will need to add math and phonics/reading instruction to* ***Five in a Row**.*

Visit fiveinarow.com for additional information on the latest products.

Made in the USA
Middletown, DE
23 April 2022